MAN'S QUESTIONS—

GOD'S ANSWERS

MAN'S QUESTIONS-

GOD'S ANSWERS

Sotirios J. Noussias

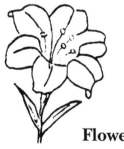

Flower Publishing   Canton, Ohio

Printed in USA by Thomson-Shore
Edited by Kay Ballard
Cover Art by Steve Henry
Typesetting by Alabama Book Composition

Published by Flower Publishing
P.O. Box 8498
Canton, Ohio 44711-8498
U.S.A.

Publisher's Cataloging in Publication
   (Prepared by Quality Books Inc.)

Noussias, Sotirios J.
      Man's questions—God's answers / Sotirios J. Noussias.
            p.   cm.
      Includes index.
      LCCN: 96-85003
      ISBN 0-9652284-0-1

      1. Bible—Commentaries.   I. Title.

BS491.2.N68   1997   220.7
                                          QBI96-40081

Dedicated to:

You. It doesn't matter who you are, or what you have done in your life. This book is an introduction to and your opportunity to meet and to have a personal relationship with the One, True, and Living God. This God is your Creator and the Creator of all things visible and invisible, both on earth and in heaven.

Special Thanks to:

My loving Lord and God for all His wonderful blessings and for this opportunity to spread His Good News.

My loving wife Tula for being wonderfully patient and supportive during the nearly four years that it took me to write this book.

My loving daughter Jaime for her dedication, time, and work in transposing my handwritten manuscript.

INTRODUCTION

Does serving God require that we bow down to mortal men and conduct our worship and our charity according to man-made rituals and commandments? If we are to believe this, should we not at least look to see if what we are being told is true? Could it be that commandments of men are being taught as doctrines of God? Is it God's Will that we know His "Truth," or does He want us to keep our minds and our mouths shut and to just follow the paths of our parents, whether they lead us to Him or not? Do not be deceived!

God gave each of us a free mind so that we could freely choose to seek, to know, to love, and to follow Him. Those that sincerely seek to know God will find Him, and those that find Him will love and follow Him. Loving God, contrary to the belief of many, has nothing to do with religion. True, pure, and unadulterated "Love" involves friendship, trust, and loyalty, and is something that cannot be bought or forced upon anyone. It is something that develops between friends as they enjoy sharing their thoughts, goals, and ideas with each other.

Did you know that, just as we enjoy spending time with our friends, God enjoys spending time with His friends? God created man for His Pleasure, and will give eternal life to and spend eternity with His friends. God has personally revealed this and His entire Master Plan to us in His Written Word, the Holy Bible. God did this so that we would not live in fear, but would have peace in knowing where we stand as far as He is concerned and in knowing that there is a glorious future just ahead.

Unfortunately, the spirit enemy of mankind has worked, and is working in many to prevent mankind from knowing God's "Truth." The enemies of God are not only those that have opposed and are outwardly opposing the Holy Bible, but are also those that have perverted and are perverting God's Word with their pride and greed-driven man-made doctrines, which go against God's Will.

Who is God? Who or what is God's "Truth?" Is there proof? What does the Holy Bible really say? Why has the Holy Bible been attacked unlike any other book in the history of mankind?

These questions and many more will be answered for those that are willing to take time out from their sports and favorite pastimes, and devote a few hours to sincerely seeking the knowledge of God. God declares that people will be destroyed for lack of knowledge. This book can prevent that from happening to you.

This book was written to give you, the reader, an in-depth understanding of God, His Word, and His Master Plan for all mankind. This is possible only by taking an orderly look at the past, the present, and the foretold future of mankind. If for whatever reason you do not feel that you will read this entire book, begin with Part VII, which is entitled Prophecy. This will at least enable you to know, and to prepare for what is about to take place in this world. Afterwards, you will want to read this book in its entirety from the beginning, in order to fully understand God's "Truth."

NOTE

Unprescribed drugs, including alcohol, work to block the Voice of God from entering one's mind and heart.

CONTENTS

PART I
THE ETERNAL PAST—THE GREAT FLOOD

PART II
THE POST-FLOOD ERA—THE JEWS ENTER ISRAEL

PART III
THE NATION OF ISRAEL—THE ROMAN EMPIRE

PART IV
THE BIRTH OF JESUS—THE TRANSFIGURATION

PART V
THE TRANSFIGURATION—THE ASCENSION OF JESUS

PART VI
THE CHURCH AGE

PART VII
PROPHECY

THE BOOKS OF THE HOLY BIBLE
and their abbreviations

Old Testament

Book	Abbr.	Book	Abbr.
Genesis	Gen.	Ecclesiates	Eccl.
Exodus	Ex.	Song of Solomon	Song
Leviticus	Lev.	Isaiah	Is.
Numbers	Num.	Jeremiah	Jer.
Deuteronomy	Deut.	Lamentations	Lam.
Joshua	Josh.	Ezekiel	Ezek.
Judges	Judg.	Daniel	Dan.
Ruth	Ruth	Hosea	Hos.
I Samuel	I Sam.	Joel	Joel
II Samuel	II Sam.	Amos	Amos
I Kings	I Kin.	Obadiah	Obad.
II Kings	II Kin.	Jonah	Jon.
I Chronicles	I Chr.	Micah	Mic.
II Chronicles	II Chr.	Nahum	Nah.
Ezra	Ezra	Habakkuk	Hab.
Nehemiah	Neh.	Zephaniah	Zeph.
Esther	Esth.	Haggai	Hag.
Job	Job	Zechariah	Zech.
Psalms	Ps.	Malachi	Mal.
Proverbs	Prov.		

New Testament

Book	Abbr.	Book	Abbr.
St. Matthew	Matt.	I Timothy	I Tim.
St. Mark	Mark	II Timothy	II Tim.
St. Luke	Luke	Titus	Titus
St. John	John	Philemon	Philem.
The Acts	Acts	Hebrews	Heb.
Romans	Rom.	James	James
I Corinthians	I Cor.	I Peter	I Pet.
II Corinthians	II Cor.	II Peter	II Pet.
Galatians	Gal.	I John	I John
Ephesians	Eph.	II John	II John
Philippians	Phil.	III John	III John
Colossians	Col.	Jude	Jude
I Thessalonians	I Thess.	Revelation	Rev.
II Thessalonians	II Thess.		

PART I

THE ETERNAL PAST—
THE GREAT FLOOD

THE ETERNAL PAST— THE GREAT FLOOD

ONE GOD

The fact that various people worship different gods in different parts of the world does not change the fact that there is only ONE, TRUE, LIVING, LOVING, and ALL POWERFUL GOD. All other gods do not have the breath of life in them. They cannot give life, and are therefore nothing more than foolish imaginations, without power and without purpose. That the True God is the God of the Holy Bible is evidenced by the fact that only God could have revealed what took place before the existence of man, and could have foretold what would happen to man from the time of his creation through the end of this Age, into the next Age, and into Eternity. Everything that God said was going to happen has happened, and will happen exactly as He said it would. When one looks at the facts, he will see that there is no other god like the True God. The True and Living God is a Just God Who has a definite plan and purpose for all those that put their faith in Him. Knowledge of God and of His Master Plan is the most important and the only life-saving knowledge that one can obtain while on this earth. This knowledge can be found only in the inspired Word of God, the Holy Bible.

ONE SOURCE OF TRUTH

The Holy Bible is the only book that reveals the One and Only True God. The Jews of Judaism, the Christians of Christendom, and the Muslims of Islam all believe that the God of creation, mentioned in the first part of the Holy Bible, is in fact the One True God. However, they do not agree as to His True Identity. History, science, archaeology, ancient manuscripts, and fulfilled ancient prophecies reveal God's True Identity and prove beyond a doubt that the Holy Bible is the written Word of God.

Yes, God Himself is the Author of the Holy Bible. How? "Holy men of God spoke as they were moved by the Holy Ghost" (II Pet. 1:21).

OLD AND NEW TESTAMENTS

The Holy Bible is comprised of two main sections. The first section is the Old Testament, which was originally written in the Hebrew and Aramaic languages. This portion of God's WORD tells us about life before the human race, and sets the foundation that is necessary for a complete understanding of God and of His Master Plan. In the second portion of God's Word, which is called the New Testament, we will see the fulfillment of God's greatest prophecies. These prophecies were made and recorded thousands of years earlier in the Old Testament. God intended for us to see these fulfilled prophecies, so that we could know without a doubt that He is the True God, and that the Holy Bible is His WORD.

NOTE

As we begin our journey, I would like to mention that we are going to cover a lot of material in a brief manner. Because of this, you will be given the name of the book of the Holy Bible, the number of the chapter, and the number of the verse from which the information given was derived. This will enable you to easily locate the scripture (in parenthesis) and read it for yourself in more detail. God instructed man to search the scriptures (John 5:39), so that he does not get led astray by false teachings. The Holy Bible begins with two accounts of the creation. The first chapter gives us a broad description, while the second chapter gives us a more detailed account of how our male and female human race originated.

FROM THE ETERNAL PAST

The first verse of the Holy Bible tells us that in the beginning, or from the eternal past, God created the heavens and the earth (Gen. 1:1). As we can see, God begins His WORD by revealing to us that He existed from the eternal past. The word "God" that is used in this passage is derived from the Hebrew word "Elohim," which is a plural noun. As we will learn, God's Oneness is made up of

One Mind, One Soul, and One Spirit Body. Elohim is the general name of God used in connection with creation and other acts of God. Angels are referred to as sons of Elohim, because they were created by Elohim to serve and to worship Him. God tells us in His WORD that the angels sang and shouted for joy when the earth was created (Job 38:4–7). This means that God created the angels before He created the earth.

EARTH BECOMES WASTE

The second verse of the Holy Bible tells us that "the earth was without form and void" (Gen. 1:2). This could have been translated: "the earth became waste and empty." How could this be? God's WORD declares that the earth was not created "in vain" (Is. 45:18). The Hebrew word for "in vain" is the same word used in the second verse of the Holy Bible meaning "waste." God did not create the earth in the wasteful condition in which it appears in verse two. If He had, the angels surely would not have sung together and shouted for joy. Let's learn why and how the earth was brought from its perfect condition in verse one to its chaotic condition in verse two.

LUCIFER

Lucifer, whose name means "light-giver," was a specially created cherub. This angelic being was created full of wisdom, in perfect beauty, and was adorned with precious stones. He also had musical instruments prepared in him when he was created. Lucifer was anointed by God to serve Him, which means he was near God's Throne. Lucifer was perfect until unrighteousness was found in him (Ezek. 28:15). The moment Lucifer sinned against God, he became Satan the devil. The name Satan means enemy or adversary. Note that God did not create the devil. Lucifer, the perfectly created head angel, became the devil when he decided to rebel against God. God gave individual minds both to angels and to humans, with the freedom to choose their path in life. Lucifer was in charge of spreading God's Light, which is the Knowledge of God, to the first inhabitants of the earth. When he became jealous of God and wanted to be like God, he led these inhabitants away from God. The earth was then brought to the wasteful and empty condition found in the second verse of the Holy Bible.

SIN OF PRIDE

God tells us in His Word that Lucifer's heart became exalted, or proud, due to his beauty, and that he corrupted his wisdom (Ezek. 28:17). In order to understand this, we must first consider the fact that it is in one's heart where the true image of one's mind is found. This image or hidden man of one's heart is known as his soul. Due to the fact that one's heart is at the center of one's mind, the condition of one's soul is determined by the thoughts and desires of one's mind. A wise man's heart is surrounded by, centered in, and inspired by Godly thoughts and desires. Instead of thinking about God, Satan began to think about himself. He said in his heart that he would raise his throne above the stars of God, and would be likened to the Most High (Is. 14:13–14). His throne was no longer good enough for him. He no longer wanted to exalt God, but rather to exalt himself so that he could be worshipped as God.

SATAN'S SPIRIT SPREADS

As an angel of light, Lucifer spread the Knowledge of God. As an angel of darkness, Satan became the father of "the lie," and began to deceive and to turn others away from the True God. He did this by accusing God, and by getting others to focus on self instead of on God. Satan through his lies was able to deceive and to lead one-third of God's angels in a failing attempt to exalt his throne above the stars of God (Rev. 12:4). This revolt marked the beginning of a spiritual war that would enter into and continue within the human race.

EARTH RESTORED

As we continue with the second verse in the first chapter of Genesis, we read that the earth was not only waste and empty, but that it was covered with water. Here we learn that the earth had been flooded. In verse three, God said "Let there be light," as His Holy Spirit moved upon the face of the waters. The Holy Spirit is the Ever-Present, All-Knowing, and All-Powerful Spirit Body of God, Who makes manifest what is spoken by God. Verses 9, 11, 14, 20, 24, and 26 all begin with the words: "And God said, Let." The word "let" is a word of command which God used as He directed

His Holy Spirit to renew the earth for a new race of inhabitants, the human race.

TWO KINGDOMS

God does not reveal to us the number of years that Lucifer ruled the earth before he became Satan the devil, or the number of years that elapsed after this event before He renewed the earth and created our human race. After defeating Satan and his followers, God allowed them to remain until a predetermined future date, in order to give the human race the opportunity to individually choose between serving Him and serving Satan. Those that abide in God's Holy Spirit will become His children, and will inherit eternal life in His Kingdom. Those that continue to follow Satan's spirit, which is the spirit of this world, will be his children, and will spend eternity in his kingdom. The existence of Satan is a fact that must never be taken lightly.

THE CREATION OF MAN

After the earth was restored, God said: "Let us make man in our image and after our likeness" (Gen. 1:26). Notice God said, "Let us" make man. As was mentioned, God's Fullness is made up of One Mind, One Soul (True Image), and One Spirit. The "Oneness" of these Realities is confirmed by the fact that God said, "in our image and after our likeness." God did not say, "In our images" and "after our likenesses." As we will clearly understand, God has one image and one likeness. In Gen. 2:7, we read that the LORD God formed man from the dust of the ground.

THE LORD GOD

Notice the word "LORD" appears in front of God in the previous verse. This name appears as "YHWH" in the original Hebrew, and is used approximately 7,000 times in the Holy Bible. This name, which was once considered too sacred to be spoken, came out as "Yayweh" when the vowels were added, and would later be translated into English as Jehovah, which means the True God Who reveals Himself. "LORD" is the name of God used in connection with the creation of man, and with God's early communications with man.

MAN COMES ALIVE

After the LORD God formed man from the dust of the ground, He breathed the breath of life into man's nostrils, and man became a living soul (Gen. 2:7). God imparted life to man's body of dust by breathing into his nostrils, at which time man's spirit was formed within his body (Zec. 12:1). Man's spirit was created in the image and after the likeness of the LORD God. God is the Spirit (John 4:24) of Love (I John 4:8). As we will learn, God chose to reveal Himself to the world through the True and Eternal Image of His Eternal Mind of Love. Man's spirit mind also has an image which reveals one's true identity, and is known as man's soul. Every spirit mind and soul are one, and belong to the Giver of Life, the LORD God (Ezek. 18:4). When man's physical body dies, his spirit returns to God (Luke 8:55).

CREATION VS. EVOLUTION

It was the LORD God Who imparted and gave life to man and every living thing. This agrees with the law of biogenesis, which states that life comes only from other life. Thus, life cannot come from non-life. There are many who do not want to accept this truth. This group includes those that want to live as they please, without having to acknowledge and answer to their Creator. For this reason and for the lack of Godly Knowledge, many choose to believe in evolution, which is nothing more than an unproved scientific theory. It takes blind faith to believe that the heavens with their awesome solar systems, and the earth with all its living plants and living creatures, including mankind, all came together without plan or purpose. Can one honestly believe that a bunch of dead elements came together without any intellect and just happened to form God's vast universe, which is far beyond the human mind's ability to comprehend? The truth is that the LORD God created all things, including scientific knowledge. He alone understands all things. God's Word tells us that those that turn towards man for the answers to life's problems, and turn their hearts away from the LORD God are cursed (Jer. 17:5). Man was created to turn to his Creator for all his needs, and not to man-made theories, philosophies, ideologies, and religions. Those that repent (change their minds) and choose to call upon the

Name of the LORD God, which He revealed to us, will be saved from this curse.

MAN AND WOMAN

The LORD God took the man whom He had created, put him in a garden which He had planted in Eden, and told him to dress (cultivate) it and to keep (guard) it. There, the LORD God made every tree that is pleasant to the sight and good for food to spring up. In the middle of this garden was the "tree of life," and also the "tree of the knowledge of good and evil." The LORD God commanded the man to eat freely of every tree except the tree of the knowledge of good and evil, of which he was emphatically told that he may not eat, for in the day that he would eat of it, he would surely die (Gen. 2:17). The LORD God then brought all the birds, the cattle, and the beasts that He had created to the man, to see what he would call them, and that became their names. Seeing that the man did not have a suitable helper, the LORD God caused the man to fall into a deep sleep, and took out one of his ribs. From this rib, the LORD God formed a woman, and brought her to the man. The man and his wife were both naked, and they were not ashamed.

ADAM

The day the LORD God created man and his wife, He called their name Adam (Gen. 5:2). They were both called Adam and the LORD God told them to multiply, and to replenish or refill the earth (Gen. 1:28). This confirms the fact that the earth was inhabited before it was made waste and empty, and prior to its renewal and the creation of the human race. The LORD God also told them to subdue the earth, and to have dominion over all living things in the land, in the sea, and in the air. Man was given rule over all of the LORD God's lesser creatures.

THE SABBATH

The heavens and the earth, along with everything in them, were finished in six days (Gen. 2:1–2). The Hebrew word translated as finished also means made ready. The LORD God finished His creation and rested from His labor on the seventh day, which He blessed and made holy. When the LORD God looked at everything that He had created and prepared, He saw that it was very good (Gen. 1:31). Now that the earth was renewed and the human race was created, the LORD God would continue to personally talk to and develop a personal relationship with His creation.

A BEAUTIFUL LIFE

When Adam was first created, he looked towards the LORD God with faith and obedience. As long as Adam trusted and yielded to the Word of God, he had perfect health, peace, and happiness. Imagine what a beautiful life this first couple had. They could joyfully come into God's presence, and talk freely to the LORD without any guilt or shame. With their eyes and minds focused on the LORD God, they were led by God on the perfect road of life, and were given access to the "tree of life." The Hebrew word "life," used in the tree of life, means to remain alive, to sustain life, and to be well. As long as Adam and his wife had access to this tree, they would never age or become sick. They would live forever in perfect health. This tree, as we will learn, still exists and will be accessible to those that obey the Word of the LORD God. Man has always been rewarded for listening to and being obedient to the Word of God. Those that choose to walk with the LORD God receive the LORD's blessings, which are called fruit of the Spirit (Gal. 5:22–23). These blessings include love, joy, peace, longsuffering, gentleness, goodness, faith, meekness, and temperance.

SATAN'S GOAL

As we learned, Satan and his followers were allowed to temporarily remain in the world to test man. Satan, being jealous of God, was probably filled with rage when he saw the renewed earth and the loving relationship that the LORD God had with His newly-created man. In his wisdom, Satan knew that if he could get Adam's mind off God, and get Adam to obey him by disobeying God, he could gain control of man's spirit and become his new master. Man can serve only one master (Matt. 6:24). Satan knows he is a defeated foe, and is working hard to deceive and to destroy as many souls as he can before he himself is destroyed. He is doing this by deceiving many into disregarding God's commandments, which are written in the Holy Bible.

ADAM SINS

Satan entered into and used the serpent as the vessel through which he would confront man. The serpent was at that time the most cunning beast in the garden (Gen. 3:1). Satan planned to destroy man by getting him to obey him, and to disobey the LORD God by eating of the forbidden fruit. One day the serpent asked Adam's wife if God had told her that she could not eat of every tree. She told him that she could eat fruit from all the trees, except the fruit from the tree in the middle of the garden, and that if she even touched this fruit, she would die (Gen. 3:3). Satan first accused God of being a liar by telling her that she would not die. He then lied and tempted her by telling her that if she and Adam ate of this fruit, they would become as gods, knowing good and evil. Instead of remaining loyal to God for all His blessings, and rejecting Satan's temptation, the woman allowed Satan's words to enter her heart. She did this by dwelling on Satan's lie, which was that she and her husband could become like gods by eating of the forbidden fruit. She then hardened her heart towards God and yielded to Satan's temptation. After eating of the fruit, she gave some to her husband and he also ate of it (Gen. 3:6). Adam was not deceived (I Tim. 2:14). He ate of the fruit to please his wife. One must never put wife, husband, parents, children, relatives, friends, or anyone else before the LORD God.

SHAME AND FEAR

The first thing that happened after Adam and his wife sinned is that their eyes were opened to the fact that they were naked. Being self-conscious of their naked bodies, they made aprons of fig leaves and covered themselves (Gen. 3:7). Along with shame, fear entered the human race. Man's perfect peace was now gone. Later, when the LORD God called unto Adam, he was afraid and was hiding because he was naked (Gen. 3:10). When asked about the forbidden fruit, Adam blamed his wife, and his wife blamed the serpent. God would punish them both because they both disobeyed Him. When it comes to the LORD God's judgment, all excuses and blaming others will be in vain. We will all be judged by God's WORD, and should therefore not believe everything we hear. Instead, we should search the scriptures daily, as did the early church (Acts 17:11), to check whether what we hear is indeed according to God's Word. Sadly, many do not take the time to do this, and are therefore being led astray by false teachers, who are only concerned with filling their bellies (Rom. 16:18). God also tells us in His WORD that people are destroyed for lack of knowledge (Hos. 4:6). This is why those that receive God's "Truth" are commanded to tell others, so they too may be saved from God's coming judgment.

GOD CURSES SERPENT

God began His judgment by placing a curse on the serpent which Satan possessed in order to deceive man. The LORD God told the serpent that he would now have to crawl on his belly, and eat dust for the rest of his life. Evidently, the serpent could stand up and walk when it was first created, and before it became a vessel for Satan the devil (Gen. 3:14).

GOD JUDGES SATAN

The LORD God told the serpent that He would put hate between him and the woman, and between his offspring and the woman's offspring. The LORD God said that the woman's seed would trample upon the serpent's head and that the serpent would bruise its heel (Gen. 3:15). This would happen when the LORD God would come into this world through the seed of Adam's wife, and defeat Satan and death. He would then give those that believe in Him the power to do the same. The apostle Paul said that the God of peace would soon crush Satan, and that the feet of those that follow God would trample upon Satan and his demons (Rom. 16:20).

WOMAN PUNISHED

The LORD God then told the woman that He would multiply her sorrow, and that she would now have birth pangs during her pregnancy. She was also told by the LORD that the man would now be the head of the family, and that her desires would be to please her husband (Gen. 3:16). Adam now called his wife Eve, which means the mother of the multitudes. Due to the fact that the woman sinned first and caused the man to sin, the man became the spiritual head of the family. Many men have twisted this scripture for the purpose of manipulating their wives into doing things against their will, and against the Will of God. A wife must put the LORD God before her desires, and also before the desires of her husband.

MAN PUNISHED

The LORD God told Adam that because he obeyed his wife instead of Him, the ground would be cursed. Man would now have to face obstacles and struggles during his life. He would now have to sweat in order to make a living for his family, and would then die and return to the ground from which he was made (Gen. 3:17–19). As the head of his household, the man was given the responsibility of leading his family in the path of righteousness, according to the Will of God. As illustrated in the case of Adam, a man's desires, as well as his wife's and family's, must never be put before the Will of God.

DEATH PENALTY

The LORD God told man that if he ate of the forbidden fruit he would surely die. The LORD God does not lie. He drove man out of the garden of Eden (Gen. 3:24), which meant that he could no longer have access to the tree of life, which sustained man's physical life and well-being. Thus, from the moment in which man sinned and was removed from the garden, he began to age and to lose his perfect health.

A LOVING GOD

The LORD God showed His Love for man by seeking Adam and Eve after they had sinned. He could have destroyed them, but the truth is that He never stopped loving man. It was and is the disobedience to His Will, known as sin, that the LORD God hates. God saw that Adam and Eve were both sorry and ashamed for what they had done. They were also afraid of God, which is the beginning of all wisdom (Prov. 9:10). Because of this, the LORD God forgave them. As we will learn, God Personally provided the

"Way" through which all mankind could once again be clothed in the Righteousness of God, and enter freely into His Presence.

MAN'S SECOND CHANCE

Yes, the LORD God gave man a second chance to live with Him in perfect peace and happiness for all eternity. As we learned, the LORD God told man that he would surely die if he ate of the forbidden fruit. God never lies. While on this earth, man's physical body will one day die. At this time man's ghost, which is his spirit mind and its image, known as man's soul, will return to the LORD God. If, at this time, one's soul is clothed in the Righteousness of God, he will be rewarded with a new, glorified body, which will be able to partake of the tree of life and live in perfect peace and happiness with the LORD God for all eternity. The souls of those that either rejected or neglected to receive the Righteousness of God will face the second death. This means that they will be eternally separated from God, and shall have their part in the lake of fire (Rev. 21:8), where there will be torment, day and night, for ever and ever (Rev. 20:10).

JUSTIFICATION

In order for a man's soul to be justified, which means to be found righteous in the eyes of God, it has to be free from all sin. In order for this to happen, one must repent, which means to change one's mind about sin, turn from his evil ways, and accept the LORD God's "Way," while he is still alive on this earth. Only then can one's soul be found righteous, and be justified to enter into the Eternal Kingdom of the LORD God upon one's physical death.

COATS OF SKIN

After Adam and Eve repented of their sin, the LORD God forgave them, and clothed them with coats of skin before removing them from the garden (Gen. 3:21). In order for these coats of skin to be made, the innocent blood of animals had to be shed and exchanged for the sin of man. The LORD God taught man that the life of all flesh is in the blood, and it is the blood that maketh an atonement for sin (Lev. 17:11). To "make atonement for" means to "cover one's sin." This was possible at that time only by offering the LORD God a sinless life, in the blood of a spotless animal sacrifice, in exchange for the covering of one's sin.

SIN ENTERS ALL MANKIND

Due to the fact that Adam was the first man on this earth (I Cor. 15:45), the sin in his life, which was in his blood, would enter into and infect the human race. As a result of Adam's sin, his offspring would never be able to trace back a spotless family relationship to the LORD God. Thus, all mankind became infected through Adam (Rom. 5:12). Everyone would now have to be washed by a blood sacrifice, in order for their soul to be found righteous when it returns to God. Even though God never received pleasure in animal sacrifices (Heb. 10:6), He instituted it to teach man the consequences of sin, and to prepare mankind for the LORD God's Ultimate Sacrifice, which would become the only "Way" through which man could be justified.

CAIN AND ABEL

Cain and Abel were sons of Adam and Eve. Cain, a tiller of the ground, offered the LORD God a fruit offering for the forgiveness of his sin. Abel, a keeper of sheep, offered his best lamb as a sacrifice for his sin. The LORD God accepted Abel's offering because it contained a spotless life, which was in the blood of this innocent lamb. The LORD God refused Cain's offering because it was not a blood offering. After this, Cain killed his brother Abel in a rage of anger and jealousy (Gen. 4:8). The LORD God then told Cain that the voice of his brother's blood crieth unto Him from the ground, and because of this, he would be cursed from the earth which received his brother's blood. The earth would no longer yield its fruit unto Cain. Cain's grandson would also commit a murder, as man began to grow worse and worse.

SETH AND ENOS

Eve then gave birth to another son, who the LORD God told her would replace the seed of Abel. This son was named Seth. Seth had the image and likeness of his father Adam, who repented of his sin and loved the LORD God. Seth would later have a son whom he would name Enos. This name denotes weakness and helplessness. At this time, as things grew worse, mankind realized that they needed the LORD God's help, and began to call upon the name of the LORD (Gen. 4:26). God has always desired to be man's friend, and for man to willfully use his mind to seek Him. The LORD would then begin to reveal Himself to man as a Rewarder to all that sincerely seek Him (Heb. 11:6).

NOTE

The Lord God gave man a mind so that he could use it to know Him. Man can serve the LORD God only by using his mind to meditate on God's Word and to communicate with God's Spirit (Rom. 7:25). This is why drunkenness and drug abuse are abominations to the LORD God. Satan's spirit encourages these because they weaken man's mind and conscience. As a result, many commit crimes and acts that they would not normally commit.

SATAN'S SPIRIT SPREADS

As Satan's spirit spread, men became more and more disobedient to the LORD God, their Creator. As we learned, the LORD God told Satan that he was going to get crushed by the seed of Eve. Satan therefore planned to utterly destroy the human race before he himself would be destroyed, as the LORD God had told him. In his wisdom, Satan knew that only God Himself could destroy him, and that He would use a righteous virgin to enter into this world. To prevent this from happening, Satan led some of his fallen angels in an attempt to completely destroy Eve's seed, the human race. Satan's angels began to possess the bodies of men, and to marry the women, after whom they lusted (Gen. 6:2). These women bore evil-spirited children, who became mighty and controlled the earth (Gen. 6:4). When the LORD God saw how polluted the human race had become, He was grieved and felt like destroying man until He looked at Noah, who found grace in His eyes (Gen. 6:8).

NOAH

Noah was the only righteous man that walked with the LORD God in this time of corruption. It seems that Noah and some of his family were the only ones who were not physically contaminated by the corrupt seed of Satan. After seeing that every imagination of the thoughts of man's heart was only evil continually, the LORD God told Noah that He would destroy the people and everything on the earth with a great flood. He instructed Noah to build an ark, and then to enter it along with his family, two of the various animals, birds, and creatures, and food for him and the animals. Noah did everything just as the LORD God had commanded him (Gen. 6:9–22).

THE FLOOD

After Noah did as he was commanded, the LORD God shut him and the others in the ark. For forty days and forty nights, the flood kept coming on the earth. As the waters increased, they lifted the ark high above the earth. Every person and every living thing that was left on the earth died (Gen. 7:21). When the rains stopped and the waters receded, the LORD God told Noah, his wife, his three sons, and their wives to come out, and to bring out all the animals so that they could multiply. Noah then built an altar and sacrificed burnt offerings unto the LORD God. The LORD told Noah that He would never again flood the earth, and that His rainbow in the clouds would serve as the sign of this agreement between Him and man and every living creature with man (Gen. 9:13).

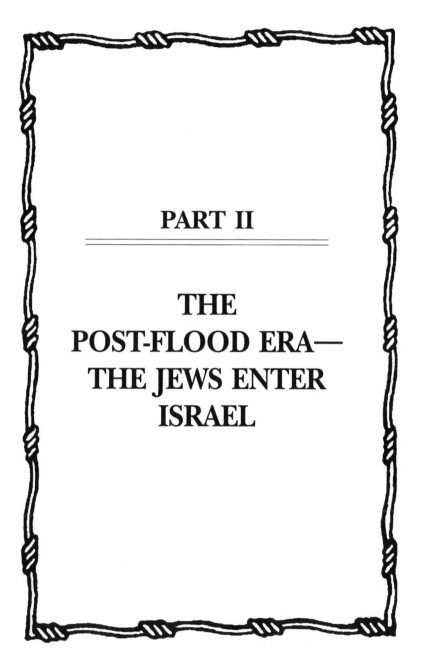

PART II

THE POST-FLOOD ERA— THE JEWS ENTER ISRAEL

THE POST-FLOOD ERA—
THE JEWS ENTER ISRAEL

BIBLE HISTORY

Historically speaking, the Holy Bible is the most ancient and also the most modern history book in the world. Archeological discoveries are constantly confirming its accuracy and its authenticity. By telling us about the time preceding the creation of man, and also about the time from the creation of man unto the near and eternal future, the God of the Holy Bible has proven beyond a doubt that He is the True God of the universe. Only by traveling historically through the Holy Bible can one attain a clear view of God's Master Plan, and have peace and joy in knowing that everything that is happening this very day is right on schedule, and is drawing us one step closer to a new and glorious age.

PEOPLE & NATIONS MULTIPLY

The sons of Noah who came out of the ark with their wives were Shem, Ham, and Japheth. As the years passed and the earth's population increased, nations began to develop. Japheth's descendants spread toward the northern coastal areas of the Caspian, Black, and Mediterranean seas. Ham's descendants moved southward and populated the Egyptian, Canaanite, and Arabian nations. The Canaanite area was to become the land of Israel. Shem's descendants initially spread eastward to the region of Mesopotamia, between the Tigris and the Euphrates rivers. It was through Shem's seed that Abraham, the father of the Hebrew nation, was to be born.

HAM'S DESCENDANTS CURSED

Noah planted a vineyard and made wine. One day, after becoming drunk, Noah was disrespected by his youngest son,

Ham. Because of this, Noah said that the Canaanites, which were the descendants of Ham, would be servants to Shem's descendants (Gen. 9:20–26). It is evident that Ham's son, named Canaan, was not worshipping the True God because Noah said, "Blessed be the LORD God of Shem." As we will learn, the original inhabitants of Israel, the Canaanites, Hittites, Jebusites, and Amorites, who were descendants of Ham, would come into conflict with the Hebrews, which were descendants of Shem. This conflict has continued unto this present day.

DIFFERENT LANGUAGES AND RACES

Nimrod, a descendant of Ham, became mighty near the year 2500 B.C. At this time, when sin began to abound once again, Nimrod began his kingdom in a plain in the land of Shimar, called Babel or Babylon. The people here wanted to make a name for themselves. Instead of wanting to please and to exalt the Name of God, they wanted the world to marvel after them. As a result of their pride, they decided to build a huge tower so that others would praise them. When God looked down and saw how they united together without acknowledging Him, He confounded their languages. When this happened, those working on the tower were changed, and began to talk different languages. This made it impossible for them to communicate with one another and to complete the tower. God then scattered them abroad upon the face of all the earth (Gen. 11:1–9).

ABRAM

Two years after the great flood, Shem became the father of Arphaxad. It was through the seed of Arphaxad, in the approximate year of 1900 B.C., that Terah became the father of Abram (Gen. 11:26). Abram married Sarai, who was barren and could not have children. Terah took Abram, Sarai, and his grandson Lot from the land of Ur and settled in the land of Haran, where Terah would die. Abram chose to obey God and because of this, God chose to reveal Himself in a personal way to Abram and to his descendants, the Hebrew people. We must all be grateful and loving towards the people and the nation of Israel, for it was through them that God chose to reveal Himself and His Master Plan to all the world. As others were worshipping false gods and idols, holy men from this nation had fellowship with the LORD God, and recorded God's Word for the benefit of all mankind.

THE LORD CALLS ABRAM

The LORD told Abram to leave his homeland, his kindred, and his father's house and to follow Him. The LORD made a covenant (an agreement) with Abram. The LORD told Abram that if he obeyed Him, He would make him a great nation, bless him, and make his name great. The LORD also told Abram that He would bless those that bless him, and curse those that curse him (Gen. 12:1–3). Without knowing where God was going to take him, Abram obeyed God. He left his home with Sarai, his wife, with Lot, his nephew, and with their herds and herdsmen. When they reached the plain of Moreh, the LORD appeared unto Abram and told him that He would give this land, which was occupied at that time by the Canaanites, unto his descendants. There, Abram built an altar unto the LORD (Gen. 12:6–7). This land is called the "Promise Land," because the LORD promised it to Abram's descendants.

NOTE

In the King James version of the Holy Bible, when you see "LORD" or "GOD" with all capital letters, this is the translation of Yayweh, which as we learned was later translated into English as Jehovah. When you see "Lord" with just the letter "L" capitalized, this is the translation of "Adonai." Adonai recognizes God as Master, Ruler, and Owner of mankind. When we see God with just the "G" capitalized, this is the translation of "Elohim." Elohim is the name of God which is used in general with angels and God's creative works. When the "Word" of the LORD came to Abram in a vision, Abram acknowledged the LORD as his Master by addressing Him as "Adonai" (Gen. 15:2).

BIRTH OF ISHMAEL

The LORD told Abram that he would have a son, that his descendants would be slaves in another land for four hundred years, and that they would then return with great wealth to the Promise Land (Gen. 15:1–15). As the years passed, Abram and

Sarai became concerned because they still did not have any children to inherit God's Promise Land. Sarai was convinced that she could not have children. For this reason, she told Abram to take her handmaid, Hagar, as a second wife, and to have a child with her. Abram did this and Ishmael was born through Hagar.

BIRTH OF ISAAC

Thirteen years later, as Abram and Sarai were approaching their death, the LORD appeared unto Abram and told him that He was El-Shaddai, which means God Almighty. The LORD wanted Abram to know that He and God Almighty are One, and that there is nothing impossible unto Him. As the LORD told this to Abram, He removed the deadness from Abram and Sarai, and changed their names to Abraham and Sarah. He then told them that they would have a son, and that through his seed, and not the seed of Ishmael, would He establish His covenant. God fulfilled His promise and Isaac was born to Abraham and Sarah (Gen. 21:3). It was through the seed of Isaac that God would reveal Himself to all mankind. God had allowed Abram and Sarai to get old before Isaac was born. This was so that they and the world would know that God alone fulfills His promises. Instead of believing that God would give them a son, Abram and Sarai tried to help God fulfill His promise in the case of Ishmael. This time, however, they were emptied of their physical self-sufficiency, and relied totally on the LORD, Who then blessed them with Isaac. Notice that it was when they looked towards the LORD for their strength that they met Him as El-Shaddai, and He became their Lord (Adonai), or Master. It was then that they were given new names, as every newly-born child of God is given when they leave the mindset of this world and enter into the Spirit of God.

SODOM AND GOMORRAH

During this time, the cities of Sodom and Gomorrah, located in the Jordan Plain, had become filled with violence and immorality. Because of this, the LORD sent two angels to destroy these cities. When the angels told Abraham about their plan to destroy Sodom and Gomorrah, Abraham began to worry about Lot and his family, who lived there. He asked the LORD if He would spare these cities if just ten righteous people were living in them. The

LORD said that He would. The two angels then went to Sodom and told Lot that the city would be destroyed. Evidently there were not ten righteous people to be found there. Lot went and warned his sons-in-law to be, but they did not take him seriously. At dawn, the two angels took the hands of Lot, his wife, and their two daughters and led them out of the city. Once out of the city, one of the angels told them to flee and not to look back. As they reached the town of Zoar, the Lord rained down burning sulfur on Sodom and Gomorrah. When Lot's wife disobeyed the angel and looked back, she became a pillar of salt (Gen. 19:26). Many people today ask how God can allow so much suffering to happen on this earth. The answer to this question is two-fold. First, God is giving sinful man the time to repent, and secondly He has spared the nations because of the righteous people dwelling in them. As we will learn, there is an event which is nearing, referred to in God's Word as the Day of the Lord, in which God's Wrath will fall on an unrepentant world.

GOD TESTS ABRAHAM

Now that Abraham was calling God "Lord," God would test his love, faith, and obedience. God told Abraham to take his son up upon a hill, in the land of Moriah, and to offer him unto Him as a burnt offering (Gen. 22:2). Abraham obeyed and led Isaac up upon this hill. Isaac carried the wood for the offering, while Abraham carried the fire and the knife. When Isaac asked his father where the lamb was for the burnt offering, Abraham told him that God would provide Himself a lamb. When they came to the place which God had told him, Abraham built an altar, laid in the wood, and then bound Isaac and laid him on the altar. As Abraham stretched forth his hand and took the knife, the angel of the LORD told him not to lay a hand on Isaac. When Abraham looked back, he saw a ram caught in a thicket by his horns. Abraham took the ram and offered it instead of his son. Abraham called the name of that place Jehovah-jireh, which means: "God will be seen" and "God will provide."

BIRTH OF ISRAEL

Because Abraham chose to obey God, God would fulfill His promise with him by making his descendants, through Isaac, heirs

to the Promise Land. Thus, Abraham became the first member of
what was to become the Jewish race and the nation of Israel. God
would now begin to reveal Himself to the entire world through
these, His chosen people, as He would meet their every need on
their journey to possessing the Promise Land. Various Old Testament Names were used to reveal the LORD as He met the various
needs of His people. Holy men of God were inspired and
instructed to record these Names and events, in order that all
mankind could know the True, Loving, and Living God, and
could know that He is able and will meet these same needs for all
those who call upon His Name. Those that call upon the Lord and
receive His Holy Spirit will have the Power to become children of
God and inherit His Eternal Kingdom.

JEHOVAH-JIREH

As we learned, the LORD (Jehovah) God is the True God
that reveals Himself. The compound names of Jehovah God used
in the Old Testament describe the various needs that the LORD
God met in the lives of His children as they journeyed to the
Promise Land. These are the same needs He is meeting in the lives
of His children today. Jehovah-jireh describes man's greatest need.
Abraham called the place in which he took Isaac and sacrificed
the ram (which the LORD provided), Jehovah-jireh (Gen. 22:14),
which means God will be seen and God will provide. The
appearing of the ram is a shadow of God's future appearance in
the flesh, and of His Ultimate Sacrifice for the forgiveness of
man's sin. It would be in the exact place where Abraham saw and
sacrificed the ram that Jesus Christ would be seen bleeding to
death, after having His Hands and His Feet nailed to the Old
Rugged Cross. Every Name of Jehovah God points to Jesus Christ
and the various needs that He Alone can meet in the lives of men.
As the Name implies, Jehovah-jireh would be seen in the Person of
Jesus Christ, Who would provide Himself as the Only Perfect
Sacrifice capable of washing away all of man's sin (Acts 4:11). The
deep meanings of Old Testament sacrifice would become clear as
God continued to reveal the knowledge of His Truth and of His
Master Plan to mankind.

ISAAC MARRIES REBEKAH

After the death of his wife Sarah, Abraham sent his chief servant to the land of Mesopotamia to bring back a wife for Isaac. This was Abraham's native land and the place where his relatives lived. Abraham did not want Isaac to marry a girl from among the Canaanites, because they were worshipping idols and false pagan gods. When Abraham's servant arrived in Mesopotamia, he prayed for God to point out the right girl for Isaac. God answered his prayer. The girl's name was Rebekah (Gen. 24:15). After Abraham's servant showered her and her family with beautiful gifts, she returned with the servant, and married Isaac who fell in love with her.

TWIN BOYS

After the death of Abraham, Isaac was concerned because his wife could not have children. After praying to the LORD for his wife to have children, Rebekah became pregnant. The LORD told her that she had two nations in her womb, of which the elder would serve the younger (Gen. 25:21–23). When she delivered, she gave birth to twin boys. The first baby boy was named Esau, and the second baby boy, which was blessed, was named Jacob.

JACOB MARRIES RACHEL

Just as Abraham wanted Isaac to marry a God-worshipping girl, Isaac wanted his son to do the same. After being blessed by his father, Jacob set out for the land of Haran to take a wife. On one of his stops, he slept at a place he called Bethel. As he dreamt, he heard the Voice of the LORD introduce Himself as the LORD God of Abraham and Isaac. The LORD told him that the land where he was lying would belong to him and his descendants. God also told Jacob that he would protect him on his trip (Gen. 28:10–15). As Jacob approached the land of Haran, he met Rachel. He told Laban, Rachel's father, that he would serve him for seven years for Rachel. At the end of the seven years, Rachel's father tricked Jacob into marrying Leah, the elder of his two daughters. Leah would bear six sons to Jacob. Because Jacob loved Rachel, he agreed to serve Laban another seven years for her. At that time there were no laws in existence that limited a man to having just one wife.

Jacob and Rachel married, and named their first child Joseph. As Jacob was returning with his family to the Promise Land, he sent them across a stream and he was left alone. At this time Jacob had a spiritual experience, in which God changed his name to Israel (Gen. 32:28).

JOSEPH REACHES EGYPT

As we learned, God told Abraham in a dream that his descendants would be slaves in another land for four hundred years, and that they would then return to the Promise Land with great wealth (Gen. 15:1–15). This dream began to be fulfilled when Joseph, who was a special child, was sold by his jealous brothers to traders on their way to Egypt. Once in Egypt, Joseph was sold at a slave market to an Egyptian military leader. As time went on, and with the Hand of God guiding him, Joseph was made a ruler under Pharoah, king of Egypt. Later, Israel, Joseph's father, and his entire family would move to Egypt to be with Joseph, and to escape a famine that hit the land. It was here that Israel and his descendants, the Israelites, developed as a nation. It would also be here that both Israel and Joseph would die at an old age.

THE ISRAELITES BECOME SLAVES

While Joseph ruled in Egypt, the Hebrews, later known as Israelites, grew in number and became mighty. After the death of Joseph, a new Pharoah (king) arose in Egypt, who had not known Joseph, and who was afraid of the growing power of the Israelites. He appointed taskmasters over them and forced them to over-work, hoping to weaken them and to keep them from multiplying. Because the Israelites continued to multiply, Pharoah ordered his soldiers to throw every newborn Israelite male into the Nile River (Ex. 1:22).

BIRTH OF MOSES

At this time, an Israelite couple gave birth to a son, whom they hid from Pharoah's soldiers for three months. When they could no longer hide the child, they put him in a basket coated with tar and laid the basket in the reeds along the bank of the Nile. When Pharoah's daughter found the boy, she felt sorry for him. She unknowingly hired the baby boy's mother to nurse the baby for her until he was old enough for her to take him home. Pharoah's daughter adopted him and called him Moses. When Moses was grown, he went out and saw how poorly his fellow Hebrews were being treated by the Egyptians. One day, as he saw an Egyptian beating a Hebrew, he lost his temper and killed the Egyptian. When Pharoah heard of this, he sought to slay Moses, who managed to escape from Egypt to the land of Midian (Ex. 2:15).

GOD CALLS MOSES

While in the land of Midian, Moses married and lived there with his father-in-law. In time, the king of Egypt died and the new king worsened the conditions of the Israelites, who cried unto God for help. For this reason, the angel of the LORD appeared unto Moses in a flame of fire and in the midst of a burning bush on Mt. Sinai. The LORD God told Moses to go back to Egypt and to tell the Israelites that "I AM" (Ex. 3:14) sent him to deliver them from their bondage, and to bring them to the Promise Land. It is important to point out here that the eternal Spirit of Jesus Christ was at this time the Image of God's Word. In other words, it was the Spirit of Christ Who made God's thoughts known to Moses through the angel of the LORD. It was also the Spirit of Christ that enabled the early prophets to foretell that Christ would come as God in the Flesh, suffer for us, and then be Glorified (I Pet. 1:11). The Spirit of Christ is God's Soul, the True Image of God's Eternal Mind of Love, Who would reveal Himself in Jesus Christ, the Son of God.

MOSES RETURNS TO EGYPT

Moses did not feel he was qualified to go to Pharoah and lead the Israelites out of Egypt. The LORD assured Moses that He would be with him, and that he should return and worship God on this same mountain, which was Mt. Sinai. The LORD told Moses, who was concerned about his speech, that his brother Aaron could be his spokesman. The LORD then told Aaron to meet his brother Moses in the desert. When Moses returned to Egypt, he met Aaron in the desert and told him everything that the LORD had told him. Afterwards, they gathered all the elders of the

Israelites together, and Aaron told them that the Lord God of Abraham, of Isaac, and of Jacob (Israel) was going to free them and bring them out of Egypt. Moses then performed miraculous signs with his rod, as the LORD had instructed him, and the people believed (Ex. 4:31).

GOD'S JUDGMENTS ON EGYPT

Aaron and Moses then went to Pharoah. They told him what the LORD God of Israel had told them, and asked him to allow the Israelites to depart from Egypt. Pharoah refused. After God sent various plagues to the land of Egypt, Pharoah still refused to allow the Israelites to leave. They were good slaves, and he wanted them to stay and build his empire. The LORD then spoke to Moses and Aaron. He told them to tell all the Israelites that on the evening of the 14th day of the month, they should sacrifice a spotless lamb and apply some of its blood on the two side posts and on the upper doorpost of their houses. They obeyed and did as they were instructed. That night, the LORD passed through Egypt and smote the firstborn in every house (Ex. 12:29). Only those in the homes that were covered with the blood of a spotless sacrifice were saved from God's judgment. Pharoah, afraid that they would all be killed, told Moses and Aaron to take all the Israelites and their belongings, and to depart from Egypt. The LORD told the Israelites that they were to commemorate this day, called "Passover," in remembrance of the night that God passed over all those that were covered with the sacrificial blood of a spotless lamb. This is a shadow of God's coming judgment on those that are not covered with the Sacrificial Blood of Jesus Christ.

THE EXODUS

On that very day of Passover, the LORD led the Israelites out of Egypt. The LORD went ahead of them in a pillar of cloud by day, and in a pillar of fire at night. By following the LORD, the two million Israelites were led out of Egypt. As the LORD guided them towards the Red Sea, Pharoah regretted his decision to allow the Israelites to leave Egypt (Ex. 14:5). He had his chariot made ready, and pursued the Israelites along with his army and every chariot in Egypt. When the Israelites reached the Red Sea, Moses stretched out his hand over the sea. The LORD then parted the sea and made a dry path for the Israelites to pass through. When all the Israelites had passed through, Moses stretched out his hand over the sea and the waters flowed back, covering and destroying Pharoah and his entire army. Just as Pharoah led his armies into the depths of the sea, Satan has led, and is leading many into the depths of hell. When one repents of his sins and commits his life to the Lord Jesus Christ (the True Image of God's Invisible Spirit), his sins are cast into the depths of the sea (Mic. 7:19). Satan knows this, and is therefore doing all he can to keep man from knowing God's "Truth," Jesus Christ.

JEHOVAH-ROPHE

When the Israelites saw how the LORD saved them from the Egyptians, they feared and put their trust in the LORD. However, their faith and praise turned to doubt and murmuring when the first water they found in the wilderness, on their way to the Promise Land, was too bitter to drink. They now began to murmur, which means to mutter complaints. Moses then cried out to the LORD, and the LORD showed him a tree which, when he cast it into the waters, made the waters sweet. The LORD then instructed Moses to tell the Israelites that if they were obedient to Him, He would not bring any of the diseases upon them that He brought upon the Egyptians, for He was Jehovah-Rophe, the LORD that healeth (Ex. 15:26). Just as the Israelites ran into bitter waters on their way to the Promise Land, we also will experience bitter things in our daily walk towards the Kingdom of God. Jesus Christ, Who was nailed to a wooden cross, heals life's bitter waters and changes them to sweet living waters. As we will learn, in a twinkling of an eye, every child of God will be given a new, glorified body and will live in perfect peace, health, and happiness for all eternity.

ISRAEL BLAMES MOSES

As the Israelites continued their journey, they murmured against Moses. They remembered how much food they had had in Egypt, and wondered if the LORD was really with them. Because of this, the LORD began to rain manna (a type of bread) from heaven every morning, and quail every evening for them to eat. They gathered twice as much bread on the sixth day, so that they could rest on the Sabbath (Ex. 16:21–22). When they reached

Rephidim, there was no water to drink, and the Israelites once again began to murmur against Moses. The LORD then told Moses to smite the rock in Horeb with his rod. When he did, water came out, and the people did drink. God was teaching man to put their faith in Him, and to come to Him with their requests.

AN ENEMY ARRIVES

Shortly after God provided water for the Israelites, they were attacked by the Amalekites. This was the first nation to oppose the Israelites in the wilderness, as they journeyed to the Promise Land. Moses told Joshua to pick out an army of men, and to go fight the Amalekites, while he stood on top of a hill with the rod of God in his hand. Joshua did as Moses commanded. When Moses held up his hands, Israel prevailed. When Moses let down his hands, Amalech prevailed. When Moses grew tired, Aaron held up one of his hands, and Hur held up his other hand, until they had defeated the Amalekites. The Lord then told Moses that He would one day completely blot out the remembrance of Amalek. As a memorial, Moses built an altar and called the name of it Jehovah-Nissi (Ex. 17:8–16).

JEHOVAH-NISSI

Jehovah-Nissi means the LORD is my banner. The LORD vowed that He would have war with Amalek from generation to generation (Ex. 17:16). These Amalekites for us today are symbolic of Satan and his servants, who oppose the purpose and the plan of God for our lives. The LORD declares that they will be totally separated from and forgotten by His children, the children of God. As in the case of Moses, when we hold up the name of the Lord Jesus Christ, we will have victory over Satan and his servants. These evil spirits cannot touch the eternal souls of those that have the "Word" of God in their hearts. As we learned, it was the Spirit of Jesus Christ Who made God's Thoughts known to Moses and to the early prophets. When the early Israelites received the "Word" of the One True God (the God of Abraham, Isaac, and Jacob) into their hearts, they were receiving the Eternal Spirit of Jesus Christ. In order to understand this, we must first understand the "Oneness" (confusedly labeled "Trinity") of God.

THE "ONENESS" OF GOD

"Hear, O Israel: The LORD our God is one LORD" (Deut. 6:4). As we learned, man was made in the image and after the likeness of God. Man has one mind, one soul (the true image of one's mind), and one body. When we look at and greet our fellow-man, we call them by their name. We can look at them and hear them speak, but we cannot know what they are really thinking. This is because we cannot see their soul and therefore cannot know their true intentions. We can judge them only by their outward appearance, words, and actions. As you can see, when we are looking at and talking with someone, we are really talking with an outer man with an inner being, which is one's soul. As we will learn, the apostle Peter referred to man's inner being as the "hidden man of the heart." God is the Eternal Spirit of Love (I John 4:8). God has One Eternal Mind, One Eternal Soul (True Image of His Mind of Love), and One Holy Spirit Body. God's Invisible Spirit Body, unlike man's physical body, is limitless. God is everywhere, knows everything, and is all-powerful. God loves man and will spend eternity with those that receive Him into their hearts. Due to the fact that God's Spirit Body is Infinite and beyond man's mental comprehension, God chose to establish a relationship with man by first revealing His Soul (the True Image of His Mind of Love) in "Word," and then in the Person of Jesus Christ so that He could pour out His Soul, as the prophet Isaiah foretold (Is. 53:12), for the forgiveness of man's sin. We will understand this more fully as we continue.

GOD'S "WORD"

Prior to the time that the Spirit of Jesus Christ, God's Soul (the True Image of God's Eternal Mind of Love), came into our worldly realm as the Son of God's Love (Col. 1:13), in the Person of Jesus Christ, God's True Image came into this world as God's "Word" (the Spirit Image of God's Thoughts), in and through His Holy Spirit Body. God would later send His Soul (the True Personal Image of His Spirit Mind of Love) in and through the Power of His Holy Spirit into the Jewess Virgin Mary to be conceived and brought into this world as the Christ, the Jewish Messiah (the Sent One of God). From that day forth, God's Soul, Jesus Christ, became known as the "Son of God;" God's Eternal

Mind of Love became known as "God the Father;" and God's
Spirit Body became known as the "Holy Spirit." This is why in the
Old Testament the LORD God was not referred to as "Father"
(except in a future reference to Jesus Christ in Isaiah 9:6), nor was
the LORD God referred to as the "Holy Spirit" (except in a future
reference to the Sent One of God's Presence, Jesus Christ, in
Isaiah 63:10). As you can now plainly see, the LORD God is One
LORD. He has One Eternal Mind, One Eternal Soul (Image), and
One Eternal Spirit Body.

TRINITY

Sad but true is the fact that the label "trinity," placed on the
"Oneness" of God, has kept multitudes from knowing God's
"Truth," Jesus Christ. For instance, the Jews of Judaism know that
the LORD God is One LORD (Deut. 6:4). When they hear the
word "trinity," many turn away, and as a result fail to recognize
Jesus Christ as their Messiah (Sent One) Who will soon return to
set up God's Kingdom in Jerusalem. Confusion over the Oneness
of God, brought on by the label "trinity," has opened the doors for
various other religions such as Islam, and for other (so-called)
Christian religions such as the Jehovah's Witnesses. These religions, along with any other religion that denies the Divinity of
Jesus Christ (the fact that Jesus Christ is God), sadly are leading
their members away from God's "Truth," and away from their
chance to have eternal life in God's Everlasting Kingdom. Over-
whelming proof of this fact will be presented as we continue. Do
not allow anyone to tell you what to believe! If you want eternal joy
and happiness for yourself, your family, and your friends, you owe
it to yourself to examine the facts, and then to make your own
decision to either accept or reject Jesus Christ and God's Free Gift
of Eternal Life. God's Loving Invitation is open for all who repent
(change their mind) and receive His Spirit.

NOTE

When God's Soul came into this world and became known as
the Son of God, God's Heavenly Spirit Mind, which became
known as "God the Father," said to Him: "Thy Throne, O God, is
forever and ever" (Heb. 1:8). You see, the mind is the head of the
soul, thus God the Father is the "Head of Jesus." This does not

mean they are separate persons. They are "One." When men hear and believe the Gospel of Jesus Christ and receive Him into their minds and hearts, His Spirit, which is the same Holy Spirit of God the Father, becomes the Head of their souls (I Cor. 11:3), and they become true children of God, through One and the Same Holy Spirit (I Cor. 12:11). This is why Jesus (this Name reflects God's humanity) Christ (this Name reflects God's Divinity) declared, "I and My Father are One" (John 10:30), "he that has seen Me has seen the Father" (John 14:19), and "My Father and your Father" (John 20:17). One cannot receive Jesus Christ without receiving God the Father, one cannot receive God the Father without receiving Jesus Christ, and one cannot receive God's Holy Spirit without receiving God the Father and Jesus Christ. This is why Jesus Christ said that He and the Father would come and dwell in the hearts of those that receive Him (John 14:23). Yes, Jesus Christ is the True Image of the Invisible God (Col. 1:15). In Him dwells the Fullness of the Godhead Bodily (Col. 2:9). Knowing that Jesus Christ is the True Image of God's Invisible Spirit, we can understand why Jesus Christ is the "Name above all names" (Phil. 2:9), why salvation cannot be found in any other name (Acts 4:12), and why Jesus Christ is the Way, the Truth, and the Life of God. Without Him, one cannot come into the Presence of His Heavenly Spirit (John 14:6). God, through Jesus Christ, will say to those that do not receive Him, "I know you not" (Matt. 25:12).

MT. SINAI

After defeating the Amalekites, the Israelites camped in front of Mount Sinai. When Moses went up the mountain, the LORD called unto him, and told him to tell the Israelites that if they would obey His Voice and keep His covenant, they would be a peculiar treasure unto Him above all people, a kingdom of priests and a holy nation (Ex. 19:5–6). Moses came down and called together all the elders of the people. He told them what God had said, and all the people agreed to do what the LORD would tell them. Moses then told the LORD that the people agreed to obey Him. The LORD instructed Moses to have the people cleanse themselves, and to be ready for Him to appear. On the third day there were thunders and lightnings, and Mt. Sinai was smoking because the LORD had descended on it in fire. The LORD then called for Moses, and gave him the Ten Commandments.

THE TEN COMMANDMENTS

Before delivering the Ten Commandments, God declared to the Israelites: "I AM the LORD thy God, which have brought thee out of the land of Egypt, out of the house of bondage" (Ex. 20:2). The LORD continued:

1. "Thou shalt have no other gods before [beside] Me."

2. "Thou shalt not make unto thee any graven image, or any likeness of any thing that is in heaven above, or that is in the earth beneath, or that is in the water under the earth: Thou shalt not bow down thyself to them, nor serve them: for I the LORD thy God am a jealous God, visiting the iniquity of the fathers upon the children unto the third and fourth generation of them that hate Me; and showing mercy unto thousands of them that love me, and keep my commandments."

3. "Thou shalt not take the name of the LORD thy God in vain; for the LORD will not hold him guiltless that taketh His Name in vain."

4. "Remember the sabbath day, to keep it holy. Six days shalt thou labour, and do all thy work: But the seventh day is the sabbath of the LORD thy God: in it thou shalt not do any work, thou, nor thy son, nor thy daughter, thy manservant, nor thy maidservant, nor thy cattle, nor thy stranger that is within thy gates: For in six days the LORD made heaven and earth, the sea, and all that in them is, and rested the seventh day: wherefore the LORD blessed the sabbath day, and hallowed it."

5. "Honour thy father and thy mother: that thy days may be long upon the land which the LORD thy God giveth thee."

6. "Thou shalt not kill."

7. "Thou shalt not commit adultery."

8. "Thou shalt not steal."

9. "Thou shalt not bear false witness against thy neighbour."

10. "Thou shalt not covet thy neighbour's house, thou shalt not covet thy neighbour's wife, nor his manservant, nor his maidservant, nor his ox, nor his ass, nor any thing that is thy neighbour's."

PURPOSE OF THE TEN COMMANDMENTS

The Ten Commandments were given so that man could have the knowledge of sin (Rom. 3:20). The first four of God's ten commandments deal with man's reverence for God, while the latter six deal with man's relationship with his fellowman. When Jesus Christ came to this earth, He summarized them into the following two: "Thou shalt love the Lord thy God with all thy heart, and with all thy soul, and with all thy mind," and "Thou shalt love thy neighbour as thyself" (Matt. 22:37–40). The Ten Commandments cannot make anyone righteous (Heb. 7:19). Without the shedding of blood there is no remission of sins (Heb. 9:22). In Old Testament times, those that sinned would offer God a blood sacrifice for the forgiveness of their sin. After mankind learned that sin leads to death and that one's sins could be forgiven only by exchanging a spotless life for a sinful life through a blood sacrifice, Christ, the Soul (Spirit Image) of God's Eternal Mind of Love, became flesh in the Person of Jesus Christ, so that God might sanctify His children with His Own Blood (Heb. 13:12). As we will learn, those that put their faith in the Shed Blood of Jesus Christ, for the forgiveness of their sins, will receive His Holy Spirit, and will become his children (through One Spirit Blood) and heirs to His coming Kingdom.

IDOL WORSHIP

When Moses returned from the top of Mt. Sinai after forty days, He found many of the Israelites worshipping a golden calf that they had built. Those that instigated this evil and rebelled against the "Word" of the LORD were put to death. (As we learned, God's Word is the Eternal Spirit of Jesus Christ.) This group, along with other Israelites, would never enter into the Promise Land because of their disobedience and their unbelief (Heb. 3:18–19). God's agreement for entrance into the Promise Land demands obedience through faith. This group of disobedient Israelites chose to bow down to an idol, a false god whom they would not have to fear, and who would not tell them what they could or could not do. Those that do not fear God, and choose to live as they please without regard for God and for their fellowman, must repent and follow Jesus Christ, if they want to enter into God's Eternal Kingdom. The choice is up to each and every individual.

THE TABERNACLE

Now that the Israelites repented and agreed to obey the LORD, the LORD commanded Moses to build a tabernacle. This tabernacle was a movable tent, approximately 150 feet long and 75 feet wide. Within the walls of this tabernacle was a sanctuary, the place where the Spirit the LORD dwelled. This tabernacle was a shadow of God's "Way," through which man could enter into the very Presence of God and inherit Eternal Life. The outer gate of this tabernacle was called the "Way." Beyond the gate was the altar of sacrifice, where the lives of spotless animals were offered to God for the remission of sin. Beyond the altar was the laver or wash bowl, where the high priest was required to wash his hands and feet. This laver is symbolic of God's sanctifying, or cleansing effect upon one's life as one receives the baptism of the Holy Spirit. This baptism is God's free gift to those who trust in the Shed Blood of Jesus Christ for the forgiveness of their sin. Beyond the laver was the door leading into God's sanctuary, which was separated into two sections by a veil or curtain. In the outer sanctuary was the Lampstand with seven oil lamps, symbolic of God's Holy Spirit. After receiving God's Holy Spirit one receives God's Light, which enables him to understand God's Word. God's Word, which is Spiritual Food for man's soul, is symbolized by the table of Shewbread just beyond the Lampstand. Beyond the table of Shewbread is the table of Incense, symbolic of prayer and worship. Only after putting God's Word in one's mind and heart can one pray effectively, call God "Father," and move beyond the veil and into the second part of the sanctuary, which was called the Holy of Holies. The Holy of Holies is symbolic of Eternal Life in the Spirit of God's Love and in the Presence of Jesus Christ.

JEHOVAH-M'KADDESH

The previous study of the tabernacle will help us to understand the meaning of the LORD's Name, Jehovah M'Kaddash (Lev. 20:8), which means Jehovah Who Sanctifies. As one approaches the altar of sacrifice with faith in the Shed Blood of Jesus Christ, he is justified, which means delivered from the penalty for sin, which is death. The Blood of Jesus Christ redeems, or pays the ransom money for one's soul. But as illustrated by the tabernacle, this is just the beginning of one's journey to the Promise Land.

When the LORD sanctifies or cleanses one, which was symbolized by the laver, He sets him apart from the world. The LORD commands His children to be holy, which is the same word as "saint." When one is truly "born again," his carnal mind switches to being a spiritual mind. God's children become new creatures by taking on the Mind (Nature) of Jesus Christ and by leaving their old nature behind. The only way one can stay sanctified is through the Word of God, and the Power of His Holy Spirit. The reason many return to their sinful ways is that they do not put and keep God's Word in their heart. God's Word declares that if one willfully sins, after having received the knowledge of God's Sacrifice, there no longer remains a sacrifice for sins (Heb. 10:26). In the time of Moses, one would have to continually offer a sacrifice for his sins. Today when one sins, he must ask Jesus Christ to forgive him, and have faith that he is forgiven through His Shed Blood. Each of God's children is to keep his mind, soul, and body blameless until He returns (I Thess. 5:23). One does not know how long he or she will live, nor does one know the exact day and hour in which the Lord Jesus will return. Whatever comes first is fine, as long as one is ready.

ISRAEL REBELS

At the LORD's command, Moses sent out twelve men, one from each of the twelve tribes of Israel, to spy out the Promise Land. Joshua and Caleb were the only two that brought back a good report about the land and its magnificent fruit. The other ten were scared, and told the Israelites that the people occupying the land were giants, and that if they would try to take the land, they would be destroyed. This caused the Israelites to become scared and to rebel against the LORD and Moses. They began to complain and wanted to return to Egypt, even if it meant being slaves. Because of this rebellion, the LORD told Moses that all the Israelites would be detained for forty years in the desert wilderness. Every man twenty years old and over, that had grumbled against the LORD, would die during this time. Only then would God allow the Israelites to enter the Promise Land.

JOSHUA GIVEN LEADERSHIP

After thirty-eight years, the entire generation of the men that rebelled against God had perished, and Israel began its final two-year march into the Promise Land. At Mount Hor, the LORD told Moses and Aaron that this was where Aaron would die. On top of this mountain and in the sight of all the people, Moses removed Aaron's garments and put them on Eleazor, who took the place of his father as high priest. As the Israelites set out for the Promise Land, they were opposed by the Midianites. With the LORD on their side, they defeated this large and powerful nation without one casualty among the Israelites (Num. 31:49). Later, when Moses was told by the LORD that he would not live to enter the Promise Land, he reaffirmed the covenant between the LORD and the Israelites. Moses did this by telling the Israelites to remember, and to teach their children that the LORD spoke to them out of the midst of the fire, and that they heard His Voice as He gave them the Ten Commandments. Moses told them that obedience to the LORD would bring blessings and prosperity, and warned them that disobedience would bring disease and failure. Upon the LORD's command, Moses gave Joshua charge before all the congregation of Israel. The LORD then allowed Moses to ascend Mount Nebo and to view the Promise Land before dying upon that mount (Deut. 32:49).

ISRAEL ENTERS PROMISE LAND

Israel mourned the death of Moses for thirty days. After this period of mourning, Joshua prepared Israel to cross the Jordan River. At this time, the LORD told Joshua that He would magnify him in the eyes of all Israel, so that the Israelites would know that the LORD would be with him, as He was with Moses. Joshua did as the LORD instructed him. He sent the priests first with the Ark of the Covenant, which was a box that held the Laws which the LORD had given Moses. As soon as their feet dipped into the water, the water from upstream stood still, and all Israel crossed on dry ground, just as they had when the LORD parted the Red Sea. Once Israel crossed the Jordan, they built a monument at Gilgal in remembrance of this miracle. It was here that the manna from heaven stopped, and the Israelites began to eat of the fruit of the Promise Land (Josh. 5:12).

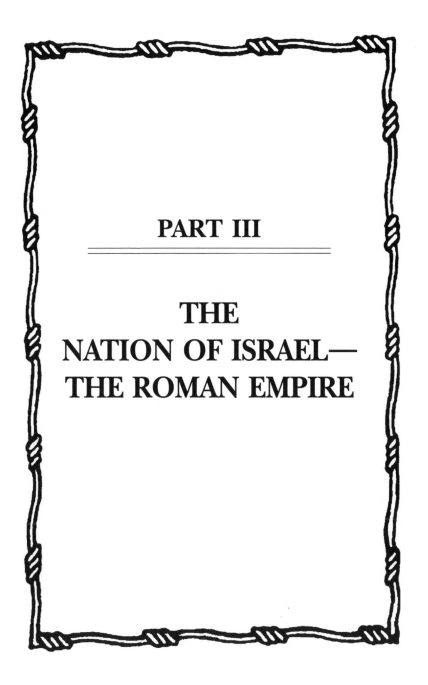

PART III

THE NATION OF ISRAEL— THE ROMAN EMPIRE

THE NATION OF ISRAEL—
THE ROMAN EMPIRE

THE LORD APPEARS TO JOSHUA

Once inside the Promise Land, the Israelites were faced with the task of overcoming the evil, corrupt, and idol-worshipping nations which dwelled in and around the Promise Land. Just ahead of them was a walled city full of enemy soldiers called Jericho. Near Jericho, Joshua lifted up his eyes and saw a Man standing before him with a sword drawn in His hand (Josh. 5:13). He told Joshua that He had come as the Captain of the LORD's army. Joshua, realizing he was talking to the LORD, fell on his face and worshipped Him. This was the Angel of the LORD that had talked to Moses. We know this for two reasons. First, the Hebrew word translated as Angel with a capital "A" means the Sent One of God's Presence, and was used to denote the Angel that talked to Moses. The Hebrew word translated angel with a small "a" means a messenger of God. Secondly, as in the case of Moses, we know that the Eternal Spirit of Jesus Christ was present with, or as, this angelic manifestation because Joshua was permitted to worship Him. In contrast, God's created angels are servants of God, and do not allow fellow servants of God to bow down to, or to worship them (Rev. 22:8–9).

WALL OF JERICHO FALLS

The LORD told Joshua that He had given them the city of Jericho, and gave him instructions on what they should do. For six days the Israelites marched once around the walled city with the Ark of the Covenant. On the seventh day they marched around the city seven times. After this, seven priests, bearing seven trumpets of rams' horns, made a long blast, and all the people began to shout. When the horns blew and the people shouted, the wall fell down flat (Josh. 6:20), and the Israelites captured the city.

In this story, Rahab, a prostitute, and her family were the only ones spared in Jericho. This was due to the fact that she helped two Israelite scouts before the battle. The LORD's intervention at Jericho illustrated His love for His chosen people. God foretold that the nations of the world would come against Israel in the future. Those that aid Israel at this time will be spared as were Rahab and her family.

VICTORY WITH THE LORD

As Israel continued their takeover of the Promise Land, their victories and defeats were based upon their obedience and their disobedience to the LORD. As the fame of the LORD God of Israel spread, the Gibeons, who were dwelling within the Promise Land, approached the Israelites and told them that they were from a distant country and that they wanted to make a peace treaty with them. Joshua agreed. Later he would learn that these people were in fact living within the Promise Land. They lied to Joshua because they had heard that the LORD God had given the Israelites the land, and were afraid that they would be destroyed. Due to the fact that Joshua had made a treaty with them, they were not killed, but were allowed to remain in the land as lumberjacks and servants of the Israelites (Josh. 9:27). When the king of Jerusalem at that time found out that the Gibeons had made peace with Israel, he joined forces with the neighboring kings and prepared to attack Gibeon. With the aid of supernatural intervention from the LORD, Joshua and the armies of Israel utterly destroyed their enemies.

NOTE

Centuries earlier, the LORD told Abraham that if his descendants obeyed the commandments of the LORD their God, He would drive out every nation that stood in their way. Abraham was also told that Israel would be cursed if the Israelites did not obey the commandments of the Lord their God (Deut. 11:23–28). The LORD God, in His Infinite Wisdom, illustrated His Love for those that hear and obey His Voice through the nation of Israel. News of God's intervention in the affairs of Israel spread the Name and the fear of the LORD God throughout the world. The LORD God then provided the "Way" through which every human being, of every nation, could choose to become a child of God and an heir to God's Eternal Kingdom. The history of Israel clearly illustrates the fact that only those that call upon the LORD (Who later revealed His Soul as Jesus Christ) and obey His commandments will be eternally blessed. It also enables one to see and to understand that God's pre-recorded history of mankind, as recorded in the Holy Bible, has been, and is being fulfilled exactly as the LORD foretold thousands of years ago.

JOSHUA DIES

The LORD gave Israel all the land that He had promised to give them. The Israelites took possession of it and settled there (Josh. 21:43). This fulfilled the prophecy that the Lord had given to Abraham hundreds of years earlier. As Joshua was approaching his death, he warned the people that if they would abandon the LORD and serve foreign gods, He, the LORD, would destroy them. The people of Israel responded by saying that they would serve the LORD, thus reaffirming their covenant with the LORD. With the death of Joshua and Eleazor, Israel would lose their strong military and spiritual unity. Every man began to do what was right in his own eyes (Judg. 17:6). Even though Israel as a whole had taken over the Promise Land, there were still inhabitants there that the Israelites did not drive out as the LORD had commanded them. The LORD wanted the Promise Land to be free from all idol worship. As a result of the Israelites' disobedience, the LORD foretold that these inhabitants would be thorns in their sides, and that their gods would be a trap unto them (Judg. 2:1–5).

ISRAEL'S NEW GENERATION

After the death of those that had seen all the great things that the LORD God had done for Israel, another generation evolved that did not know the LORD. Many of these Israelites began to follow and to worship the various gods of the people around them. This led to strife amongst the twelve tribes of Israel, which were the descendants of Jacob's (Israel's) twelve sons. As the Israelites fell into sin, the LORD raised up judges, which delivered them out of the hand of those that would corrupt them. When the judge would die, the Israelites would fall back into sin, and the LORD would raise up another judge to deliver them. One of these leaders or judges was Gideon. When the Israelites were attacked by the Midianites, they cried unto the LORD. In response to their cry, an angel of the LORD appeared to Gideon. He told him to go and strike down the Midianites and that He would be with him. The LORD said unto Gideon, "Peace be unto thee; fear not: thou shalt not die." Gideon then built an altar there and called it Jehovah-Shalom which means the LORD who gives peace (Judg. 6:24).

JEHOVAH-SHALOM

Peace is the absence of fear and mental conflict. Man's three basic fears are death, sickness, and poverty. These and all mental conflicts are the result of sin entering the human race. As we continue to learn abut God, we will understand that God's Holy Spirit is freely available and waiting to bring peace, joy, strength, patience, and self-control to those that ask the Lord Jesus Christ to come into their heart. Those that receive the Holy Spirit will have power over sin. As a result, they will live forever in a new glorified and eternal body. We will cover this in detail as we continue.

IDOLATRY

After the Midianites were subdued, the Israelites wanted to make Gideon king. Being aware that his victories were won by the LORD, Gideon told them that the LORD would be their ruler. Gideon wanted them to look towards the LORD as their King. After the death of Gideon, the Israelites once again turned to idol worship. As a result, the LORD allowed them to be severely oppressed by various nations. This caused the Israelites to remember and to cry unto the LORD for help. The LORD, upset with their disobedience, told them to cry out to the gods that they had chosen to serve, and to let those gods save them (Judg. 10:10–16). Realizing that only the LORD could save them, they rid themselves of their foreign gods and served the LORD. Many people today carry or wear a crystal, a stone, a rabbit's foot, an icon, and other idols, thinking that these objects will bring them luck. Many Greek people wear a replica of an eyeball, which they say will keep them from getting cursed by an evil eye. Today many are putting their faith in the stars, science, religion, witchcraft, and psychics, instead of putting their faith in the Lord Jesus Christ. These are the same kinds of idolatries that the Israelites were deceived into believing. Only after the Israelites destroyed their idols and turned away from the pagan gods would the LORD God come to their rescue.

FIRST KING APPOINTED

Samuel was the last judge that the LORD appointed for Israel. He was a godly man that walked in the ways of the LORD. Because of this, the LORD helped Israel regain the towns that were captured by their enemy, the Philistines. When Samuel grew old, he appointed his sons as judges for Israel. Due to the fact that these sons accepted bribes and perverted justice, the elders of Israel told Samuel that they wanted to appoint a king as their ruler. The LORD knew this would happen, and told Samuel to anoint Saul as the first king of Israel. Samuel did as the LORD commanded, but warned the people of Israel to fear the LORD and to serve Him faithfully. He also told them that if they persisted in doing evil, they and their king would be swept away (I Sam. 12:25). Due to Saul's eventual disobedience, the LORD told Samuel to privately anoint David as the next king of Israel after Saul. On this day, the Spirit of the LORD left Saul, who was still king, and was with David. With the LORD's help, David was able to slay the large Philistine soldier named Goliath, and had great success in everything that he did. Saul, fearing David's growing fame throughout Israel, attempted to kill David.

KING DAVID

After the death of Saul, the tribes of Israel were divided by the election of two kings, David and Ish-Bosheth, the son of Saul. This resulted in a civil war that eventually brought all the twelve tribes of Israel together under the rulership of King David. After gaining nationwide acceptance, David took up residence in the fortress of Zion in Jerusalem. Jerusalem thus became known as the City of David. David made arrangements for the Ark of God to be brought to Jerusalem. He told Nathan the prophet that he was bothered by the fact that he was living in a house of cedar, but the Ark of God was under a tent (II Sam. 7:2). That night the Word of the LORD came to Nathan and told him to tell David that after his death, it would be his son that would build a house for the LORD, and that the house and the throne of David would be established forever (II Sam. 7:13). God's prophets foretold that the Messiah, Jesus Christ, would come into this world through the seed of David and establish God's Everlasting Kingdom from the throne of David, which is Jerusalem. David made extensive preparations for the magnificent temple of the LORD, which would be built by his son, Solomon. David gathered all the leaders of Israel, as well as the priests and Levites, and stressed to them that the building of the temple would be a united effort. He then assigned various duties to the various tribes of Israel. These assignments included temple, government, and military duties. David then made Solomon king over Israel, and gave him all the plans for the temple that the Holy Spirit had put in his mind.

JEHOVAH-ROHI

Before David had become King, he was a musician and a shepherd. He continued to write songs to the LORD throughout his life. Many of his songs are recorded in the Book of Psalms, in the Old Testament. One of the most beloved psalms that David wrote is the 23rd Psalm. In this Psalm, David looks upon the LORD as Jehovah-Rohi, which is translated: "the LORD is my Shepherd." This name demonstrates the LORD's personal love for each and every one of His children. A good shepherd is a personal friend and companion to his sheep. Every time one looks toward the LORD for help, he is guided in the right direction. By listening to the Voice of the Good Shepherd, one is led on the path of righteousness. Jesus Christ is the Good Shepherd that leads His sheep into God's Everlasting Kingdom. The fact that David was referring to Jesus Christ as his Shepherd will become clearly evident as we continue.

KING SOLOMON

Shortly after becoming king, Solomon insured the peace of Israel by making an alliance with the king of Egypt, and by marrying his daughter. Solomon loved the LORD and walked in the statutes of his father. One night the LORD appeared to Solomon during the night and asked him what he wanted from the LORD. Solomon asked the LORD for the wisdom to govern

Israel and to distinguish between right and wrong. The LORD was pleased with his answer, and told Solomon that He would also give him riches, honor, and a long life, if he was obedient. Solomon shared his God-given wisdom in three thousand proverbs (I Kin. 4:32), many of which are recorded in the Book of Proverbs in the Holy Bible. He also wrote one thousand and five songs. He is ascribed as having written "The Song of Solomon," a short poem recorded in the Holy Bible, and as writing or having the book of Ecclesiastes written in his honor. This book talks about life's vanities, and teaches that man should fear God and keep His commandments.

SOLOMON BUILDS TEMPLE

In the fourth year of Solomon's reign as king over Israel, he began to build the temple of the LORD on Mt. Moriah in Jerusalem. The LORD told Solomon that He would reside with his people in the temple, as long as they, the Israelites, were obedient. Seven years later the temple was completed. On dedication day, the temple was filled with a cloud and the Glory of the LORD (I Kin. 8:10). When sacrifices were made at the temple, fire came down from heaven and consumed the sacrificial offerings. During this time, the Glory of the LORD could be seen above the temple.

NEW KING CAUSES DIVISION

Solomon reigned in Jerusalem and over all of Israel for forty years. At his death, Rehoboam, his son, succeeded him as king. Instead of wanting to make things better for the twelve tribes of Israel, Rehoboam said he would make things tougher (I Kin. 12:14). Because of this, only the tribe of Judah, in Jerusalem, and the tribe of Benjamin acknowledged him as king. The other ten tribes set up the kingdom of Israel under Jeroboam. Jeroboam feared that the people would honor King Rehoboam when they would go to Jerusalem to offer sacrifices at the temple of the LORD. For this reason, he set up two golden calves, built an altar in Dan and another one in Bethel, and told the people to sacrifice to these idols. Israel's priests, which were of the tribe of Levi, refused to worship these idols. They returned to Jerusalem to worship the LORD God of Israel. They were followed by many people from each tribe that were also loyal to the LORD.

Jeroboam was more interested in his power over Israel than in the eternal destiny of its people. His selfish desires led to constant war between the tribes in the north and those under Rehoboam in the south. Rehoboam reigned in Jerusalem for seventeen years before he died. His son Abijah succeeded him as king.

THE LORD PROTECTS JUDAH

Abijah's reign began with a war between his tribe of Judah and the other tribes of Israel that were led by Jeroboam. Abijah reminded Jeroboam that the LORD had established the throne of Israel in Jerusalem under David, who was a member of the tribe of Judah. Jeroboam did not care about the LORD, and thus attacked Judah. He was greatly defeated, as the tribe of Judah cried unto and relied upon the LORD for their strength. Abijah ruled in Jerusalem for three years prior to his death, at which time his son, Asa, succeeded him as king. Asa died in his forty-first year as king of Judah, and was succeeded by his son Jehoshaphat (I Kin. 15:24). As we learned, Israel was the name that the LORD had given to Jacob. The twelve tribes of Israel are the offspring of Jacob's twelve sons. From the time of Solomon's death, Israel remained divided into two kingdoms: the house of David, also known as the kingdom of Judah, and the kingdom of Israel. The kingdom of Judah was made up of the tribes of Judah, Benjamin, and Levi. The other nine tribes made up the kingdom of Israel. Overall, the kingdom of Judah remained faithful to the LORD, while the kingdom of Israel remained an idolatrous nation, which worshipped false gods and images. Jehoshaphat was devoted to the ways of the LORD. He sent his officials into the towns of Judah to teach the people the Law of the LORD. Soon those around Judah began to fear the LORD and did not make war with Jehoshaphat.

THE PROPHET ELIJAH

Three years before Jehoshaphat became king of Judah, Ahab became the king of Israel. Ahab was the most evil of all the previous kings of Israel. He worshipped idols and promoted false pagan gods. By doing so, he led most of Israel away from the One LORD God. There were still some Israelites that were faithful to the LORD. One of these was the prophet Elijah, whom the LORD would use to rescue the Israelites from idolatry, and to bring them back to worshipping Him. Elijah met with Ahab. He told Ahab to gather the prophets throughout Israel, who were sacrificing to idols, and to meet him at Mount Carmel. When these false prophets assembled, Elijah told them to prepare an altar to their god, and to put the sacrifice on the altar, but not to set fire to the wood. Instead he told them to call upon the name of their god to consume the sacrifice with fire. They prepared their altar and sacrifice, and then called upon the name of Baal, their god, from morning till evening, but there was no response. Elijah then repaired the broken down altar of the LORD, and told the people to pour water on his offering and on the wood. He then stepped forward and asked the LORD God of Abraham, Isaac, and Israel to let it be known that He is God in Israel, that he, Elijah, was His servant, and that He, the LORD, was turning the hearts of the Israelites back to Him. The fire of the LORD then fell and consumed the burnt sacrifice (I Kin. 18:38). When the people saw this, they fell facedown and cried: "The LORD, He is God." Elijah then commanded that all the evil prophets of Baal be put to death.

ELISHA THE PROPHET

When Ahab told his evil wife Jezebel what had happened, she sent a message to Elijah telling him that tomorrow he would be dead, just as the prophets of Baal who were killed. After hearing this, Elijah went to Mount Horeb. There the LORD told Elijah to anoint Hazael as king over Aram, Jehu as king over Israel, and Elisha to succeed him as the LORD's prophet. After being anointed, Elisha followed, obeyed, and learned from Elijah. Elisha followed Elijah from Gilgal to Bethel, then to Jericho, and then into Jordan. When they reached the Jordan River, Elijah took his cloak and struck the water with it. The waters parted and they crossed over on dry ground. Elijah, knowing that the LORD was preparing to take him up to heaven, asked Elisha what he could do for him before he was taken up. Elisha replied that he would like a double portion of his spirit (II Kin. 2:9). Elisha wanted to be twice as close to the LORD as was Elijah. The LORD, as part of His Master Plan, then took Elijah up to heaven in a whirlwind, to return him at a later date, as we will learn. After viewing this, Elisha tore his own clothes apart and picked up the cloak that had fallen from Elijah. He then struck the water with it. The water

parted and he crossed back over to the other side. The company
of the prophets from Jericho, who were watching, then knew that
the power of the Lord was now with Elisha.

KING JEHU

Following the death of Jehoshaphat, his son Jehoram ruled as
king of Judah (I Kin. 22:50). Jehoram married a daughter of
Ahab, and began to lead the nation of Judah away from the LORD
God and into the worship of Baal. Because of this, the LORD
brought a fatal illness upon him. His son, Ahaziah, succeeded him
as king. He like his father was an evil man. Meanwhile the
northern nation of Israel under the rule of Joram, the son of
Ahab, was continuing to lead the nation of Israel into the worship
of Baal. Thus both of the divided nations were beginning to
depart from the LORD. Elisha at this time sent a prophet to
anoint Jehu as the next king of Israel. Jehu became the LORD's
executioner. He started by executing the entire house of Ahab,
who had led the Israelites into idolatry and witchcraft. He then
executed Ahaziah and his relatives. Afterwards, he initiated the
gathering of all ministers of idol worship for the supposed
purpose of honoring their false god named Baal. After he fooled
them into gathering from every part of Israel, he executed them
all. Thus Baal worship was destroyed in all of Israel. The LORD
had warned his people concerning His judgment of the unrighteous, and the LORD is true to His Word.

DISOBEDIENCE LEADS TO OPPRESSION

Joash, the son of Ahaziah, became the next king of Judah.
Jehoiada, the high priest at that time, made a covenant that he,
the people, and the king would be the LORD's people. As king of
Judah, Joash decided to repair the temple of the LORD. Jehoiada
collected the money and had the temple redone to its original
state. As long as Jehoiada lived, Joash walked with the LORD. After
the death of Jehoiada, Joash was swayed into idolatry, and was later
assassinated. Jehu was the king of Israel when Joash became the
king of Judah. Jehu, as we learned, destroyed Baal worship, but
he did not do away with the worship of the golden calves that
his father had set up in Bethel and Dan. Jehu was succeeded as
king of Israel by his son Jehoahaz, and then by Joash, his grandson

(II Kin. 14:1), both of whom also worshipped the golden calves. Because of this, the LORD allowed them to be oppressed by the king of Syria. Zechariah, the son of Jehoiada, had warned the people that the LORD would forsake them, if they forsook the LORD.

IMPORTANCE OF ISRAEL

As we learned, the nation of Israel was established under the Inspiration of God and with the aid of God's supernatural intervention. From the day Israel became a nation, its prosperity and decline have been based entirely upon the obedience of its people to the LORD God. The LORD instructed His prophets to record the history of Israel for the benefit of all nations. As we continue, we will see and understand how God chose to use Israel to bless the entire world, and to make His Master Plan and its prophetic timeclock known to all mankind. We will soon understand the significance (to every human being) of Israel, after two thousand-plus years, once again becoming a nation.

KING AMAZIAH

Amaziah succeeded his father, Joash, as king of Judah. As king of Judah, Amaziah defeated the Edomites. When he returned to Judah, he brought idols of foreign gods back with him. He set them up as his own gods and worshipped them. The LORD sent a prophet to ask Amaziah why he would want to worship the gods of the people he had just defeated (II Chr. 25:15). If their gods had any power, why didn't they save the people from destruction? Due to this sin, God allowed Israel, under King Joash, to defeat Judah and carry away the false gods that Amaziah had brought to Judah. After the death of Joash, his son, Jeraboam II, succeeded him as king of Israel. It came to pass that Amaziah was assassinated and Uzziah succeeded him as king of Judah.

THE PROPHET JONAH

During this time, the LORD began to extend His Grace to other nations. The WORD of the LORD came to the prophet Jonah, and told him to go to the City of Nineveh, which was the home of the Assyrian king, and to preach to them. Due to the fact that Jonah did not want to go, he boarded a ship to flee from the LORD. After Jonah was thrown overboard by the crew members, the LORD provided a great fish to swallow and keep him for three days and three nights in its belly, before spitting him out onto dry ground. Afterwards, the WORD of the LORD told Jonah once again to go and preach in Nineveh. This time he obeyed. He told the people there that God had said that Nineveh would be overturned in forty days. The people believed that God would destroy them, so they began to fast and pray. The king ordered everyone to give up their evil ways and their violence. When God saw how they turned from their evil ways, He had compassion on them and they escaped destruction (Jon. 3:10). God does not want, nor does he enjoy seeing anyone perish. His desire is that all should come to repentance (II Pet. 3:9). To repent means to turn one's mind away from sin, and to follow the One True God. Jonah said that those that cling to their vanities and lies will forfeit the Mercy of God (Jon. 2:8). Many do not seek God's Truth because they don't care about God. Others are too proud or afraid to question their beliefs and traditions, in fear of being ostracized by family and so-called friends. As Jesus foretold, following Him has a price, and that price is persecution. What everyone must realize is that the amount of suffering and pain that one endures for the Name of the LORD, Jesus Christ, will be nothing in comparison to the eternal pleasures that he or she will enjoy.

THE PROPHET HOSEA

During the reign of Uzziah (Azariah), king of Judah, and Jeroboam II, king of Israel, the LORD called upon the prophet Hosea to warn the people about their spiritual adultery with idols. In order to fully understand idolatry, imagine for a moment that you are God, and that you created man. Next, imagine looking down and seeing your created beings worshipping breathless objects of gold, stone, and wood, or bowing down to other men that you created, and asking them for your forgiveness and for your blessings. How would you feel when you saw them burning incense, and praying to icons of other created being, and never personally talking with you. This is idolatry. The LORD revealed himself in the Person of Jesus Christ, by Whom, and for Whom all things in heaven and on earth were created (Col. 1:16). God's mystery, unknown to many, is the fact that God is presently establishing His Kingdom under and in the Name of His Son (Soul-True Image) Jesus Christ. As we learned, God is the Spirit of Love (I John 4:8). This is why the apostle Paul referred to Jesus Christ as the Son of God's Love (Col. 1:13). God made it known to man that Jesus Christ is the Image of His Invisible Spirit (Col. 1:15), so that man would know His Name, and how to address Him in Prayer. Man is commanded never to pray or bow to anyone or anything "beside" the LORD God, in the Name of Jesus Christ.

THE PROPHET AMOS

During this same period, the LORD called Amos, a shepherd in Judah, to go and preach in Israel (Amos 1:1). Amos spoke out about those who would give offerings at religious gatherings, but were evil and unrighteous in their hearts. He told them that they were wasting their time, because the LORD would not accept their offerings. Amos also warned the Israelites about their pride, selfishness, greed, and their disregard and their injustice towards the poor and the needy. Amos was rebuked by the high priest, and was told to leave Israel. Evidently the high priest at that time was leading those that were giving him offerings into believing that they were pleasing the LORD, while in truth they were not. The LORD then spoke through Amos, as he prophesied that Israel would be militarily defeated, divided, and forced to leave their native land.

THE PROPHET ISAIAH

Just prior to the death of Uzziah, king of Judah, the prophet Isaiah began his ministry in Judah. Isaiah spoke out about many of the social and spiritual sins of Judah. Some of these sins were: idolatry, superstitions, the practice of divination, pride, abuse of the poor, greed, drunkenness, and injustice. Isaiah foretold that the Messiah (God's Sent One), Who is Christ, would come to this earth and accurately described Christ's future earthly mission. As we learned, it was the Eternal Spirit of Christ in the prophets that made it possible for them to foretell the future. Isaiah's prophecies were made 700 years before the birth of Jesus Christ. In addition to his prophecies about Christ's first appearance, Isaiah described future events which have not yet been fulfilled. There is not one prophecy that God's prophets spoke that has not been, or that will not be fulfilled exactly as the prophets spoke it. This is because Bible prophecy is the written history of future events. Only God Almighty can write history with 100 percent accuracy before it happens. The study of the Bible's accurate and detailed prophecies will prove beyond a doubt that the LORD God of the Holy Bible is the True God, that He is in control of this world, and that His Master Plan will be fulfilled exactly as He said it would through His prophets.

THE PROPHET MICAH

After the death of Uzziah, king of Judah, in 739 B.C., his son Jotham succeeded him as king. The WORD of the LORD came to the prophet Micah at this time, and he began to speak to the people of Judah (Mic. 1:1). The WORD of the LORD came to him in a vision. In this vision, he saw the resulting punishment of Samaria and Jerusalem for their sins. These sins included witch-craft and the bowing down to the works of human hands. As we learned, the Word of the LORD (the Image of God's Mind) through the Holy Spirit revealed God's Thoughts and would later reveal God's "True Being" by becoming flesh in the person of Jesus Christ (John 1:14). The Spirit of Jesus Christ, in God's Love, told the early prophets to record these events in order to save mankind from God's coming judgment on this world. Jesus Christ will soon return to judge and to rule over this earth. He is the only Image of God's All-Powerful and Eternal Holy Spirit. Those that bow down and pray to statues, pictures, icons, and other images will be judged, unless they rid themselves of all these things and put their full faith in the True Lord and Savior, Jesus Christ. He is the only Mediator between man and God's Invisible Spirit (I Tim. 2:5). Those that are praying to idols are not only deceived, but are also disobedient to God. Mankind will be judged according to the Word of God. Those that do not live according to God's Word are in the same boat as those that reject God's Word.

KING AHAZ

Ahaz succeeded his father, Jotham, as king of Judah (II Kin. 16:1). The prophet Isaiah came to Ahaz with a warning that Israel and Syria would invade Judah. He told Ahaz that the LORD told him to tell him that he would have nothing to fear if he put his trust and faith in the LORD. Instead of trusting in the LORD, Ahaz trusted in his own military strength and was badly defeated. As a result of his disobedience, Judah became weak, and had to turn to and rely upon Assyria for protection from the Edomites and the Philistines, who had once again invaded Judah. It is clear that the LORD's LOVE and Protection are conditional. As we will learn, those that call upon the LORD in the Name of Jesus Christ will be saved from God's coming judgment upon this earth.

HEZEKIAH

After the death of Ahaz, his son Hezekiah succeeded him as king of Judah (II Kin. 18:1). Hezekiah began his reign in the third year of the reign of Hoshea, king of Israel. In the first sixteen days of his reign, he repaired and cleansed the Temple of the LORD. Every unclean thing in the temple was taken out, and worship services were resumed. Israel, on the other hand, failed to listen to the prophets' warnings, and did the things that the LORD had forbidden them to do. They worshipped idols and false gods, and also practiced divination and witchcraft. Divination is the use of a psychic to foretell one's future. This practice is against the Will of God. As a result of their sin, Israel was taken over by Assyria, and the people of Israel were taken into exile in Assyria. The king of Assyria then brought people from Babylon and other countries, and settled them in Samaria (II Kin. 17:24).

ASSYRIA FAILS TO ENTER JERUSALEM

In the fourteenth year of King Hezekiah's reign, Assyria attacked Judah. Hezekiah agreed to pay Assyria three hundred talents of silver and thirty talents of gold to withdraw and to leave them alone. Later Assyria decided to take over Jerusalem and sent Hezekiah a message boasting how they had defeated many nations and how that the gods of these nations did not protect them. Hezekiah prayed to the LORD. As a result, the LORD told Isaiah that He would defend and save Jerusalem (Is. 37:21–35). That night the angel of the LORD went out and put to death one hundred and eighty-five thousand Assyrian soldiers. The next morning when the king of Assyria awoke and saw all the dead bodies, he returned in disgrace to Nineveh and stayed there. Those that mock the Lord Jesus Christ are warned to repent and to change sides. Those that do not heed and turn to Jesus Christ will be excluded from His Utopian Kingdom, which is coming to this earth. This is the Kingdom that people pray for when they recite the Lord's Prayer. Those that are excluded will be responsible for their own fate, and will not be able to rightfully blame God, Whose kingdom is presently open to all.

MANASSEH

Manasseh, Hezekiah's twelve-year-old son, succeeded him as king of Judah (II Kin. 21:1). Manasseh put a stop to the spiritual revival that his father began in Judah. As he grew older, he bowed down to false gods, practiced sorcery and divination, shed innocent blood, and led Judah into idol worship. Because of this, the LORD said through the prophets that He would forsake Judah, and would allow its people to be looted and plundered by their enemies. Isaiah prophesied that the people of Judah would be taken captive by the Babylonians, and that Judah would be restored by Cyrus, the king of Persia. This would come to pass one hundred and fifty years later. Isaiah also prophesied about the future time when Jesus Christ would destroy the evildoers, and establish God's Eternal Kingdom of Love, Peace, and Joy.

NAHUM AND JOSIAH

King Manasseh was taken prisoner by the king of Assyria. In his deep distress, he humbled himself and prayed to the LORD. After this, the LORD brought him back to his kingdom in Jerusalem. Manasseh then ordered all false gods to be removed from Jerusalem, and told the people of Judah to worship the LORD. During this time, the prophet Nahum prophesied about the fall of Nineveh, which was an enemy of Judah at that time. After the death of Manasseh, his son Amon ruled for two years before being assassinated. Amon's son Josiah was then made king of Judah.

ZEPHANIAH AND JEREMIAH

King Josiah cared more about the LORD than any other king (II Kin. 23:25). Josiah tried to restore proper worship in Judah, but his efforts would not save Judah from the LORD's judgment.

During Josiah's reign, the LORD called the prophets Zephaniah and Jeremiah. He told them to warn the people of Judah and of Israel about God's future judgment upon them for worshipping false gods, the sun, the moon, and the stars. They were also consulting psychics, which is against the Will of God. As a result, Jeremiah foretold that Judah would be overthrown by the Babylonians, and that the Jews would be taken and held captive in Babylon for seventy years. This would happen after the death of Josiah, who died from an arrow wound he received when he, against God's Will, led Judah in a losing battle against Egypt. Josiah's son, Jehoahaz, succeeded him as king of Judah.

NEBUCHADNEZZAR

After defeating Judah, Necho, the Pharaoh of Egypt, prevented Jehoahaz from ruling in Jerusalem. He did this by taking him captive and by making his brother, Eliakim, king. Necho changed Eliakim's name to Jehoiakim (II Kin. 23:34), and allowed him to reign as long as he paid him the silver and gold that he demanded. Thus in 609 B.C., Judah was really controlled by Egypt, with Jehoiakim being nothing more than a puppet king. The prophet Jeremiah warned Necho that the LORD would bring punishment upon Egypt, and that they would be attacked and defeated by Nebuchadnezzar, the king of Babylon. Just four years later, in 605 B.C., Nebuchadnezzar defeated Egypt, as Jeremiah had foretold. Nebuchadnezzar then invaded Judah, and made Jehoiakim his puppet. Nebuchadnezzar made the Jews his slaves and took them to Babylon, along with various articles he had taken out of the LORD's temple.

THE PROPHET DANIEL

Daniel was among the captives that were chosen by King Nebuchadnezzar's officials to be trained, and to serve in the king's palace (Dan. 1:4–6). God gave Daniel the ability to understand visions and dreams of all kinds. In the second year of his reign, Nebuchadnezzar had a dream that greatly disturbed him. He called for his magicians, enchanters, sorcerers, and astrologers, and commanded them to tell him what he had dreamt. They asked the king to tell them his dream, and they would then interpret it. Nebuchadnezzar refused, and told them that if they could not tell him what he had dreamt and explain it to him, all the wise men in Babylon would be put to death. When Daniel heard of this, he approached the king and asked him for time to interpret his dream. He then returned home and prayed for God to reveal his mystery to him. That night Daniel received a vision in which the LORD revealed the king's dream to him. Daniel returned to the king, told him his dream and its meaning, and gave God the glory. This dream foretold the rise and fall of every world empire leading up to the return of Jesus Christ to this earth. The LORD God wanted mankind to know that He is in control of this world, so that man could live in peace and in the hope of His return.

DANIEL'S VISION

In his vision 2,500 years ago, Daniel saw an image which represented the future world empires leading up to the establishment of God's Kingdom upon this earth. This image had a head of gold, which symbolized the Babylonian empire. Below, or next in line, were the arms of silver, symbolic of the Medo-Persian empire, which would defeat Babylon in 539 B.C. Next, the stomach and thighs of bronze symbolized the Grecian empire which, under Alexander the Great, would defeat the Medes and Persians in 331 B.C. Next, the two legs of iron symbolized the Roman Empire, which under Julius Caesar conquered the Greeks in 63 B.C., and had its two headquarters in Rome and in Constantinople. Next, the ten toes of iron mixed with clay would symbolize the Revived Roman Empire. This empire is the present European Union, which will one day control the world from ten regions. It will be the final one-world government, and will control the world at the time of Christ's return. Evidence of this will be given as we continue.

KING ZEDEKIAH

After the death of Jehoiakim, the puppet king of Judah, Jehoiachin succeeded him as king. He reigned only three months before Nebuchadnezzar entered Jerusalem, and took him and ten thousand other citizens of Jerusalem as slaves to Babylon. Nebuchadnezzar then made Mattaniah, the third son of Josiah, his puppet king and changed his name to Zedekiah (II Kin. 24:17).

During this time, Jeremiah sent a letter to the exiles in Babylon, telling them that the LORD revealed to him that they would be in exile for seventy years, and that He would then bring them back to Jerusalem. God tells us in His Word that the exile of Judah's people was caused by their refusal to turn to the LORD. Jerusalem was the place of God's temple. This is where the Spirit of the LORD had dwelled with His people. The people however did not listen to Him, nor to His prophets, whom they mocked and despised. The LORD let them know that he disapproved of their sin by casting them from His Presence, just as He had warned them through the prophets. While the Jews were in exile, the LORD continued to send them messages of guidance through the prophets, and was anxious to welcome them home when they returned. Jesus Christ is the same yesterday, today, and tomorrow (Heb. 13:8). His Arms are anxious to welcome all those that sincerely call upon His Name.

THE PROPHET EZEKIEL

The prophet Ezekiel was among the ten thousand captives that were taken to Babylon by Nebuchadnezzar. In the year 592 B.C., the WORD of the LORD came to Ezekiel and he began to prophesy (Ezek. 1:3). The LORD used the prophets as messengers to guide, to warn, and to demonstrate to Israel and the world that He is the True God. The LORD did this by foretelling the outcome of future events. The true prophets spoke the Words that the LORD put in their minds. That is why they would begin their speech by saying, "Thus saith the LORD." Ezekiel spoke out against the shedding of innocent blood. He also spoke out against the false prophets. The LORD described false prophets as those that predict things in the name of the LORD that do not come to pass. Many false prophets, such as the "Jehovah's Witnesses," have, on more than one occasion, falsely predicted the time of Christ's return. Those that follow these and other false prophets are being led astray. As we learned, Jehovah God is the English translation of Yayweh, and means the True God Who reveals Himself. Jehovah revealed himself to man as Jesus Christ. True children of God are witnesses of Jesus Christ, Who will soon return as King of kings and Lord of lords (Rev. 19:16). As we will learn, Jesus Christ will return to rule and reign over God's Everlasting Kingdom from Jerusalem.

JERUSALEM, CAPTURED AND DESTROYED

As we learned, Zedekiah was a puppet king, controlled by Babylon's King Nebuchadnezzar. In the ninth year of his reign, he rebelled against Nebuchadnezzar (II Kin. 25:1), who then burnt and destroyed Jerusalem in 588 B.C. Nebuchadnezzar captured Zedekiah and killed his son before his eyes. He then put out Zedekiah's eyes and put him in a prison in Babylon, where he would die. Ezekiel and Jeremiah both prophesied that the Jews would be scattered into other nations, as a result of their sins against the LORD. They both prophesied, 2,500 years ago, that in the latter days, the northern tribes of Israel and those of Judah would once again be gathered, brought back, and reunited in their homeland. The fact that Israel became a nation in 1948, that the Jews captured Jerusalem in 1967, and that the Jews have returned and are returning to Israel from every nation of the world, is the greatest sign that we are indeed living in the latter days of this age, that the Holy Bible is indeed the Word of God, and that the God of Abraham, of Isaac, and of Jacob, in the person of Jesus Christ, is indeed the True God of the universe.

JEHOVAH-TSIDKENU

Jeremiah prophesied that a future King would one day reign in Jerusalem and described Him as Jehovah-Tsidkenu which means "The LORD our Righteousness" (Jer. 23:5–6). God is Holy and in order for man to enter into and remain in the presence of God, he would have to be found righteous. When Jesus Christ returns to this earth as King of kings, the unrighteous will be eternally removed and separated from Him. Knowing that the blood of all mankind was contaminated by Satan's spirit, God knew that the only way to save mankind would be for Him to offer man the opportunity to replace his sinful mind (nature) with the Righteous Mind of Jesus Christ, the True Image of God's Invisible Spirit. As we will learn, God is presently offering to impart His Spirit to those who will publicly confess Jesus Christ as their Lord and Savior with their mouth, and believe in their heart that He rose from the dead (Rom. 10:9). Only those that believe, ask God in the Name of Jesus Christ into their hearts, and receive God's Holy Spirit, will be clothed in the Righteousness of Christ. It will be this group that will enjoy God's soon to come Kingdom of

Love upon this earth. We will consider this in more detail as we continue.

SHADRACH, MESHACH AND ABEDNEGO

In Babylon, King Nebuchadnezzar erected a nine-foot-high image of gold, and ordered everyone to fall down and worship this image when the sound was given (Dan. 3:4). Whoever refused would be thrown into a fiery furnace. Three Jews named Shadrach, Meshach, and Abednego refused to fall and worship the image, and were reported to the king. When they were brought before Nebuchadnezzar, they were given the choice to either bow down to the image or be thrown into the burning furnaces. They told the king that they would not worship the image of gold. This angered the king, who then commanded that the temperature of the furnace be increased, and that the three Jews be thrown in. The fire became so hot that when the Jews were thrown into the furnace, the flames killed the soldiers who threw them in. When Nebuchadnezzar viewed the scene, he saw four men walking around inside the fire, and the One appeared like the Son of God. The king then called for the three Jews, and they came out of the furnace untouched. The king then acknowledged the power of the Most High God, and made a decree that anyone who would speak against the God of Shadrach, Meshach, and Abednego would be cut to pieces. Those that trust in Jesus Christ are putting their trust in the Living God (I Tim. 4:10). Those that put their trust in idols, wealth, their own abilities, religion, or in any person or thing *beside* Jesus Christ, need to change their minds and turn to Jesus Christ in order to inherit eternal life in God's never-ending Kingdom.

JEHOVAH-SHAMMAH

Fourteen years after the fall of Jerusalem and the destruction of the LORD's Temple, which was originally built by Solomon, the prophet Ezekiel, who was still in exile in Babylon, was taken to Jerusalem by God in a vision. In this vision Ezekiel was given a tour of a future rebuilt Jerusalem. As he was standing in front of this new temple, the voice of the LORD, from inside the temple, told him that this would be the place of His Throne forever. At the end of this vision, Ezekiel was told that this Holy City would be called

Jehovah-Shammah, which means, "The LORD is Present" (Ezek. 48:35). Unlike the previous Names of God, this final name pictures God's Everlasting Throne instead of His Person. We will understand this as we continue.

KING BELSHAZZAR

In the first ten years after the death of King Nebuchadnezzar, the king's throne changed leadership five times. The fifth and last king of Babylon was Belshazzar. During a large banquet, Belshazzar ordered that the gold and silver goblets that Nebuchadnezzar had taken from the LORD's temple be brought to him. He and his friends then drank wine from them as they praised their idols. Suddenly the fingers of a human hand began to write on the wall as Belshazzar watched. The king became frightened and asked his wise men to read the writing on the wall. After they failed to read the writing, Daniel was brought in to read it. Daniel read the writing and told Belshazzar that it said that his reign would be brought to an end, and that the Babylonian kingdom would be divided and given to the Medes and to the Persians. That night Belshazzar was killed and Darius the Mede took over the kingdom (Dan. 5:31). Three years later in 539 B.C., Cyrus, the king of the Medo-Persian Empire, entered into and took over the Babylonian Empire. This fulfilled the writing on the wall, and was the beginning of the fulfillment of one of the prophecies that Isaiah had told approximately one hundred and fifty years earlier. In this prophecy, Isaiah foretold that Judah would be restored by a Persian king named Cyrus.

KING CYRUS

In the first year of his reign, Cyrus was moved by the LORD to send the exiled Jews back to Judah to build a new temple for the LORD in Jerusalem (Ezra 1:1). As the Jews were preparing for their return to rebuild the LORD's temple, they were given gold and silver by their neighbors in Babylon. King Cyrus also returned the gold and silver temple articles, which Nebuchadnezzar had taken from the LORD's temple. In the second year of the return of the Jews to their land, the temple foundation was laid. This came to pass seventy years after the Jews were first taken into captivity by Nebuchadnezzar. This was the exact fulfillment of

Jeremiah's prophecy, in which he foretold that the Jews would be held captive in Babylon for seventy years. At this time, many of Judah's former enemies did not want them, the Jews, to have Jerusalem, and therefore fought to stop the construction of the LORD's temple.

THE PROPHETS HAGGAI AND ZECHARIAH

In 521 B.C., Darius became king of Persia. During this period, the prophets Haggai and Zechariah prophesied to the Jews in Judah and in Jerusalem in the Name of the God of Israel (Ezra 5:1). Zerubbabel, the governor of Jerusalem, listened to these prophets and resumed the construction of the LORD's temple. King Darius issued a decree prohibiting anyone to interfere with the work of the LORD's temple (Ezra 6:7). The prophet Haggai delivered a message from the LORD to Zerubbabel and to Joshua, the high priest. He told them that because the people were preoccupied with fixing up their own homes and had neglected the LORD's home, the LORD would withhold the rain and cause a drought in the land. The prophet Zechariah told the people that the LORD Almighty said that He would return to them, if they returned to Him. The people harkened to the prophets, and the LORD's temple was completed in 516 B.C. The Holy Bible makes it clear that God will hear and bless only those that come to Him. The LORD illustrated this when He told Daniel that his prayers were heard from the first day that he set his heart on Him and began to keep himself from evil (Dan. 10:12).

KING XERXES

King Darius died in 486 B.C. and his son Xerxes became the king of the Persian empire. Xerxes's Hebrew name was Ahasuerus. The Holy Bible in the book of Esther tells of a series of events that happened during the reign of Ahasuerus, who is believed to be King Xerxes. During his reign, he chose and made Esther his queen. A Jew by the name of Mordecai heard that two of the king's officers were planning to kill the king. He reported it to Queen Esther and, as a result, the king was rescued. Some time later, a man by the name of Haman was honored and given the highest seat of all the king's princes (Esth. 3:1). The king commanded all his servants to bow down and reverence Haman. Mordecai, obeying the LORD's Commandment, would not bow to Haman. Haman was furious and planned to use his authority to execute Mordecai and all the Jews that were throughout the whole kingdom of Ahasuerus. In the meantime, the king was planning to honor Mordecai for saving his life. When Haman's plan to kill Mordecai was made known to the king, Haman and his people were executed, and the Jewish race was saved. Those that love their God and creator are not to bow down to any human being, regardless of their man-made and man-given titles.

THE PROPHET MALACHI

During this time, the WORD of the LORD to Israel came through the prophet Malachi (Mal. 1:1). Malachi assured the Jews that the LORD loved them, and spoke out against their spiritual faults. Many were cheating the LORD by holding back their best animals, and offering their crippled and diseased animals as sacrifices to God. Secondly, the priests were not giving glory unto the Name of the LORD, which caused many to stumble at keeping God's Law. Also many were robbing God by not paying their tithes. The tithe was basically the first tenth of one's increase from his flocks and crops. As we learned, Jacob, whose name was changed to Israel, had twelve sons. The descendants of those sons formed the twelve tribes of Israel that left Egypt for the Promise Land. The tribe of Levi did not receive an inheritance in the Promise Land. Instead they were put in charge of all the temple sacrifices and services, and were supported by the tithes of the other tribes. When Jesus Christ died upon the cross, the Age of the Law came to an end, and the Age of Grace began. Jesus Christ became man's High Priest and His Blood became the final and Only Sacrifice that could wash away all of man's sin. Jesus Christ paid the price for everyone that receives Him into their heart. Those that do, are to personally serve Him by sharing and helping to spread His Gospel and by helping the less fortunate. The tithe today belongs to Jesus Christ. This is because the Spirit of Jesus Christ is presently living in the hearts of man and not in man-made temples (Acts 17:24). Pastors that demand 10 percent from their congregations are wrongfully demanding what belongs to God. Jesus Christ commanded His apostles to freely give (Matt. 10:8). Spreading God's Word was never intended to be the career opportunity that it has become. Those that are being taught God's Word are to give what they can cheerfully give to those that teach, without neglecting to personally give to the spiritual and physical needs of their fellowman. While on this earth, Jesus taught that those that help the poor will be storing up treasures in heaven (Luke 18:22).

EZRA

Artaxerxes, king of Persia, granted Ezra, a scribe in the law of Moses, his request to lead the second group of Jews back to Jerusalem from Babylon (Ezra 7:6). Ezra was given gold, silver, and many other supplies to be used in the LORD's temple. Upon his return to Jerusalem, Ezra taught the Law as it was given to Moses, and encouraged the people to walk in the Way of the LORD. According to the original Law, it was unlawful to intermarry outside the Jewish race. This law was to prevent God's chosen people from worshipping foreign gods. Unfortunately this is exactly what happened, and for this reason, the LORD's judgment fell upon the nation of Israel.

NEHEMIAH

Nehemiah, a close servant of King Artaxerxes, received word from Jerusalem that the walls of the city were still broken down, and that his fellow Jews were in great distress (Neh. 1:3). When the king found this out, and saw that Nehemiah was saddened, he made him governor of Jerusalem and sent him there to rebuild its city walls. The enemies of the Jews became angry upon learning that the walls of Jerusalem were being rebuilt, and conspired to come and to fight against Jerusalem (Neh. 4:8). The Jews at this time were slaves in their homeland, and were surrounded by many of their former enemies who were also governed by the king of Persia. Nehemiah ordered one half of the workers to carry swords and spears, and to protect the other half as they worked on the wall. After the wall around Jerusalem was completed, more people, including priests and servants, resettled inside the city. There they reviewed the sins of their forefathers, and vowed to faithfully follow the Law of God as it was given through Moses. After this, Nehemiah returned to Artaxerxes. When he did, the people became lax in their spirituality, causing Nehemiah to return to Jerusalem and to correct them. Once the wall was around the city, the people felt secure in themselves and no longer relied upon the LORD. This is true of so many today. When they need something, they turn to God, and when they are blessed, they cease to communicate with Him, Who blessed them. The hearts of those that truly love God are stayed on Jesus Christ (God's True Image) and on His Written Word, the Holy Bible, during both good and trying times.

END OF THE OLD TESTAMENT

Nehemiah returned to Jerusalem for the second time in the approximate year of 425 B.C., It is at this time, during the Persian Empire, that the Old Testament Scriptures come to a close. It would be approximately four hundred years before Biblical history would once again be resumed in the scriptures of the New Testament. However, there are various other writings that record and give us a clear chronological view of the empires, and of the plight of the Jewish people during this period of time.

THE GRECIAN EMPIRE

As we learned, the Old Testament closes with Nehemiah bringing religious reform to the Jews, who had returned to their homeland during the Persian Empire. It was during this period of time that the Persian Empire began to weaken. Greece became the next world power in 334 B.C., at which time "Alexander the Great" defeated the Persians. Alexander treated the Jews well. When he died in 323 B.C., the Grecian Empire was divided between its generals. General Seleccus took over the land north of Jerusalem, which was called Syria. General Ptolemy of Egypt took control of Jerusalem, and encouraged many Jews to relocate to the Egyptian city of Alexandria. With Greek being the language of the day, the Old Testament was translated into the Greek language by Hebrew scholars. In 204 B.C., "Antiochus (Seleccus) the Great," king of the land north of Jerusalem (Syria), took control of Jerusalem away from Ptolemy. Under Seleucid rule, the Jews in Jerusalem were forbidden to worship the LORD. This caused the Jews to rebel until they regained their religious freedom, at which time they rededicated the LORD's temple.

THE ROMAN EMPIRE

In 63 B.C., the Romans, under General Pompey, invaded and captured Jerusalem. In 48 B.C., Julius Caesar gained control of the rising Roman empire, and appointed Antipater as ruler over the Holy Land. After the death of Antipater, his son Herod succeeded him and was given the title: "King of the Jews." As the Romans defeated various nations, they would govern them by appointing their own rulers over them. The Romans conquered the Grecian Empire piece by piece, and finished them off when Octavian, the adopted son of Julius Caesar, defeated the armies of Cleopatra. Octavian, who was given the name of Augustus Caesar, was the first emperor of the official Roman Empire under the "Pax Romana." The New Testament begins during the reign of Augustus Caesar and the reign of Herod, who was the appointed King of Judea under the authority of Augustus Caesar.

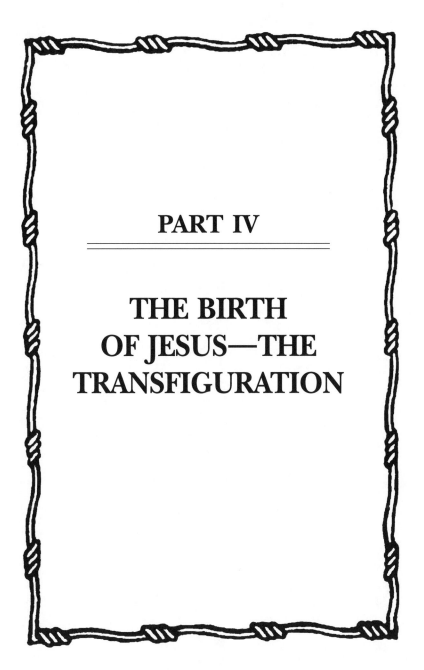

PART IV

THE BIRTH OF JESUS—THE TRANSFIGURATION

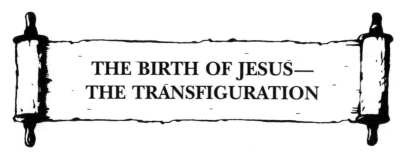

THE BIRTH OF JESUS—
THE TRANSFIGURATION

ANNOUNCEMENT OF JOHN THE BAPTIST

In the time of Herod, Zechariah was serving as a priest in the temple of the LORD. One day when he went into the temple, the angel Gabriel appeared to him. Gabriel told Zechariah that his wife Elizabeth, who had been barren, would bear him a son who would be called John, and who would prepare a people for the coming of the Lord (Luke 1:5–17).

ANNOUNCEMENT OF JESUS CHRIST

During the sixth month of Elizabeth's pregnancy, the angel Gabriel was sent from God to a virgin named Mary. Mary was engaged to a man named Joseph whose ancestors were of the lineage of King David. Gabriel told Mary that because she found favor with God, she would bear a son and call his name Jesus. He also told her that Jesus would be called the Son of the Most High, and that he would reign on the throne of David and over the house of Jacob forever. Mary then asked Gabriel how this could happen, since she was a virgin. He told her that the Holy Spirit would come unto her, and the power of God would bless her by impregnating her with the Son of God. He added that nothing shall be impossible with God (Luke 1:26–37). After Mary had become pregnant, an angel of the LORD appeared to Mary's fiancé, Joseph, and told him that the baby which was conceived in Mary was of the Holy Spirit, and that he should not be afraid to take Mary as his wife. The angel made it clear to Joseph that this was no ordinary baby and that this child, which was of God's Holy Spirit, would save his people from sin. The birth of Jesus Christ would fulfill the prophecy that Isaiah the prophet spoke 700 years earlier, when he prophesied that a virgin would give birth to a son called Emmanuel, which means "God with us" (Matt. 1:18–24).

BIRTH OF JESUS CHRIST

At the time just prior to the birth of Jesus Christ, Caesar Augustus, the emperor of Rome, issued a decree that all the world should be taxed. Everyone was required to go to his own city to be taxed. Joseph, being of the house and lineage of David, left Nazareth with Mary and entered into a city of David, called Bethlehem of Judea. While they were there, Jesus Christ was born in a manger because there was no room in the inn (Luke 2:1–7). At this time, the angel of the Lord appeared unto the shepherds in the field. He told them that unto them was born that day, in the city of David, a Savior which is "Christ" the Lord. Christ is the English translation of the Greek Name for Messiah, and means "of God" or "God's Sent One." "Christ" recognizes Jesus's Divine Existence, and "Jesus," which means Savior, identifies Christ's Human Existence. As we learned, Christ existed from the eternal past (Mic. 5:2), and was later sent by the Power of His Holy Spirit into this world to save mankind (Gal. 4:4).

THE WISE MEN

After the birth of Jesus Christ, wise men from the east arrived in Jerusalem and asked the whereabouts of Him that was born "King of the Jews." They said that they had seen His star and come to worship Him (Matt. 2:1–2). It is important to understand that at this time, the Jews were anticipating the arrival of their Messiah. According to the prophets, this coming King, the Sent One of God, would save Israel and its people from foreign control and persecution. When Herod, the king of Judea under Caesar Augustus, learned of the wise men's search for the newly born King of the Jews, he was greatly troubled. He gathered together the chief priests and scribes, and asked them where Christ was to be born. They told him that according to the prophets, the Christ was to be born in Bethlehem. Herod then called the wise men and sent them to Bethlehem to find the Christ. Herod told them that when they found Him, they should return and tell him, so that he too could go and worship Him. When the wise men found Christ, they fell down and worshipped Him, and gave Him gifts of gold, frankincense, and myrrh. God warned them in a dream not to return to Herod, so they departed into their country by another route.

JOSEPH'S DREAMS

After the wise men left, an angel of the Lord appeared unto Joseph in a dream and told him to take Jesus and Mary, and to flee to Egypt until further notice. This was due to the fact that Herod wanted to kill Jesus, for fear that Jesus would take over his throne as King. When Herod found out that the wise men had left without telling him where Jesus was, he ordered that all the baby boys in Bethlehem be killed, hoping one of them would be Jesus. After Herod died, an angel of the Lord appeared in a dream to Joseph, while in Egypt, and told him to take Jesus and His mother Mary, and to go into the land of Israel. Fearing the new king, Herod Archelaus, son of Herod, Joseph went into Galilee and dwelt in a city called Nazareth.

THE CHILDHOOD OF JESUS

The Holy Bible does not give us a lot of information about the childhood of Jesus, but we are told that as he grew, He became strong, filled with wisdom, and that the "Grace" of God was upon Him (Luke 2:40). This tells us that Jesus gave pleasure, joy, and delight as a child, and that He showed loving kindness towards others. Even though Jesus is God, He is meek and lowly in heart (Matt. 11:29). He is humble and easy to approach and talk to. We can only spiritually approach Him now, but we will be able to physically approach Him when He returns. Christ did not come into this world to judge and condemn this world. He saw that man was headed for destruction, and in His Love for mankind, He chose to physically come into this world to save mankind. Christ, the Eternal Image of God, chose to come into this world and to shed His Blood on the cross in order to reward those that choose to believe, accept, and follow Him with Eternal Life. While on earth, Jesus taught man how to live. At twelve years of age, Jesus was in the LORD's temple amazing the teachers with His understanding and His answers. When Mary found Him in the temple, after being separated from Him, Jesus told her that He had to be in His Father's house, in order to take care of His Father's business (Luke 2:49). Even as a child, Jesus was teaching mankind the truth about God. During His human life on earth prior to the beginning of his full-time ministry, Jesus was a carpenter by trade (Mic. 6:3). Jesus experienced the trials and hardships of human life, and therefore can relate to our needs. At the age of thirty, the accepted age of rabbis, Jesus Christ began His full-time ministry, in which He revealed and proved beyond a doubt that He is the Way, the Truth, and the Life of God (John 14:6).

HISTORY UPDATE

During His thirty-year wait, Jesus learned firsthand what it is like to experience both the good and the bad things of human life. Unlike the hypocrites, Jesus taught "do as I do" instead of just "do as I say." Jesus began His full-time ministry during the time in which Tiberius Caesar was the emperor of the Roman Empire. Under the authority of Tiberius Caesar were: Pontius Pilate, governor over Judaea; Herod-Antipas, ruler over Galilee; Herod Philip, ruler over Ituraea and Trachonitis; and Lysanias, ruler of Abilene. Annas and Caiaphas were the Jewish high priests at this time (Luke 3:1-2).

THE MESSAGE OF JOHN THE BAPTIST

The appearance and the ministry of John the Baptist was foretold 700 years in advance by the prophet Isaiah. Isaiah prophesied that a voice would proclaim and prepare the way for the appearance of the LORD (Is. 40:3-5). John the Baptist was that voice. He prepared the people by telling them to repent and turn from their sinful ways. As an outward sign he would baptize or immerse in water those that repented. Baptism was an old Jewish ritual that was practiced for centuries and was symbolic of purification. John told the people that One Mightier (Jesus Christ) than he would come and baptize them with the Holy Ghost and with fire (Matt 3:11). John foretold that those that would receive Jesus Christ as their Lord would be baptized with the Holy Ghost, and that those would not would be cast into fire (Luke 3:9). John the Baptist was predestined to introduce Jesus Christ to the world (John 1:6-7). The Holy Bible tells us that this was necessary because no man had seen God at any time. Only Christ, God's Soul (True Image), Who is in the Bosom of the Father (God's Eternal Mind of Love) could make God known (John 1:18). Notice the words "Who is in the Bosom of the Father." This confirms the fact that Jesus Christ is the Soul, or the Man of God's Heart. Knowing that God is the Spirit of Love (I

John 4:8), we can further understand why the apostle Paul referred to Jesus as "the Son (True Image) of God's Love" (Col. 1:13).

THE PHARISEES

While John was baptizing people in the Jordan River, the Jews sent priests and Levites from Jerusalem to ask him who he was. These priests were members of the largest Jewish religious-political party called the Pharisees. The Pharisees believed that the way to reach God was by following a bunch of man-made rituals and traditions, which were incorporated into Old Testament Law. They were more concerned about keeping the rules than having a relationship with God. The Pharisees were also self-righteous and judgmental hypocrites. When they asked John who he was, he told them that he was the voice of one crying in the wilderness, that the prophet Isaiah mentioned. He also told them that One Greater than he would come, Whom they did not know, even though He stood among them (John 1:19–28).

THE BAPTISM OF JESUS

The next day, when John saw Jesus coming towards him to be baptized, John said: "Behold the Lamb of God which taketh away the sin of the world" (John 1:29). John bore witness that he saw the Holy Spirit descend as a dove and remain upon Jesus, and that this was the sign given to him to know that Jesus was the Sent One, the Son of God, Who baptizes with the Holy Spirit (John 1:30–34). As far as we are told, up until this time, Jesus chose to experience human life as a normal human being without using or demonstrating the infinite power of His Holy Spirit. Jesus was now ready to reveal Himself, and then to provide Himself as the Perfect Sacrifice for the forgiveness of man's sin. For this reason, Jesus referred to Himself as the "Son of man." As we will soon understand, to those who choose to believe in Him, He grants the Holy Spirit Power to become children of God (John 1:12).

SATAN—MAN'S ENEMY

As we begin to study the ministry and the earthly mission of Jesus Christ, it is most important to remember that man's biggest

enemy is Satan and the influences of his wicked thoughts or spirits
(Eph. 6:12). As we learned, when Satan sinned by rebelling
against God, he was thrown out of God's Heaven, along with the
angels that sided with him. This is because God hates sin, which is
disobedience to His Will. When God created man, Satan saw how
much God loved man. Because of this, Satan hated man, and set
out to destroy man's perfect relationship with God. He did this by
getting man's mind to turn from desiring and working to please
God, to desiring and working to please one's self. This is the spirit
of Satan that entered into and began to control man's mind, thus
becoming man's new master. Due to the fact that Adam was the
father of the human race, Satan's spirit was passed down through
him to every generation (Rom. 5:12).

SHEOL

The Hebrew word "Sheol" was used in the Old Testament to
describe the place where souls went after leaving the body upon
one's physical death (Job 17:16). Hades is the Greek translation of
the word Sheol. Hades, a dwelling place of disembodied spirits,
was divided into two sections or compartments.. The righteous
souls went to the comfort zone, and the unrighteous souls went to
the torment zone (Luke 16:22–23). When Jesus began His
ministry, the Old Testament believers that obeyed the Law of
Moses and had their sins covered, by offering the LORD a blood
sacrifice, were abiding in the comfort zone of Hades. As we
learned, animal sacrifices could only cover sin, but they could not
take away sin (Heb. 10:4–5). Only God could cleanse man of his
sin, free him from Hades, and grant him entrance into His
Everlasting Kingdom.

JESUS CHRIST—MAN'S SAVIOR

The Person of Jesus Christ has been so misunderstood and
misrepresented that many people never think of Jesus Christ as
their Savior. Jesus came to do what no man could do. He came to
fight and defeat Satan, and then to give us the power to do the
same. The first thing that Jesus did after he was baptized was to go
out and fight Satan, face to face. When they met, Satan began to
tempt Jesus, just as he had done to Adam and Eve. He took Jesus
to a very high mountain and showed him all the kingdoms of the

world and the glory of them. Satan then told Jesus that he would give Him all of them if Jesus would fall down and worship him. Jesus told Satan, "You shall worship the Lord your God and Him only shall you serve" (Matt. 4:10). Jesus defeated Satan by refusing every temptation that the world had to offer.

NOTE

Before we continue, it is important that we understand how Satan could offer Jesus Christ the kingdoms of this earth. In order to understand this, we must first consider the fact that at the time of man's creation, his spirit mind, which is the head of his body, was at perfect peace with, and obedient to the Lord God, his Creator. As we learned, when man disobeyed God, Satan's spirit entered into and corrupted man's mind. The minds of men began to think of ways to please their fleshly lusts instead of ways to please God. Satan's spirit of greed and pride led to crime, immorality, disease, and death. Satan is a liar. Every kingdom of the world became his, only in the sense that his spirit became the spirit of this world. When God took on a body of flesh, Satan tried to tempt Jesus with worldly lusts. Jesus told him: "Get thee behind me, Satan" (Luke 4:8). Jesus proved that His Spirit is more powerful than any worldly temptation. Those that receive God's Holy Spirit, by accepting and following Jesus Christ, will overcome this world. This group will rule and reign over this earth with Jesus, after He returns and removes Satan and his followers from it. As you can now see, everything belongs to Jesus Christ. All of Satan's offers of fun, wealth, and fame are only temporary.

SATAN'S WORLD

When Satan corrupted man's mind, God had the choice either to destroy man, or to provide a way to restore or renew man's mind. Due to God's great love for man, God chose the latter. In order to accomplish this, God would have to come into this world, live a perfect human life, and then impart His Perfect Human Mind (Nature) into the minds of man. Man would then have the power to know and to reject every evil thought and temptation that was against the Will of God. In the meantime, God would allow Satan to reign in this world for a predetermined time. Up until Judgment Day, man would have the freedom to choose his master. Those that choose, receive, and abide in and with the Spirit of Jesus Christ will become children of God and will inherit all things. Those that fail to receive God's Holy Spirit will continue to live and work for the temporary pleasures and things of this world until Judgment Day arrives. At this time, Satan and all those that are led by his spirit will be eternally separated from those that chose to accept God's "Way" of Eternal Life, Jesus Christ. Do not be deceived! Satan can promise you fame, pleasure, and fortune, but his temporary rewards lead to eternal damnation. Yes, Satan's present reign, as prince of the world (John 12:31), is coming to a rapid end. Satan's spirit has been the cause of every evil thing in this present world. Unfortunately, many people do not understand this and have blamed God for the sufferings of humanity. Those that are presently committing crimes and living unrighteous lives are children of Satan (I John 3:10). These folks must call upon God in the name of Jesus Christ, ask Him to cleanse them of their sins, and invite Him to come and live in their heart as their Lord and Savior. If they fail to do so, they will be eternally separated from Jesus Christ, along with Satan and his followers. When that day comes, there will be no turning back, and no one to blame but oneself.

JESUS CLEARS THE TEMPLE

Jesus went up to Jerusalem for the Jewish celebration of Passover. When Jesus entered the temple and saw that it was being used as a business place by sellers of animals for sacrifices and changers of money, He made a small whip and drove off all the animals. He then poured out the money changers' coins, overthrew their tables, and told those that were selling to leave and not make His Father's house a trading house. After Jesus disrupted these businesses, the Jews asked Jesus for a sign to show them by what authority He had done this. Jesus then told them to destroy this temple and He would raise it up in three days. The Jews thought Jesus was talking about the temple which had taken them forty-six years to build, but in reality, Jesus was speaking to them of the Temple of His Body (John 2:13–22). As Jesus Christ continued his ministry, He was hated more and more by the evil people, both inside and outside the religious system of that day. This was because Jesus was exposing their evil activities and rebuking their hypocritical ways. The righteous people loved Jesus, but the evil people hated Him. This is also true today.

NICODEMUS

While in Jerusalem, Jesus was approached one night by a ruler and member of the Pharisees named Nicodemus. Nicodemus told Jesus that many believed that He was sent from God. Jesus answered by telling Nicodemus that unless a man is "born again," he cannot see the Kingdom of God (John 3:3). Nicodemus then asked Jesus how one can be born again. Jesus told him that unless one was born of water and of Spirit, he could not enter into the Kingdom of God (John 3:5). Jesus clarified this by letting Nicodemus know that one is born of water from his mother's womb, and that one is born of Spirit when he receives God's Holy Spirit. Jesus then told Nicodemus that God so loved the world, that He sent His only begotten Son into the world, not to judge the world, but rather to save the world. One is saved by receiving God's Free Gift of the Holy Spirit. This happens after one hears and believes the Gospel of Jesus Christ, confesses with His mouth that Jesus Christ is the Son (the True Image of God's Eternal Spirit), and receives God's Holy Spirit. Notice that Nicodemus came at night. He was among the Pharisees that believed that Jesus was the Son of God, but would not confess their belief publicly, for fear of being thrown out of the synagogue and losing their position in society. Jesus let Nicodemus know that in order for him to be born again he would have to publicly confess his faith. John the Baptist prepared the way for Jesus by preaching a baptism of repentance for the forgiveness of sins (Mark 1:4). To repent means to turn one's mind away from its former way of thinking and towards the True God. As an outward sign, John would publicly immerse those that repented in water. Jesus did not Personally baptize his followers with water (John 4:2), but would later, as foretold by John the Baptist, baptize His followers with the Holy Spirit.

IMPRISONMENT OF JOHN THE BAPTIST

John the Baptist was hated by the evil people of his day. This was due to the fact that he spoke out against them, regardless of who they were. John the Baptist spoke out against all the evil things that Herod Antipas (the second son of Herod the Great) had done, including an affair with Herodias, his brother Philip's wife. As a result of this, Herod shut John up in prison (Luke 3:19–20), and later had his head cut off. Jesus taught man that he should not fear those that can physically kill the body and not the soul, but that they should fear God, because He Alone has the power to destroy both the body and the soul in hell (Matt. 10:28). Jesus Christ told His followers that He is the Giver of Eternal Life and that no one can take His sheep out of His Hand (John 10:28). As long as one keeps God's Word in his or her heart, Satan cannot accuse them of being sinners and claim them as his children. This is why Satan and his demons are working hard to prevent as many as possible from knowing God's Truth, Jesus Christ.

WOMAN OF SAMARIA

After John the Baptist had been imprisoned, Jesus departed from Judaea and headed north towards Galilee. Between Judaea and Galilee was Samaria, the old capital of the kings of Israel. At this time, Samaria was populated by the exiles from many nations, many of whom intermarried with the northern tribes of Israel. For this reason, there was great animosity between the Jews and the Samaritans, who were not considered pure by the Jews. As Jesus was passing through this region, He stopped at Jacob's Well and asked a Samaritan woman for a drink. The woman was shocked, because Jesus was a Jew and at that time the Jews did not associate with the Samaritans. In their discussion Jesus told the woman that salvation was from the Jews. The woman told Jesus that she knew that the Messiah would come, Who would be called Christ. Jesus then told her that He was the Jewish Messiah (John 4:25–26). When the woman returned to town and told the people, they came and many believed that Jesus was indeed Christ, the Sent One of God, the Savior of the world (John 4:39–42). Jesus opened His arms not only to the Jews but to all people. Salvation is from the Jews, because it can be had only through faith in Jesus Christ, Who was delivered into this world through the Jewess Mary.

JESUS HEALS THE SICK

When Jesus reached Galilee, an official begged Him to heal his son who was ill and at the point of death. Jesus told the man to go and that his son would live. As the man went towards his home, his servants met him and told him that his son liveth. When they told him the time his son began to recover, he realized it was at the exact hour in which Jesus had told him that his son would live. Because of this, this official and all his household believed in Jesus Christ (John 4:46–54). Jesus healed all that were sick and came to Him, so that all mankind would believe that He was the Sent One of God, the Savior of the world.

JESUS DESCRIBES HIS MISSION

While Jesus was in Nazareth, the town in which He grew up, He entered the synagogue to read from the Scriptures. He read out of the book of Isaiah (Is. 61:1–2), where it was written that the Holy Spirit would anoint One to preach the gospel to the poor, to heal the brokenhearted, to proclaim release to the captives (those physically and spiritually bound by the devil), to preach recovering of sight to the blind (those physically blind and those blind to God's Truth), to set at liberty those who are oppressed (those broken down by life's calamities), and to preach the acceptable year of the Lord (the time of God's Kingdom). When Jesus finished reading, He declared that He was this Anointed One of Whom Isaiah wrote. Those in the synagogue became furious because they did not believe Jesus, Whom they knew as a youth (Luke 4:16–30). Jesus then moved to Capernaum, a city of Galilee.

JESUS CASTS OUT UNCLEAN SPIRIT

At Capernaum, Jesus entered the synagogue on the Sabbath and taught the people with authority. The people were astonished at His doctrine because His Word was with Power. A man with an unclean spirit (a devil-possessed mind) feared that Jesus would destroy them, and cried out to Jesus, "Let us alone." He told Jesus that he knew that He was the Holy One of God. Jesus responded by ordering the unclean spirit to be silent, and to come out of the man. The unclean spirit then convulsed the man and cried with a loud voice as he came out of him. The people were amazed that even the unclean spirits obeyed Jesus. At once the fame of Jesus spread throughout the surrounding regions of Galilee (Mark 1:21–28).

NOTE

God's angels are His messengers or ministering spirits. (Heb. 1:14). Angels were created with the freedom of choice. As we learned, Satan and the angels that chose to follow him were cast out of God's Heavenly Kingdom when they rebelled against God. Jesus Christ said that He was there and saw Satan fall from heaven (Luke 10:18). The fallen angels are presently the evil spirits of this world, known as devils or demons. This explains how they recognized Jesus Christ, and also why they feared Him. You see, Jesus Christ is One with God Almighty, the Father of all spirits. As God, Jesus has authority over all spirits. When God saw that Satan, who was created full of wisdom, and his fallen angels were deceiving mankind and leading him to hell, He took on a body of flesh and came into the world to save mankind. Satan tried to defeat God, after God had taken on a human body, by tempting Jesus with the lusts of this world. Jesus not only defeated Satan, but also has enabled mankind to overcome Satan by granting His Holy Spirit to those that ask. Those that receive Jesus Christ into their hearts receive the Power to break all their addictions and to say no to Satan and all his evil influences and temptations. Millions have been set free from alcohol addiction, drug addiction, sexual perversion, and every other kind of sin by inviting Jesus Christ into their hearts and receiving His Holy Spirit, which is the Holy Spirit of God Almighty. Remember, Jesus Christ is the True Image of, and One with God's Ever-present, All-knowing, and All-Powerful Holy Spirit.

JESUS HEALS ALL

As the fame of Jesus Christ spread, many that were possessed with devils were brought to Jesus, and He cast out the unclean spirits with His Word. Whatever Jesus spoke was fulfilled. The Word of God always accomplishes, without exception, exactly what it sets out to accomplish (Is. 55:11). We must always remember that the Lord God is the same yesterday, today, and tomorrow.

This means that God operated in the same way in the Old Testament as He did in the New Testament, and in the same way as He does today. Jesus Christ in the Old Testament was the revealed Image of God's Word. From the time that God revealed Himself in and through Jesus Christ, Jesus Christ made God known both in Word and in Person. By knowing that one's word comes from his living and breathing soul (the true image of one's mind), and by understanding that Jesus Christ is the Essence of God's Soul (the True Image of God's Eternal Mind of Love), we can understand how God created all things by Jesus Christ (Eph. 3:9). At the time of creation, Jesus spoke the Will of His Invisible Spirit Mind, which He would later introduce to mankind as God the Father. Then, through the Power of His, God's Holy Spirit, everything that He spoke was made manifest. Jesus Christ, as the Man of God's Heart, is God, and does the Perfect Will of His Eternal and Invisible Spirit Mind. Whatever Jesus Christ speaks, happens by the power of His Holy Spirit, Who is also the Holy Spirit of God the Father, Christ's Eternal Mind of Love. Yes, God's Essence is One Mind, God the Father; One Soul, God the Son; and One Spirit, God the Holy Spirit. It is Jesus Christ Who directs His Holy Spirit to do the Will of His Heavenly Spirit Mind. This is how and why Jesus could heal everyone that was brought to Him, and could command evil spirits and sicknesses to depart (Matt. 8:16). Jesus Christ is the Name of the LORD God Almighty and whatever He speaks, happens.

FAME GROWS

As the fame of Jesus Christ grew among the people, the influence of the Pharisees began to dwindle. People were now coming from every surrounding city to see and to hear Jesus preach, and to receive their healing. The people began to realize that the Pharisees and all the religious people at that time could not heal them. Jesus Christ on the other hand healed everyone that came to Him. There was not any disease that Jesus did not heal. Even those that were blind, crippled, deformed, mentally ill, and paralyzed were all healed. When Jesus performed His first healing, He stated that unless the people see signs and wonders they would not believe (John 4:48). Jesus wanted everyone to believe in Him then, and He wants everyone to believe in Him today. This is why Jesus Christ is still healing people in every part of the world today. According to His Master Plan, Jesus will soon reward every born-again believer both past and present with a new glorified body. In order for one to be born again, he must receive God's Holy Spirit while he is alive on this earth. This is why it is so important for everyone to take the time to meet God now. As Jesus said, what good is it for one to gain the whole world and lose his own soul (Matt. 16:26). All material or worldly things are only temporary, but God is Eternal. The devil and his followers want you to put your faith in the temporary things of this world, instead of in God. Do not be deceived! Ask Jesus into your heart today and tell your family and friends to do the same, so that they too can be with you for all eternity. This is why those that truly love someone will tell him or her about Jesus.

JESUS PERSECUTED

As Jesus continued His earthly ministry, He identified Himself more and more as the Living God. In Capernaum, a paralytic was brought to Jesus for healing. As the Pharisees and scribes listened, Jesus told the man that his sins were forgiven. The scribes, most of whom were Pharisees, were the experts and teachers of the Law of Moses. Knowing that God alone can forgive sins (Mark 2:7), they thought within themselves that Jesus committed blasphemy, which is a disrespect of God that was punishable by death. Jesus, Who can see the deep thoughts of man, told them that He could have told the man to arise and walk. He chose not to because he wanted everyone to know that He, the True Image of God, is He Who forgives sins (Matt. 9:1–8). As Jesus began to identify Himself as the Living God, the Pharisees, scribes, and other religious sects of that time began to persecute Him. Persecute means to pursue in a hostile manner, to harass, to trouble, and to afflict. They began to accuse Jesus of breaking God's Law by eating with sinners, by not fasting, and by healing the sick on the Sabbath (John 5:17).

PHARISEES REJECT JESUS

Why would the Pharisees, supposedly the most righteous Jewish sect of that time, desire to persecute Jesus? We must first consider the fact that the members of this sect were praised by men. They sat in the highest and best seats at all occasions, and enjoyed the praises of men. When Jesus appeared, He not only refused to go along with their systems, but also spoke out against them. Jesus told them that they were hypocrites, who sought praise instead of directing man to praise God. The Pharisees had taken on the spirit that Satan brought into this world. These Pharisees enjoyed their lifestyles and the praises of man, and they did not want Jesus Christ to spoil their party. Despite their threats, Jesus continued performing miracles and revealing the Power of God to mankind. As the Pharisees saw the large crowds following Jesus, they were afraid that they would soon lose their present positions in society. At this time, the Pharisees were so much into their traditions, rituals, and laws that they did not have the Holy Spirit of God's Word in their hearts. Because of this, they failed to recognize and accept Jesus Christ as the Messiah of Whom the Holy Scriptures testify. Unfortunately, many are making the same mistake today. Only God's Holy Spirit, which accompanies God's Word, can teach and prepare us for what is about to happen.

JESUS REVEALS HIMSELF

When Jesus told the Pharisees that God was His Father, making Himself equal with God, they sought the more to kill Him (John 5:18). Due to the fact that they put their man-made rituals and traditions before the very Word of God, they were unfamiliar with the over one hundred prophecies contained in the Holy Scriptures that described Jesus Christ and His earthly mission. Because they failed to recognize Jesus as "God with us," they could not understand under whose authority Jesus could heal the sick, give sight to the blind, and forgive man of his sins. Despite the threats and persecutions that Jesus faced, He continued His mission by revealing Himself to all, and by choosing twelve apostles to spread His Gospel throughout the world. This Good News was, and is His Promise of Eternal Life to all those that believe His Gospel and receive Him during this present "Age of Grace."

THE TWELVE APOSTLES

Not all the Jews rejected Jesus. The Jews and non-Jews that believed and followed Jesus Christ during His earthly ministry were called disciples of Jesus Christ. Disciples of Jesus Christ are presently His Body of "born-again" believers. Their duty today, as in the past, is to learn, obey, and share the Good News or the Gospel of Jesus Christ, as they journey through life upon this earth. During Christ's earthly ministry, a great crowd of His disciples and others gathered to hear Jesus speak and to be healed of their diseases (Matt. 6:17). From among these disciples, Jesus, Who came into this world as a Jew, through the seed of Abraham, chose twelve Jewish apostles. Jesus chose twelve Jewish apostles because there are twelve tribes of Israel, and each apostle will one day rule over one of the twelve tribes (Matt. 19:28). The names of these twelve apostles were: Simon-Peter, James, John, Andrew, Philip, Bartholomew, Matthew, Thomas, James the son of Alphaeus, Thaddaeus-Judas, Simon, and Judas Iscariot, who would betray Jesus.

NOTE

The way the apostles described Jesus Christ when they first met Him makes it clear that they thought Him to be the Messiah. For example: After Andrew found Jesus, Andrew told his brother Simon-Peter that they had found the "Messiah," translated into English as "Christ," the Sent One of God (John 1:41). After Philip met Jesus Christ and joined the other disciples of Christ, he told Nathaniel that they found Him of Whom Moses in the Law and the prophets did write (John 1:45). Yes, the first four of the ten commandments refer to Jesus Christ. Man is not to have any other gods, beside Jesus Christ, the True Image of the LORD GOD. It is important to note that these ordinary men had God's Word in their hearts, while the religious priests did not. The lesson to be learned from this is that rituals and traditions should never be substituted for the reading and teaching of God's Word, the Holy Bible.

SERMON ON THE MOUNT

One day a great multitude of people came to hear Jesus and to be healed of their diseases. At this time, Power came forth from Jesus and healed all those that touched Him (Luke 6:19). This was the situation just prior to Jesus Christ's speech, known today as the Sermon on the Mount (Matt. 5–7). Let us take a look at a few of the many spiritual topics covered in this famous speech. Jesus began by pointing out the qualities and the blessings of those that choose to follow Him and inherit the Kingdom of Heaven. Jesus described His followers as humble, repentant, meek, and pure of heart. He referred to them as the "salt" and as the "light" of this earth. During their earthly lives, these people as salt will preserve righteousness, and as light will show others the "Way" of God. Jesus proceeded to tell the people that He did not come to destroy, but rather to fulfill the Law of Moses and to fulfill the prophecies of the prophets.

THE NEW COVENANT

Jeremiah prophesied 600 years before the birth of Jesus Christ that the Old Covenant, which was the Old Testament agreement between the LORD and Israel, would be fulfilled and that the LORD Himself would make a New Covenant with the house of Israel (Jer. 31:31). The LORD God, through His WORD, the Eternal Spirit of Jesus Christ, established the Old Covenant with Israel. The LORD then came into this world, in the Person of Jesus Christ, and established His New Covenant with Israel and all the world. The Old Covenant offered man a way to temporarily cover his sins through animal sacrifices. The New Covenant, which applies to this present, and soon to end, "Age of Grace," offers all mankind the "Way" to become One Spirit Blood with God. Those that receive and are led by the Holy Spirit of Jesus Christ are children of God and will inherit eternal life.

JESUS CLARIFIES LAW

In His Sermon on the Mount, Jesus clarified God's Commandments to the people, and made them aware that they were accountable not only for their deeds, but also for their inner thoughts. For example, Jesus said that man should not commit adultery in deed or in thought, and that any man who looks at a woman lustfully has committed adultery in his heart. In other words, immoral fantasies in one's mind are spiritual adulteries. As Jesus continued His sermon, He taught man to pray in purity and humility, and gave him the Lord's Prayer as an example of how he should pray.

THE LORD'S PRAYER

Jesus instructed man not to pray in order to be seen by others as the hypocrites, but to go into their room, shut the door, and pray to their "Father" in secret (Matt. 6:6). The Lord's Prayer is recorded both in the Book of Matthew and in the Book of Luke. Jesus instructs us to address our prayers to our "Father" in heaven. The LORD God, in the Old Testament and through Christ (His Spirit Image), said: "For as the heavens are higher than the earth, so are My ways higher than your ways, and My thoughts (God's Heavenly Spirit Mind) than your thoughts" (Is. 55:9). In reality, Jesus Christ was introducing His Heavenly Spirit to mankind as God the Father. Due to the fact that Jesus Christ is One with His Heavenly and Spirit Mind of Love, known as God the Father, Jesus was drawing mankind unto Himself. You see, it is God's desire to head up all things, both in the heavens and upon the earth in Jesus Christ (Eph. 1:9–10). The Good News or the Gospel of Jesus Christ is that those that choose to believe in and follow Jesus Christ become children of God and will inherit eternal life in His Kingdom. When we pray, "Thy Kingdom come, Thy will be done, on earth as it is in heaven," we are praying for Jesus Christ, the Son (True Image) of God's Love, to come to this earth and to set up God's Everlasting Kingdom, in which everyone will love one another and do God's Will. This new and glorious age will begin after Jesus Christ releases God's vengeance on the evil, and returns to this earth as King of kings, to rule and to reign over the nations of this world from Jerusalem.

JESUS CHRIST

Jesus Christ is, and has always been in the bosom of God the Father (John 1:18). Jesus Christ, the Essence of God's Soul, is the Man of God's Heart. He revealed God's Image to man when He came and was born into this world by the Virgin Mary. Only after taking on a human body did God's Eternal Soul become known as the Son of God, and God's Eternal and Heavenly Mind become known as God the Father. Christ always existed with and as God. He was in the beginning, and all things were made by Him (John 1:1–3). He created not only man, but also everything visible and invisible. Isaiah the prophet prophesied 700 years before the birth of Christ, "for unto us a Child is born, unto us a

Son is given" (Is. 9:6). This portion of God's Word proceeds to tell us of Christ's future and Kingly reign on this earth. This will take place when Jesus Christ returns as Judge and King. Jesus was rejected in part by the Jews because they were expecting the Sent One of God to immediately set up God's Kingdom. They failed to study and to recognize from the Scriptures that the Christ on His first appearance would be the Sacrificial Lamb, as described in the 53rd Chapter of Isaiah. Jesus Christ first came into this world to shed His Blood for the payment of man's sin (Gal. 4:4). This is why John the Baptist, when he saw Jesus approaching, introduced Him as "the Lamb of God, which taketh away the sin of the world" (John 1:29). We will understand this more fully as we continue.

ONE MASTER

Jesus stated, in His "Sermon on the Mount," that no one can serve two masters. One will work either for God, or for worldly things. One will fast for God, or for personal praise. One will give in private, or in public. One will lay up treasures in heaven, or on this earth. One will live in peace, or in fear. One will judge oneself, or others. One will accept Jesus Christ, or reject Jesus Christ. One will help the needy, or ignore the needy. One will enter Heaven, or enter hell. One will lead others towards Christ, or away from Christ. One will love others, or hate others. One will love his enemies, or hate his enemies. One will follow Christ's path, or the world's path. One will give his heart to God, or to this world. God's Word declares that where one's treasure is, there his heart is also. We are to individually examine our lives in each and every one of the above areas.

JESUS FORETELLS DEATH

Jesus continued His mission by healing people of every sort of infirmity and by raising the dead. After Jesus healed one who was possessed with a devil, blind, and dumb, the Pharisees accused Him of casting out devils by the power of the devil. Jesus then warned them about blasphemy against the Holy Ghost. If a man refuses to acknowledge the power and the conviction of the Holy Spirit, he will remain a sinner. Afterwards, certain scribes and Pharisees approached Jesus and asked Him to prove Himself by performing mighty signs for them. Jesus refused, and told them that the only sign He would give them was the sign of the prophet Jonas (Greek form of Jonah). Jesus told them that just as Jonas was in the whale's belly for three days and three nights, He Himself would be in the heart of the earth for three days and three nights (Matt. 12:38–40). Even though they did not understand it at the time, Jesus was telling them about His future death and resurrection.

ALL EQUAL IN KINGDOM

As Jesus was talking, his mother and brethren desired to talk to Him. When someone relayed the message to Jesus, He responded by telling the crowd that whoever does the Will of His Heavenly Spirit is His brother, His sister, and His mother (Matt. 12:50). Jesus was letting everyone know that all of God's children are treated equal. Every born-again believer is a saint (I Cor. 1:2) and a priest (I Pet. 2:9). Denominational hierarchy, and the appointing and honoring of saints are definitely against God's Will. As Christians, we are all brothers and sisters in Christ, our High Priest. We are not to bow to anyone or anything else.

PARABLE OF THE SOWER

Jesus used parables to teach man spiritual truths. Parables are stories that relate to, and give purpose and meaning to one's life. In one of His parables, Jesus likened God's Word to seed that a sower went forth to sow. Some fell by the wayside, and the fowls of the air came and ate it. Seed by the wayside are those that hear God's Word, but allow the devil to take it out of their hearts before they can believe it and be saved. Some seed fell on rock, and as soon as it sprang up, it withered in the sun for lack of moisture. Seed on the rock are those that hear and receive God's Word, but when they are tempted or persecuted for the sake of God's Word, they are pulled up by the roots and fall away. Some seed fell among thorns, and the thorns sprang up with it and choked it. Seed among the thorns are those that hear God's Word, but are more concerned with the cares, riches, and the pleasures of this life. These folks do not care enough about God or about their fellowman to share God's Good News with others. Notice that the end result for each of these groups of people is death. Lastly, some seed fell upon good soil. These are the ones that will inherit the Kingdom of Heaven. These folks hear, keep, and, out of a pure heart, share God's knowledge and bring others into the family of God (Luke 8). Those that have experienced the peace and the joy of God will want to share the Gospel of Jesus Christ with their family, friends, and others. These are those that truly have the Spirit of God's Word in their hearts, and will be the ones that will live gloriously and eternally with Him.

PARABLE OF THE TARES

The parables Jesus told were prophetic in nature. In the parable of the sower, Jesus foretold how God's Word would be accepted. In the parable of the tares, Jesus likened the Kingdom of heaven unto a man that sowed good seed in his field, but while men slept, the devil came and sowed tares among the wheat. When the fruit sprang forth, the tares (weeds) appeared also. The servants then asked the householder if they should go and gather up the tares. The householder told them not to, in case they root up some of the wheat with them. He then told them to let them both grow until the harvest, at which time the tares will be burnt, and the wheat will be gathered into the householder's barn. Notice that the tares and the wheat grow side by side, the ungodly next to the Godly. When Jesus Christ returns to this earth, He will eternally separate the children of the devil from the children of God.

THE KINGDOM OF HEAVEN

While in Capernaum, Jesus told the people to repent because the Kingdom of Heaven was at hand (Matt. 4:17). God's Kingdom is presently in reach of all people who choose to receive Jesus Christ into their hearts. When Jesus Christ returns to this earth, God's Kingdom will be established, and God's Will will be done on this earth as it is in Heaven. This is due to the fact that the tares (the unrighteous) will be eternally removed from this earth. Only those that have received God's Divine Nature (II Pet. 1:4), through faith in Jesus Christ, will be a part of God's Glorious Kingdom. Those that enter God's Kingdom will keep their soul, which is their true identity, for all eternity. Did you ever wish you could live forever in a world full of Love? If so, Jesus Christ is the "Way."

THE DIVINE POWER OF GOD

As Jesus continued His mission, He did many miracles which demonstrated the fact that, as the True Image of God, His Word is the All-Powerful Word of God. The Holy Bible teaches us that Jesus Christ is the same yesterday, today, and tomorrow (Heb. 13:8). God has always directed His Ever-present, All-Knowing, and All-Powerful Spirit Body through His Soul (True Image), Who made Himself known as Jesus Christ, the Son of God. Following His sermon, Jesus entered into a ship with His disciples and departed for the other side. That evening a great storm began to fill the ship with water. The apostles became frightened and woke Jesus, Who had fallen asleep. Jesus then rebuked the winds and the sea (Matt. 8:26). Those that saw this marveled that even the winds and the rains obeyed Jesus.

LEGION

When Jesus and His disciples reached the other side of the sea, a certain man possessed with devils was there. Jesus commanded the unclean spirit to come out of the man. The man fell down and the unclean spirit, recognizing Jesus as the Son of God, begged Jesus not to torment him. Jesus asked him what his name was, and he told Jesus his name was Legion, because many devils were entered into him. These devils begged Jesus not to command them to depart into the abyss, but rather to allow them to enter a nearby herd of swine. Jesus consented, and the devils entered the swine, which then ran violently down the steep bank into the lake and were drowned. As word of this spread, people came to see what had happened. When they saw the man that had had the legion of devils sitting with Jesus, clothed and in his right mind, they were afraid (Luke 8:26–35).

DEVILS—DEMONS

There are many spiritual truths revealed in the story of Legion of which we should take notice. First, Jesus Christ made it clear to us that there are evil spirits in this world, and that He has authority over them. When Jesus commanded the evil spirits to come out of this man, they obeyed and came out. This is because they recognized Jesus Christ as the "Word" of God. Secondly, notice that these evil spirits begged Jesus not to send them to the abyss, which is the bottomless pit, but to allow them to enter the bodies of a nearby herd of pigs. These devils, knowing the torment of the bottomless pit, begged to be sent into the bodies of pigs rather than to be sent back to the pit. Those that think hell is going to be a fun spot had better think twice. Thirdly, this story teaches us that devils are capable of possessing the minds of men and animals, and illustrates the effects of this. The moment that the evil spirits entered these pigs, the pigs became violent and drowned themselves. Fourthly, notice that when the evil spirits came out of this man, he sat by Jesus in a "right mind." Knowing that there are evil spirits and that they can enter and control one's mind, we can now understand why this world has become so violent and corrupt. As we will learn, Jesus Christ predicted that this would happen, and promised to return before humanity would totally destroy itself.

DEPRESSION AND LONELINESS

In the story of Legion, we are told that these demons would drive this man into the deserts. Deserts portray places of loneliness and helplessness. We are told that while in these mental states, Legion would cut himself with stones, possibly trying to kill himself. This explains the increase in depression, suicide, and a long list of other mental and physical disorders which doctors believe begin in the mind. When one receives the spirit of Jesus Christ, he receives God's Spirit of Power, of Love, and of a sound mind (II Tim. 1:7). When Jesus Christ cast the devils out of Legion, he was clothed and in his right mind. In like manner, millions that were formerly bound to various addictions, and were depressed, suicidal, violent, immoral, and hateful, were instantly healed the moment they asked and received the Spirit of Jesus Christ into their heart, which is where one's soul is located.

JESUS RAISES LITTLE GIRL

Jairus, a certain ruler, came and fell at Jesus's feet and asked Him to come and heal his twelve-year-old daughter, who was ill and at the point of death. As Jesus approached the home of Jairus, a woman who had a blood disease for twelve years, and had unsuccessfully spent all that she had on doctors, touched the hem of Jesus's garment and was immediately healed. Jesus, knowing that Power had gone out of him, told the woman that her faith had made her whole, for she had said within herself that if she could just touch His garment, she would be made whole. When Jesus finally arrived at the home of Jairus, people were crying because the little girl had died. Jesus told Jairus not to be afraid, but to only believe. Jesus entered the house, took the girl by the hand, and told her to arise. Immediately her spirit returned and she arose (Luke 8:40–50).

ONLY BELIEVE

Jesus told Jairus not to be afraid, but to only believe. Those that come to Jesus in faith will one day be totally healed, as was this woman with the blood disease. As we will learn, there is a day that is rapidly approaching, in which the spirit of every born-again believer that ever lived will return to his or her old body, as did the spirit of this twelve-year-old girl. At this time, by the Power of God, their former bodies will be transformed into new glorious bodies. Every born-again believer that is alive at this time will also receive a new glorified body that will live for all eternity in perfect health.

HOMETOWN REJECTS JESUS

After healing two blind men and a dumb man who was possessed with a devil, Jesus returned to His hometown of Nazareth and taught in the synagogue. There, the people were astonished and wondered where Jesus got His Wisdom and His Power to do mighty works. These people knew Jesus as the carpenter, the son of Mary, and did not believe that Jesus was the Son of God. Because of their disbelief, Jesus could not perform a lot of miracles there (Matt. 13:54–58). This is due to the fact that God's promises to man are contingent upon man's belief in Jesus Christ as the Living Son of God. Those that believe that Jesus Christ is the Living Son (True Image) of God the Father (God's Invisible and All-Powerful Spirit Mind of Love) and receive His Holy Spirit, become one with Jesus Christ and with His Invisible Spirit of Love, known as God the Father. As you can now understand, no one can enter into God's Mind (God the Father) and receive His Mercy without receiving Jesus Christ (God's Soul—True Image) into his heart. This is because the "LORD God is One

LORD." God is One Mind, One Soul, and One Spirit. Those that reject or neglect to receive Jesus Christ will not enter into His Spirit Mind. To those in this group, Jesus will say, "I know you not . . . depart from Me, all ye workers of iniquity" (Luke 13:27). Jesus is called the "Door" (John 10:9), because it is only through Him that one can know, receive, and enter God's Spirit Presence.

JESUS SENDS APOSTLES

As Jesus looked upon the great multitudes of people, He had compassion for them. He gave His twelve apostles the power and the authority to cast out devils, and the power to cure diseases. Jesus told them to go to God's chosen people, the Jews, and to tell them that the Kingdom of Heaven is at hand (Matt. 10:5–15). Before sending His apostles out to preach the Good News of God's coming Kingdom, Jesus warned them that they would be persecuted and hated for His Name's sake. Jesus told them not to fear man and what man could do to them physically, because man could not harm their soul. Jesus warned His apostles to fear only God, and to guard their minds against the evil spirits that want to take God's Word out of their heart. As Jesus taught in His parables about the Sower and the Tares, there are evil spirits around God's children. Satan's spirits work to prevent the Gospel of Jesus Christ from entering the minds and hearts of man. These demons deny Christ, tempt people to live in sin, and work to deceive people into getting so caught up with the cares, riches, and pleasures of this life that they put the Love of God behind worldly loves. As you can now understand, Satan and his demons use various methods to keep man's mind away from God.

CHRISTIAN PERSECUTION

Jesus said that He would confess, in the Presence of His Heavenly Spirit, all those that confess Him before men upon this earth (Matt. 10:32). He foretold that in many instances, man's foes would be those among his own household. Many that hear the Gospel of Jesus Christ, and ask Jesus into their heart, will face persecution from their parents and other family members that care more about family traditions than about pleasing God. The Holy Spirit opens one's eyes to God's "Truth." He turns one's mind from darkness to light, and from the power of Satan unto the Power of God. As we learned, it is through Jesus Christ that one can receive forgiveness of sins and become a member of God's family (Acts 26:18). The Holy Spirit enables one to see and to know the glory and the hope of having Jesus Christ as Savior (Col. 1:27). God, through the Power of His Holy Ghost (Holy Spirit), gives one the strength to follow Christ, even while being persecuted. Jesus said that He who loses his life on account of Him will find it (Matt. 10:39). The suffering one endures on this earth, due to his or her faith in Jesus Christ, will be nothing in comparison to God's eternal rewards.

THE LORD PROVIDES

Jesus took His apostles to a desert place. The time was just prior to the Feast of Passover, and there were many people from the surrounding areas on their way to the Jerusalem Temple to celebrate this feast day. When the people learned that Jesus was there, they came unto Him. Jesus talked to them about the Kingdom of God, and healed those that had need of a healing. By evening, great crowds had gathered to see Jesus. Jesus ordered the crowds to sit down on the grass. He then took five loaves of bread and two fish, and looking up to heaven, blessed the food. Afterwards, Jesus handed bread and fish to His disciples to serve the great crowds of people. God multiplied the five loaves and the two fish, and about 5,000 men, besides women and children, ate until they were full (Matt. 14:13–21). Notice that God supplied man's needs through the hands of Jesus Christ. There is no other way to receive God's Blessings. After everyone ate, perceiving that the people wanted to make Him a King, Jesus told His disciples to get into the ship and to head for the other side, while He sent the multitudes away. After doing so, Jesus caught up to the disciples by walking upon the water.

THE BREAD OF LIFE

The next day, the people entered ships and found Jesus on the other side. Jesus, knowing that the people had followed Him because they had eaten of the loaves and were filled, told them that they should not work for the food that perishes, but for the eternal food which endures unto everlasting life. This Food that Jesus gives to those that work for Him is His Holy Spirit. When the people asked Jesus what they should do to work the work of God, Jesus told them to believe in Him, Whom God the Father sent. He told them that He is the Bread of Life that was sent from Heaven, and that those that come to Him shall never hunger, and those that believe in Him shall never thirst. Jesus added that on the last day, He would raise every one that believes in Him to everlasting life (John 6:22–40). The work of Christ's disciples is to share the Good News of Jesus Christ, so that others might be saved.

KNOWING JESUS CHRIST

The Jews began to murmur against Jesus Christ because He told them that He came down from Heaven. Jesus told them not to murmur, because no one can come to Him unless they are drawn by His Heavenly Spirit. Those that are drawn and come in faith to Jesus Christ will be the ones that He will raise up when He returns. Jesus told them that those that are drawn by God would also be taught by God, and that everyone who has been taught by God will come to Him. Jesus was telling them that if they knew God the Father, they would believe and follow Him, but because they did not know God the Father (Christ's Heavenly Spirit), they could not know Him (John 6:41–45). These Jews did not recognize Jesus Christ because they did not study the Scriptures, and were not being led by Christ's Heavenly Spirit. God declares in His Word that all Scripture is giving by the Breath of God (II Tim. 3:16). If these Jews had the breath of God's Word in their hearts, they would have been led by God's Holy Spirit, and they would have known that Jesus Christ was the "Sent One" of God.

NOTE

In order for one to understand the deep truths of God, one must willingly read and hear God's Word, and allow God's Holy Spirit to convict and teach them. It is the Holy Ghost Who opens one's eyes and enables him to recognize God's "Truth." It is important to realize that Jesus was talking to the most religious sect of that time, and that He flat out told them that they did not know Him because they did not know God. The Pharisees did not have the "Word" of God in their hearts. They participated in various rituals and ceremonies, but they did not know God. They were deceived into believing that they were close to God by participating in rituals and ceremonies. Ironically they were persecuting God Himself. These religious hypocrites put their religion before God Himself. If they had put God's Word, which is accompanied by God's Holy Spirit, into their hearts, they would have known that Jesus Christ is the True and Living Image of God's Invisible Spirit.

HYPOCRITES

The scribes and Pharisees came to Jesus and told Him that His disciples did not obey their traditions. Jesus responded by telling them that they disobeyed God in order to keep their traditions. Jesus then pointed out one of their traditions which went against God's commandment to honor one's father and mother. This tradition said that it was good for children to tell their parents that their gift from them would be given to God instead. In reality, the Pharisees were teaching the people that it was better to give them their money than to honor their parents with gifts. Jesus proceeded by telling them that the prophet Isaiah described them rightly as hypocrites, that honor God with their lips, but their heart is far from God. Jesus told them that they were wasting their time worshipping God, as long as they falsely taught their rules as commandments of God (Matt. 15:1–9).

MAN'S SPEECH

Jesus told the people that it is not what goes into a man's mouth that defiles or makes a person unclean, but that which comes out of one's mouth that defiles him. One's words and deeds including evil thoughts, murders, adulteries, fornications, thefts, false witnesses, and slander come out of the heart. It is important to know that all the teachings of Jesus Christ point to a man's heart or soul. Jesus demonstrated that He does not like hypocrites by rebuking those that were putting on a holy outward appearance, while being full of evil on the inside. Jesus called the Pharisees hypocrites, and warned the people that if they did not open their eyes and stop following these blind guides, they would fall into the pit with them (Matt. 15:10–20). Jesus then said that we will all have to account for every idle word that comes out of our mouth (Matt. 12:36). As servants of God, we are to spread His

Word and His Spirit of Love to others. We are all to judge our own speech, in order to see whose spirit we are spreading.

GOD OF ISRAEL

Jesus departed into the coasts of Tyre and Sidon. There, a Syro-Phoenician woman came crying to Him, and asked Him to heal her daughter who was devil possessed. Jesus, knowing that she was not Jewish, tested her faith by ignoring her. When she persisted, He told her that He was sent only unto the Jews, which are God's chosen people. As the woman continued to plead with Him, Jesus commended her for her great faith and healed her daughter (Matt. 15:21–28). Jesus taught that salvation is of the Jews (John 4:22). He wanted everyone to know that He is "One" with the Old Testament God of Israel, and that He came into the world, through the seed of Abraham, to bless all the nations and peoples of the world. God chose to use the Jews to reveal Himself to the world. All Bible prophecy revolves around the Jews, the nation of Israel, and more specifically around the Holy City of Jerusalem. God loves everyone that comes to Him through faith in His Son (True Image), Jesus Christ, Who came into this world as a Jew. It is one's faith and not one's nationality that God cares about. In Jesus Christ we are all equal (Gal. 3:28).

GOD'S REVELATION TO PETER

When Jesus came into Caesarea Philippi, He asked His disciples who they thought He was. Simon Peter told Jesus that He was the Christ, the Son of the Living God. Jesus then told Simon Peter that he was blessed because God the Father (Christ's Heavenly Spirit) revealed this to him (Matt. 16:13–17). As we learned, the Pharisees did not recognize Jesus as the Son of God. They were unwilling to put aside their traditions, study God's Word, and allow God's Holy Spirit to show them God's "Truth," Jesus Christ. Do not be deceived! Salvation and all of God's Blessings come from the Hand of Jesus Christ, by and through His Ever-present, All-Knowing, and All-Powerful Holy Spirit.

THE ROCK

After Peter confessed that Jesus Christ was the Son of God, Jesus told Peter and the disciples that this confession would be the rock, or the foundation, of His church, and that the gates of hell shall not prevail against it (Matt. 16:18–19). Those that confess that Jesus Christ is the Son of God and follow Him will be saved from the torments of hell and will enjoy eternal life with Jesus Christ and all His followers. Jesus is He Who welcomes His believers into His Heavenly Presence, and is also He Who rejects those that rejected Him. Jesus said that those who come to Him shall not be cast out (John 6:37). Jesus wants man to come to Him. He did not tell man to go to a priest, or to an icon, or to a statue of the Virgin Mary. Jesus said that He is the Way, the Truth, and the Life, and that no one can come unto the Father (the Presence and the Knowledge of His Heavenly Spirit) but by Him (John 14:6). Knowing this truth can set you free from the control of the many man-made religions. In order to know and to enter into God's Presence, one must call upon Him in the Name of Jesus Christ in prayer. The work of all true servants of God is to lead people to Him in the Name of Jesus Christ.

JESUS FORETELLS CRUCIFIXION

After discussing His true identity, Jesus began to tell his disciples about His future death and resurrection. Jesus told them that He would have to go to Jerusalem and suffer many things from the elders, the chief priests, and the scribes. He told them that he would be put to death, and that He would rise on the third day (Matt. 16:21). Jesus let His disciples know that He would be crucified. He did this by telling them that if any man chooses to follow Him, he should deny himself and take up His cross. Jesus did not tell man that it would be easy to follow Him, but rather that they would have to deny themselves and carry their cross. The cross is the symbol of the pain, suffering, denial, and the persecution that precedes total victory.

JESUS TRANSFORMED

Jesus told a crowd that He will return in the Glory of His Heavenly Spirit, and with His holy angels. Jesus warned that when

He does, He will be ashamed of those that were ashamed of Him and of His Word. Jesus added that some that were standing there in the crowd would not taste death before they saw the Kingdom of God come with Power (Mark 8:38–9:1). The Kingdom of God, which is Righteousness, Peace, and Joy in the Holy Spirit (Rom. 14:17), came in part on the day of Pentecost, and will come in full when Jesus Christ returns in the near future to rule this earth. On the seventh day, after Jesus had said that some of them would live to see the coming of the Kingdom of God, Jesus brought Peter, James, and John up onto a high mountain, and was transfigured before them. Jesus took them into the future, and gave them a glimpse of how He will appear when He returns to rule this earth from Jerusalem.

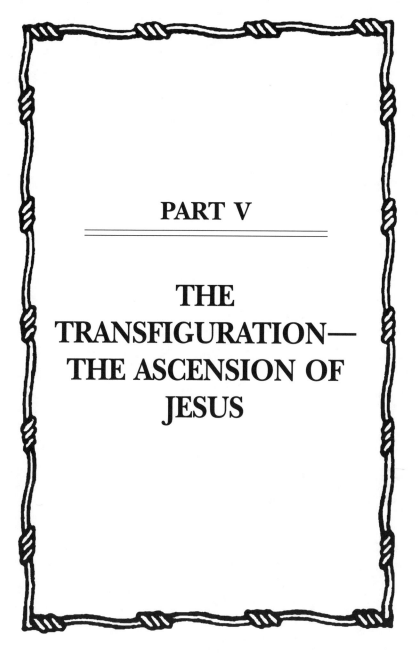

PART V

THE
TRANSFIGURATION—
THE ASCENSION OF
JESUS

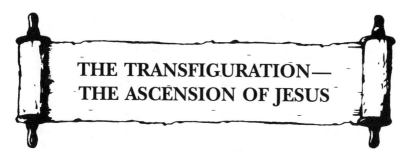

THE TRANSFIGURATION— THE ASCENSION OF JESUS

A GLIMPSE INTO THE FUTURE

When Peter, James, and John saw Jesus in His Future State of Being, He was seen talking with the prophet Elias and with Moses. His face was shining as the sun, and His garments shone whiter than anything on earth. Then a cloud came and overshadowed them. A Voice came out of the cloud and told them to hear Jesus because He was His Beloved Son (Mark 9:2–9). Jesus told His apostles not to tell anyone about what they had witnessed until after He had risen from the dead. Christ, the Living Word of God, let His apostles know that He is One with, and the True Image of His Heavenly Spirit. He showed them that, as in the Old Testament times, He would again talk to them through His multitude of angels that would come down as a cloud. As we will learn, this is how Jesus would appear to Paul. Many make the mistake of putting limitations on the Essence of Christ. As a result, they fail to comprehend His Fullness. Jesus is everywhere in Spirit. The Word of Jesus Christ is the Word of God (John 1:14). The Person of Jesus Christ is the Person of God (Matt. 1:23). The Spirit of Jesus Christ is the Spirit of God (Rom. 8:9). Jesus Christ said He would return in His Glory (His Face will shine as the sun and His garments whiter than anything on earth), in the Glory of His Father (with Power and Authority over all), and in the Glory of the Holy angels (Christ is the Brightness of God's Glory cloud (Heb. 1:3), which is made up of His angels, who are illuminated by His Brightness).

DETECTING FALSE TEACHINGS

The apostles Peter and John warned the people to beware of the teachings of false prophets. They said that any teaching that denies the fact that Jesus is the Son (True Image) of God is of the devil (I John 2:18–24). The apostle John labeled Satan's spirit "the spirit of antichrist," because it goes against Jesus Christ. A Holy Spirit-led preacher is one who teaches that Jesus Christ came "ek" (out) from God (I John 4:3), and is One with God. God's Word declares that the LORD God is One LORD (Deut. 6:4), and that He Alone is the Savior (Is. 45:21). God's Word also tells us that Jesus Christ is this Savior, and that there is no other name than the name of Jesus Christ in which salvation can be found (Acts 4:12). The Name of Jesus Christ is far above every name in this world and in the world to come (Eph. 1:21). Jesus Christ created all things in the heavens and on the earth, both visible and invisible (Col. 1:15–16). God tells us in His Word that those that deny these truths have the spirit of antichrist and are of the devil.

THE THREE HEAVENS

The Greek word translated as heaven, in the previous verse, is plural and has been correctly translated as heavens in some versions. As we get deeper into the knowledge of God, we must keep in mind the fact that the Holy Bible teaches us that there are three heavens. God's throne is in the north side of the highest, or third heaven (Is. 14:13). The third heaven is also the home of God's holy angels. The second heaven is below God's third heaven and above the first heaven. The first heaven is the air we breathe into our bodies. The second heaven is where Lucifer's throne was set up when he was appointed to rule over the earth. As we learned, in an attempt to raise his throne into God's heaven, Lucifer led a revolt against God. It was at this time that he turned from being an angel of God into Satan the devil, the father of all lies (John 8:44). Because he was cast down from God's Heaven, he is using every lie he can to prevent man from entering into and enjoying God's Kingdom. The present war between Satan and Christ began before the creation of man. Christ, God's Eternal Soul (True Image), was there and saw Satan fall as lightning from God's third heaven (Luke 10:18). Satan and the angels that followed him are the devils of this present age. They have been allowed to temporarily exist, in order to give man the opportunity to choose their master. Without a choice, true love cannot be expressed. Every human being chooses his master, either knowingly or unknowingly, while he is upon this earth.

NOTE

Man's inability to understand and explain the True Identity of Jesus Christ separates the three major groups that believe in "One True God." Of these three groups, the true Christian believes that Jesus Christ is the Sent One of God. The Judaian believes that Jesus Christ lived on this earth but does not believe that He is the Messiah, the "Sent One" of God. The Muslim believes, as did the prophet Mohammed, that Jesus Christ was among the great prophets, or messengers of "Allah" (the Muslim name of God). Man's inability to understand the true identity of Jesus Christ has also led to the spread of false doctrines within various so-called Christian denominations, which deny the fact that Jesus Christ is One with the Heavenly Spirit of God, known as the "Father." The truth is that God has always existed and has always operated as "One." God's Fullness is made up of God's Three Realities and NOT Three Separate Persons, as many have been misled to believe. Sadly, God's Oneness was labeled Trinity by the Roman church. This label has led many to believe and to teach that God the Father, God the Son, and God the Holy Spirit got together one day and decided that Jesus would come into this world, etc. This is erroneous!

THE FULLNESS OF GOD

Due to the Greatness of God, and due to the fact that God wants us to know Him, in His Wisdom God revealed Himself to us in three distinct but united Realities. Above all, God is the Spirit (John 4:24) of Love (I John 4:8). God's Eternal Spirit Mind of Love became known to man as "God the Father" when God's Eternal Soul became known to man as "God the Son," in the Person of Jesus Christ. In order for God, Who is Spirit, to reveal Himself to man, He sent His Soul (the Exact Image of His Mind) into the world, first in Word and then in the Person of Jesus Christ, so that man could acknowledge and receive His Heavenly Spirit into their minds and hearts. God's Fullness is as follows: God the Father is God's All-Powerful and Heavenly Spirit Mind of LOVE. God the Son is God's Soul, the Revealed Image of God's Spirit Mind of LOVE, in Word and in the Person of Jesus Christ. God the Holy Spirit is the Ever-present, All-Knowing, and All-

Powerful Spirit Body of God the Father and of God the Son. This is the True Oneness of God that was confusedly labeled "Trinity."

THE DISTINCTION OF SOUL AND SPIRIT

God's Word declares that man was created in the image and after the likeness of God (Gen. 1:26). Man's outer body was originally formed from the dust of the ground, and became a living soul when God breathed the breath of Life into Adam's nostrils (Gen. 2:7). The Old Testament Hebrew word "soul" means a living creature. Thus in the Old Testament times, man was viewed as a living soul, made up of an outer body and an inner spirit, which would leave man's body and go to Sheol (habitation of disembodied spirits) upon one's physical death. The New Testament scriptures also teach that a man's body without the spirit is physically dead (James 2:26). The difference is that in the New Testament, man is viewed as a being made up of an outer body, an inner soul, and an inner spirit (I Thess. 5:23). As you can see, man's inner spirit of the Old Testament is divided in the New Testament into an inner soul and an inner spirit. This dividing asunder of soul and spirit is not actually a division, but a distinction between one's spirit mind and one's spirit soul (one's true image). Only by understanding this distinction between soul and spirit can one truly understand the Perfect Unity of God the Father and God the Son. The Soul, or Son of God, Jesus Christ, is the Revealed and Living Image of God's Invisible Spirit Mind, known as God the Father. Even though God's Mind and God's Soul can be viewed as Two Separate Realities, they must also be viewed as One, because they are interwoven. The Soul (Image) of God has the Mind of God, and the Mind of God has the Soul (Image) of God. This is why Jesus Christ said that He and His Father are One (John 10:30); that he who has seen Him has seen the Father (John 14:9); that He was in the Father, and the Father was in Him (John 14:11); and that he who hates Him hates His Father also (John 15:23).

MAN'S SOUL

Unlike God, man is not self-existent. Man's mind is from God, and his soul belongs to God (Ezek. 18:4). The apostle Peter talked about man's soul as the "hidden man of the heart" (I Pet. 3:4).

One's soul is the true identity and the exact image of one's mind, which others cannot see. Only God can see one's soul. As a matter of fact, this is the part of a man that God sees when He looks upon a man. This is because one's soul is the true "hidden man" behind one's outward appearance. It is one's soul which directs the words and the actions of one's outward or physical body. Man's soul is inspired by and conforms to the image of the spirit it chooses to follow. The "spiritual father" of each man is the spirit that dwells with and inspires one's mind or human spirit to make certain decisions. The will of the mind is then passed on to and inspires one's soul or inner man, who in turn directs and leads the body to speak and to act accordingly.

FREE MORAL CHOICE

Even though man's soul belongs to God, the mind of each soul has the freedom to choose its master. Every soul will fall into one of two categories. Each soul that hears and believes the Gospel of Jesus Christ, and receives Him as Lord and Savior, will receive and have the Holy Spirit living and working inside him, both to will and to do God's will (Phil. 2:13). The souls in this category have Jesus Christ as their Master. The souls in the only other category are those that reject or neglect to receive Jesus Christ as their Master. The souls in this category have Satan as their master, and are inspired by his worldly spirit of antichrist. Instead of following Jesus Christ, these souls are driven by pride, fame, and the bodily and material lusts of this world, which include money, immoral sex, drugs, material possessions, and worldly pleasures. Whenever one physically dies, his soul is eternally placed on the side of and with the master he chose to serve. The decision one makes regarding Jesus Christ will determine the eternal destiny of one's soul. This is why God looks upon each man's heart. The story of Samuel and David clearly illustrates this fact.

SAMUEL AND DAVID

Over 1,000 years before the birth of Jesus Christ, the elders (the men of authority in Israel) gathered and decided that they wanted a king to reign over them. Instead of wanting the LORD God to be their King, they wanted a king like all the other nations

(I Sam. 8:7). As we learned, Samuel was a prophet, a priest, and the last of the major judges prior to the reign of kings in Israel. Saul became the first king of Israel. After he disobeyed God, the LORD sent Samuel to Bethlehem to anoint one of Jesse's sons as the next king of Israel. When Samuel got there, his attention went to Eliab, one of the sons of Jesse. From Eliab's appearance, Samuel surely thought that he would be the one that the LORD would want him to anoint as the next king. The LORD then told Samuel that Eliab was not the one, and that He does not look upon a man's outward appearance as man does, but looks instead upon the heart (I Sam. 16:7). When the LORD looked upon the sons of Jesse, He chose David, because he was a man "after" God's heart (Acts 13:22). The LORD then told the prophets that the coming "Christ" or "Messiah" would be brought into this world from the lineage of David.

GOD'S SOUL

One thousand years later in this same town of Bethlehem, the Virgin Mary, who was of the lineage of King David, gave birth to the Man "of" God's heart, Jesus Christ, known as the Son of God. Man, created after the likeness of God, has only one soul (hidden man of his heart). One's soul is the true image of one's mind. Jesus Christ is God's True Image Who is in the bosom or the heart of God the Father (God's Spirit Mind of Love) (John 1:18). As we learned, God's Holy Spirit is the Ever-present, All-Knowing, and All-Powerful Spirit Body of God the Father and of God the Son. Many become confused with God's Oneness because they do not realize that God is One Holy Spirit Body, with One Mind (God the Father) and with One Soul—True Image (God the Son). Jesus Christ is the True Image of the Invisible God (Col. 1:15). Jesus Christ clearly claimed His Pre-existence and His Oneness with God when He said that He was the Root (the Pre-existent God) and the Offspring (the Incarnate God) of David (Rev. 22:16). Jesus Christ personally testified to the fact that He was the Lord that David spoke about in the 110th Psalm (Matt. 22:41–45). This was 1,000 years before Christ took on a Body of Flesh and Blood.

REVIEW

God taught us in the story of Samuel and David that He can, and that He does look upon our soul. He did this because He loves us and does not want us to suffer the second death, which is the eternal separation of one's soul from Him. Satan, knowing from experience that God does not allow sin in His Heavenly Presence, tried to eternally destroy God's loving relationship with man. After deceiving Adam and Eve, Satan may have thought that he had succeeded in forcing God to annihilate mankind. Little did he know that the Great God of Heaven was only using him as part of His Master Plan of creating a loving and obedient family with whom He could share His endless pleasures. In order to accomplish this, God sent His Soul, the Image of His Holy Spirit Mind, into this world as Jesus Christ, the Son of God, and provided the "Way" through which mankind could be cleansed of all of his sin and granted entrance into His Heavenly Presence, where no evil, pain, or sorrow can enter. God declares in His Word that where a tree falleth, there it shall be (Eccl. 11:3). Those that choose to accept God's "Way" while on this earth will become children of God, and will keep their souls for all eternity. Those that fail to accept God's "Way" will be eternally separated from the Light of God.

MIRACLE POWER

When Jesus returned to the multitude, a certain man came to Him, kneeled down, and asked Jesus to heal his son. He told Jesus that he brought his son to the disciples, but that they could not cast the dumb and deaf spirit out of him. Jesus told the man that if he could believe, all things are possible to him that believeth. This man told the Lord Jesus that he believed, and to help him with his unbelief. Jesus then ordered the dumb and deaf spirit to come out of the boy and to never return. Notice when Jesus told this man to "believe," this man cried out for Jesus to help his unbelief. This man knew that the faith needed to heal his son could come only from Jesus. He then humbled himself and completely yielded himself to Jesus. When the disciples asked Jesus why they could not cast out this evil spirit, Jesus told them that this kind of spirit can come out only by prayer and fasting (Mark 9:14–29). Prayer is communicating with God, and fasting is denying and devoting one's self totally to God. Fasting was done by men of God throughout the Bible. Those that fasted would pray continually while abstaining from food. The apostle Paul fasted often (II Cor. 11:27). Jesus said that man cannot live by bread alone (Luke 4:4). Man must feed not only his outward body but also his soul. God's Word is food for the soul. Today many believers fast and pray when a serious need arises, or when they just desire to get closer to Jesus. A one- to three-day fast with nothing but water and the Word of God is a common practice among believers. Let your heart tell you when and how long to fast.

AS LITTLE CHILDREN

The disciples asked Jesus which of them were greater in the Kingdom of Heaven. Jesus called a child unto Him and told His disciples that unless they turn and become like children, they would never enter the Kingdom of Heaven. Jesus added that he that humbles himself like that child is the greater (Matt. 18:1–4). Children enjoy playing without ever thinking about how great or famous they are. They also look towards and depend upon their parents for love, food, protection, and all of their needs. This is how we are to look towards God. The spirit of antichrist tells man to put his trust in oneself, in others, in man-made religions, in the government, in idols, etc. God, through Jesus Christ, tells us to put our trust in Him. He does this in Love, because it is not His Will that anyone should lose his soul, but that everyone would inherit eternal life.

WARNING TO OFFENDERS

Jesus Christ gave a strong warning to anyone who ever thinks about offending one of His children. He said it would be better for that person to have a great stone fastened around his neck, and to be drowned in the depth of the sea (Matt. 18:6). God and His angels rejoice when one that was lost comes to Jesus Christ. This is why those that cause one of His children to turn from Him will be thrown into everlasting fire. Jesus Christ warned the people that all of God's children have their own angels which look upon the Face (Countenance) of God the Father in Heaven. God's angels know God's Anger, and at the Great Harvest will cast those that came against the children of Jesus Christ into everlasting fire.

FAITH IN JESUS CHRIST

The apostle John saw someone who was not in their group casting out demons in the Name of Jesus Christ, and told him not to do so. Jesus told John not to forbid him, because no one who does a mighty work in His Name will soon be able to speak evil of Him (Matt. 9:38–40). Jesus added that he that is not against Him and His followers is on their side (Mark 9:40). It is one's faith in the Name of Jesus Christ that is accompanied by God's Power, and not the name of some man-made denomination. As many as receive Christ, He gives them the Power to become the sons of God, even to those that believe in His Name (John 1:12). Jesus baptizes each and every one that comes to Him with One and the Same Holy Spirit. There are no denominations in the eyes of Christ.

JUDGE RIGHTEOUS JUDGMENT

At about the midst of the Feast of Tabernacles, Jesus went up into the temple to teach. He taught the people to judge one's doctrine, not by appearance, but by righteous judgment (John 7:24). Jesus said that he that talks from his own will and of himself seeks his own glory (John 7:17–18). While on earth, Jesus glorified His Eternal and Heavenly Spirit known as God the Father. In doing this, Jesus was teaching man to look up to God and not to pray to anyone or anything on this earth. He commanded man not to address any religious person on this earth as "Father" (Matt. 23:9). Knowing that Jesus is God's Heavenly Image, man can now pray "Father, in the name of Jesus Christ . . ." Any church or religious doctrine that is in disagreement with God's Word, the Holy Bible, and which glorifies itself instead of Jesus Christ is not of God. A Godly church leads and teaches its members to love God, in the Name of Jesus Christ. An ungodly church spreads prejudices and causes division by teaching its members to love their church. They and their members proudly claim to be the only true church that can save one's soul through their man-made rituals. Not True! Religion cannot save one's soul. Only Jesus Christ can save one's soul. This kind of church spreads Satan's spirit of pride. The deceived members of these churches that are trusting in their denominations for salvation, instead of in the Lord Jesus Christ, must repent and turn to Jesus Christ in order to be saved.

REPENT AND BE SAVED

Early one morning, as Jesus was teaching in the temple, the Pharisees brought unto Him a woman that was caught committing adultery. They asked Jesus if they should stone her, as was commanded in the law of Moses. Jesus told them that he among them that was without sin should cast the first stone. Being convicted by their own conscience, those that gathered then departed. After the woman's accusers left, Jesus told her that He also did not condemn her, but to go and sin no more (John 8:1–11). As we are beginning to understand, Jesus did not come to destroy men's lives, but to save them (Luke 9:56). It is God's Will that all people turn away from their evil ways and follow Him into eternal life. As we just learned, Jesus wants us to recognize and to rightfully judge false doctrine, but He does not want us to condemn an individual. If we see a person that is living an immoral and sinful life, we are not to condemn him, but rather to lead him to God through the Gospel of Jesus Christ. Jesus said that there is joy in heaven when one sinner repents (Luke 15:7). Those that lead sinners to Jesus Christ will one day be rewarded.

GOSSIPERS AND FALSE ACCUSERS

The Holy Bible teaches us that elderly women are supposed to behave holy, and are not to be false accusers or slanderers (Titus 2:3). The Greek word used for slanderer means devil. Many do not realize that those that slander and spread gossip and rumors are included in the group that will not make it to heaven. Just as Jesus Christ spread God's Holy Spirit through His Spoken Word, which is the Word of God (John 14:10), gossipers spread the spirit of their father, the devil. We are all to ask ourselves this question: Are we children of God, who spread His Word and Spirit, or are we children of the devil, who spread lies and gossip? Jesus Christ said that each and every one of us will one day be held accountable for every idle word that we ever spoke (Matt. 12:36). Woe to the self-righteous hypocrites that slander, hate, and offend a child of God.

JESUS QUESTIONED

When Jesus told the people that He was the "Light of the World," and that those that followed Him would have the Light of Life, the Pharisees accused Him of not telling the truth. Jesus told them that His testimony was true because He was not alone, but with the Father. The Pharisees asked Jesus where His Father was. Jesus told them that they did not know Him or His Father, and that if they knew Him, they would know the Father also. Jesus told them that He was from above, and that if they did not believe that He was the "I AM," they would die in their sins. If, on the other hand, they did abide in His Word, they would be His disciples, they would know the "Truth," and the Truth would set them free (John 8:12–32). One can be set free from the bondage of false religious teachings only by knowing God's "Truth," Jesus Christ. He is the True Image of the Living God, and the only Source of God's Blessings.

NOTE

It is through God's Word that one obtains faith in Jesus Christ and is set free from the bonds of Satan. Satan's spirit of antichrist denies Christ's declaration that He is "One" with God's Eternal Spirit known as God the Father. This is why Jesus said that those that believe in Him and His Word are of God, and that those that disbelieve His Word are of their father, the devil (John 8:44). Notice that Jesus said it is those that abide in His Word that shall be set free. After one believes in the Gospel of Jesus Christ, he is to breathe in the Spirit of His Word and live accordingly. The Words of Jesus Christ have eternal life (John 6:68). Therefore, those that put and keep God's Word in their heart will live eternally.

A CHILD OF GOD

Many falsely believe that everyone is a child of God. God declares in His Word that every soul receives its life from Him and belongs to Him. This is true, but only those that have received and are abiding in His Holy Spirit can rightfully call Him "Father." This is possible only by inviting and receiving the Spirit of Jesus Christ, which is "One" with the Spirit of God the Father, into one's

mind and heart. As we learned, the children of Satan will be
eternally separated from the children of God at the end of this
age. Those that have been "born again" will be on God's Side, and
all others will be on Satan's side.

"I AM"

When the Jews questioned Jesus about Abraham, Jesus told
them: "Before Abraham was I AM" (John 8:58). As we learned,
God chose to reveal Himself through Abraham and his seed, the
Jewish nation of Israel. When the Angel of the Lord called Moses
to go to Pharoah, and to lead the Israelites out of Egypt, He told
Moses that He was the God of Abraham, the God of Isaac, and the
God of Jacob. Moses asked God how he should answer the
Israelites after he tells them that the God of their forefathers sent
him, and they ask him: "What is His Name?" God told Moses to
tell them that "I AM" sent him (Ex. 3:14). After Jesus Christ
proclaimed to be One with the Lord God of Abraham, the Jews
became furious and picked up stones to throw at Him, but Jesus
went through the midst of them and left the temple.

JEWS REJECT THEIR MESSIAH

Christ, as the Word of God, told the early Israelites that He is
God and that only He could tell them the end from the beginning
(Is. 46:9). Most of the Pharisees and those of the other sects of
Judaism rejected Jesus because they did not have His Holy Spirit
dwelling in them. This is due to the fact that they failed to put
God's Word into their hearts and therefore were not being led
and enlightened by God's Holy Spirit. This is proof that God's
Word is the only Way to enter into the Knowledge of God's
"Truth." The mistake that these Jewish leaders made is that they
replaced the Word of God with worthless traditions and rituals.
This is why they could not see that the Old Covenant between the
LORD and Israel was about to be fulfilled, and that the LORD
Himself, in the Person of Jesus Christ, would make a New
Covenant with Israel, as the prophet Jeremiah had foretold (Jer.
31:31). They also failed to recognize Jesus Christ from the over
one hundred prophecies that foretold, among other things, the
exact time and place of His birth. Because the Pharisees did not
have the Word of God in their hearts, Jesus told them that they

were not of God. If they were, they would have known that He proceeded forth from God (John 8:42). While on this earth, Jesus commanded man to know when His return would be near (Matt. 24:33). This Godly knowledge cannot be obtained through religious rituals, but only through the Holy Spirit of Jesus Christ, Who accompanies and inspires those that put the Word of God in their minds and hearts.

ETERNAL LIFE

When asked what one must do to inherit eternal life, Jesus answered by commanding man to love the Lord their God with all their soul, strength, and mind; and to love their neighbor as themselves (Luke 10:27). Jesus was then asked who one's neighbor is. Jesus illustrated in a parable that a good neighbor is one that stops to help another in need. Jesus practiced what He preached. After Jesus stopped to restore the sight of a blind man, the Pharisees accused Him of being a sinner because He had healed this man on the Sabbath. No wonder Jesus called these religious Pharisees snakes. Just as Satan used a serpent to deceive Eve, Satan's spirit entered into and was using these religious hypocrites to deceive man into believing that following them and their traditions was the way to eternal life. Not so! Calling upon Jesus Christ is the only "Way" to enter into the Holy Spirit Presence of God, and keeping God's Word in one's mind and heart is the only way to abide in God's Holy Spirit. Jesus told mankind that following Him is not easy, but the reward is great. He will lead many away from family tradition, and by doing so will cause division (discord) between the father and his son, the mother and her daughter, and the mother-in-law and her daughter-in-law (Luke 12:53). This is the price (a small one) that many will have to pay in order to inherit eternal life in God's Glorious Kingdom.

THE GOOD SHEPHERD

Jesus told the people that He was the Good Shepherd, and that those that hear His Voice and follow Him shall become one flock, to whom He would give eternal life (John 10:27–28). Jesus foretold that there would be wolves or false prophets who would come to steal, to kill, and to destroy His sheep. These false prophets are servants of Satan, who is a murderer and the father of all lies (John 8:44). Satan's spirit of antichrist (against Christ) is based on the lie that Jesus Christ is not God, and therefore one does not need Him. Satan uses false prophets to spread his spirit in the realm of religion. He also uses others outside religion to captivate and keep man's mind off Jesus Christ and the Word of God. He does this by inspiring people to give their hearts to the pursuit of worldly fame, wealth, and pleasures, instead of giving their hearts to Jesus Christ and pursuing the Will of God for their lives. As long as one follows Christ, Satan and his followers cannot touch his soul. They may physically kill him, as they did Jesus, but like Jesus, he will be raised into eternal life. Satan is a murderer and wants to lead as many souls as possible into eternal hell. Do not be deceived! God's Gift of Eternal Life is available only through and in the Name of Jesus Christ (Rom. 6:23). Those that receive God's Holy Spirit through faith in Jesus Christ and His Word, which is the Word of God, also receive the Holy Spirit Image of Jesus Christ. One cannot receive God's Holy Spirit without also receiving the Holy Spirit Image of Jesus Christ, because they are "One." This is why Jesus Christ is the only "Way" to know God. His Word is the Word of God, His Person is the Person of God, and His Spirit is the Holy Spirit of God. As we learned, when God's Soul became known as God the Son, God's Eternal Mind became known as "God the Father" and God's Ever-present, All-Knowing, and All-Powerful Spirit Body became known as the Holy Spirit.

COVETOUSNESS

Covetousness is dedicating one's heart to acquiring worldly wealth and possessions. Many have been deceived into believing that he with the most things wins. Jesus warned about this kind of thinking, and taught that a man's life does not consist in the abundance of the things which he possesses (Luke 12:15). Jesus told his disciples a parable about a rich fool. When this rich man's ground brought forth more fruit than his barns could hold, he thought within himself, and told his soul to tear down his barns and build bigger ones, in which he could store his goods. He could then have enough money to just lie around, eat, drink, and be merry. God called this man a fool, for that night his soul would be demanded to return to God and then who would get all his possessions? Jesus taught that everything which one lays up for one's self upon this earth will be lost when one dies. Only the things done and given under the inspiration and for the glory of God, in the Name of Jesus Christ, will last forever. These good deeds will become stored-up treasures for those that inherit the Kingdom of God (Luke 12:13–21).

HOW MAN OPERATES

Notice in this parable that Jesus said that this rich man thought within himself, and then told his soul what to do. Each decision is made in one's mind and is then revealed to one's soul which directs the body to act accordingly. As you can see, one's mind is the head of one's soul, who is the living image in the heart of one's mind. After receiving the decision, which is the will of the mind, the soul then leads the body in accordant word and action. One's mind and soul make up one's spirit life that temporarily dwells in and animates one's human body. As illustrated in this parable, everyone's soul belongs to God (Ezek. 18:4), and God can require one's soul at any time. If the soul if unacceptable to God, it is eternally separated from Him. This is known as the second death. Jesus taught that there are two eternal sides, and that those on the torment side will never be able to cross over to His Side; neither can anyone on His side cross over to the torment side (Luke 16:26).

IN THE IMAGE OF GOD

Now that we understand how man, who was created after the likeness of God, operates, we can better understand the Oneness and the Fullness of God. The Truth is that Jesus Christ is God's Eternal Soul. He is the Living Image in the Heart of God's Eternal and Spirit Mind of Love, known as God the Father. Jesus is One with, and always does the Will of God the Father (John 8:29). God the Father and God the Son are Spiritual Titles that distinguish between the Realities of God, and are not to be thought of in the human sense of procreation. In His Eternal Mind of Love, known as God the Father, God Willed that His Soul take on a body of flesh and blood, so that man could know Him and come to Him. God's Soul, Who is the Image of God and always does the Will of God, then directed God's Holy Spirit to bring Him into the world as a man, at which time Jesus Christ was conceived and came into this world through the Virgin Mary. It is through hearing and believing this Gospel of Jesus Christ that one receives the Power to know God and His Love for mankind. Jesus Christ said that no man can come into the Father but by Him (John 14:6). In other words, if one wants to enter into God's Eternal Mind of Love and become a child of God, one must receive Jesus Christ into his or her heart.

LAZARUS

After Lazarus became ill, his sisters sent for Jesus. By the time Jesus arrived with His disciples, Lazarus had died and his body had lain in the grave for four days. Jesus told Martha, the sister of Lazarus, that whosoever liveth and believeth in Him shall never die. Martha told Jesus that she believed that He was the Christ, the Sent One of God. Jesus approached the grave and ordered that the stone covering the tomb be taken away. Jesus then lifted His Eyes and thanked His Heavenly Spirit, Whom He introduced and made known to the world as God the Father. Jesus did this aloud so that the people could hear Him, and believe that He was the Son, the True Image of the Invisible God. Jesus then called for Lazarus to come forth. Lazarus came back to life and walked out of his tomb. Many of the Jews then believed that Jesus was the Son of God (John 11:1–46). Because of this, the chief priests held a meeting and talked about putting Lazarus to death (John 12:10). Jesus Christ not only proclaimed to be One with the Eternal Spirit of God the Father, but also demonstrated that His Word was accompanied and made manifest by the Power of God's Holy Spirit.

REPENT

Jesus taught man that unless he repents, which means to change one's mind and turn from sin, he will be lost. God gives us all an opportunity to repent before we are cut down, like a fruit tree that does not produce fruit (Luke 13:3–7). Jesus spoke a parable about a son that took his inheritance and spent it all on harlots and wasteful living. When a famine swept throughout the country and this son became in need, he repented and humbly returned to his father. When his father saw him returning from a distance, he ran to welcome him with open arms. He rejoiced because his son was dead, and was now alive (Luke 15:11–24). This parable teaches that when one willfully rejects God's Path, he is lost and dead unless he repents and turns to God. This parable also teaches that God is like a loving parent who forgives his repentant children and welcomes them with open arms. God's angels in heaven rejoice over each sinner that repents (Luke 15:7–10).

PHARISEES DECIDE TO KILL JESUS

The Pharisees met and discussed the fact that if they let Jesus continue, all men would believe in Him and they would lose their standings in the community. To prevent this from happening, they decided to kill Jesus. During this meeting, the Holy Spirit came upon Caiaphas, the high priest. Caiaphas then predicted that Jesus would die for their nation, and would gather together into one body all the children of God. Not understanding the meaning of this, the Pharisees proceeded with their decision to have Jesus put to death (John 11:47–49). As we can clearly see, God is presently establishing His Eternal Kingdom. He is doing this by gathering His children unto Himself in the Name and through the Spirit of Jesus Christ.

JESUS FORETELLS RESURRECTION

Before going up to Jerusalem to celebrate the Passover, Jesus told His disciples what would happen to Him. He told them that He would be betrayed unto the chief priests and scribes, who would condemn Him to death and deliver Him to the Romans to be mocked, whipped, and crucified, after which He would rise from the dead on the third day (Matt. 20:17–19). He then told them that all the things that the prophets wrote concerning Him would be accomplished, but they did not understand what He was talking about (Luke 18:31). One can know and understand prophetic events only through the Spirit of God's Word. God gave man a mind and commanded him to learn of Him (Deut. 31:12). Unfortunately, many never take the time to seek God and will be lost for lack of knowledge (Hos. 4:6).

PASSOVER

As we learned, Passover is a holy day set aside by God in remembrance of the day in which He freed the Israelites from their slavery in Egypt. On this day, God instructed each family to sacrifice a lamb and to apply its blood to their doorpost. That evening God's angel delivered God's judgment on every home in Egypt, except on those that were covered with a blood sacrifice, which God's angel passed over. Only after God executed this judgment did Pharoah allow the Israelites to depart from Egypt. Each year, lambs were sacrificed in remembrance of this day. It is important to realize that God came into this world as a Jew, and that each Jewish holiday is related to Jesus Christ. Passover is a shadow of the coming day when God's judgment will fall on unrepentant mankind. At this time, only those that are covered (through faith) with the Sacrificial Blood of the Lamb of God, Jesus Christ (John 1:29), will be saved.

MARY ANOINTS JESUS

Six days before Passover, Jesus went to Bethany to see Lazarus. Mary, the sister of Lazarus, took a very costly ointment and anointed the feet of Jesus and then wiped his feet with her hair. Judas Iscariot, the disciple who would betray Jesus, remarked that this was a waste of money. Jesus told him that Mary had kept this ointment for His burial (John 12:2–8). Mary was led to do this by God's Holy Spirit. God uses people in ways that even they do not understand. All these things, which might seem insignificant to many, are mentioned in God's Word to show mankind that God does have a detailed Master Plan and that He is in full control.

THE TRIUMPHAL ENTRY

As Jesus approached Jerusalem, He sent two of His disciples into the next village to bring Him a certain donkey and its colt. This was done so that the prophecy of Zechariah (Zec. 9:9), which was made 600 years earlier, would be fulfilled. This prophecy foretold that the King of the Jews would come to them humbly and mounted on a donkey and its colt (Matt. 21:1–2). As Jesus began His Triumphal Entry into Jerusalem on the Sunday prior to His crucifixion, known today as Palm Sunday, many people spread down palms, which were a sign of beauty and prosperity. It is probable that Jesus rode the donkey for the difficult part of the journey, and then mounted the colt at the descent of the Mount of Olives. As Jesus approached Jerusalem, a multitude of His disciples began to shout and praise God for their coming King, the prophesied Sent One of God (Luke 19:36). Jesus made His humble entrance into Jerusalem through the eastern gate. This is the entrance through which the sheep for temple sacrifice were led into the city.

LONG AWAITED KINGDOM

As we learned, David's kingdom was at one time the largest empire in the world. The kingdom later became divided between the north and the south, and was then conquered by the Assyrians and the Babylonians. The dispersion, or the scattering of the Jews throughout the world followed. Even though many Jews returned and were in Jerusalem during the time of Jesus, Jerusalem was under the rule of the Roman Empire. For this reason, many Jews were anxiously awaiting God's Sent One, Who would come from the lineage of David, re-establish the Davidic kingdom, and reign as King of the world from Jerusalem, as foretold by the prophets (Jer. 33:20–22, Is. 9:7). Those who believed that Jesus was the Sent One believed that He would overthrow the Roman Empire and set up God's Kingdom at that time. They were saddened when they realized that Jesus Christ, the Sent One of God, came to this earth for the first time "as a lamb to slaughter," as foretold by the prophet Isaiah (Is. 53:7).

ONE FATHER

As Jesus spoke to the multitudes about the hypocrisy of the scribes and Pharisees, He commanded them not to address any man on earth as "Father." He told them that there was only One Father, and that He was in Heaven (Matt. 23:9–10). Jesus, being One with the Father, proceeded forth from the Father so that He could draw to Himself those that love Him. To these He will grant eternal life in His Kingdom. Knowing that He would soon be returning to Heaven, Jesus did not want mankind to follow and to trust in future Pharisees, but to always look towards Him for all their needs. As we learned, one can enter into God's Heavenly

Spirit only by calling upon God in the Name of Jesus Christ. Those that call any earthly priest "Father" should repent, and stop doing this. This is a direct commandment of the Lord Jesus Christ. Jesus told the apostle John concerning the churches that He hates the deeds of the Nicolaitanes (Rev. 2:6). Nicolaitane means victory over the laity. Christ hates systems of hierarchy which rule over the laity, and has warned those that hold this doctrine to repent (Rev. 2:16). Those that put man-made doctrines and traditions before the Word of God are following man instead of God. An obedient and humble servant of God would forbid anyone to call him "Father" and would lead his fellowman to the True Father, in the Name of and through faith in Jesus Christ. God's Word declares that every perfect gift is from above (James 1:17). This is why Jesus Christ, in His great Love for mankind, taught man to look up when praying and not towards any human being.

CHRIST'S WARNING

In His Love for man, Jesus publicly exposed the evils of the Pharisees because they were leading people towards destruction and away from the Kingdom of God. Jesus looked upon the hearts of the Pharisees and publicly told them that while they looked Godly from the outside, inwardly they were full of evil (Matt. 23:25). By doing this Jesus warned man that he should always put the Will of God before the will, doctrine, and traditions of man. One is not to follow, do, or believe anything that is contrary to the Word of God. One's love of God is demonstrated by one's obedience to His Word. Jesus Christ described those that love Him as those that obey His Commandments (John 14:21).

GOD'S GREATEST COMMANDMENTS

Jesus told us (mankind) that God's greatest commandment is to love the Lord our God with all our heart, soul, mind, and strength. Jesus said the second greatest commandment is to love our neighbor as ourself (Mark 12:30–31). Both the first and the second of God's greatest commandments to man are to "love." Any person or organization that spreads racial, cultural, religious, political, or ethnic hatred is not of God. Members of hate groups, whether they realize it or not, are members of Satan's kingdom. Satan hates God and is therefore trying to destroy God's creation, which includes humanity. The devil's spirit leads one to hate Jesus Christ and to hate his fellowman. If you belong to any group that spreads hate towards blacks, whites, Jews, Muslims, Christians, or any other people, get out and turn to Jesus Christ. As we will learn, there is a glorious and eternal future for all that do.

JUDAS JOINS CONSPIRACY

Two days before the feast of Passover, Jesus told His disciples that He would be betrayed and crucified. The chief priests and scribes at this time were trying to figure out how to arrest Jesus, without causing an uproar among the many people who gathered to celebrate Passover and to see Jesus. Judas Iscariot, one of Jesus's twelve apostles, offered them the solution to their problem. He did this by agreeing to conveniently deliver Jesus Christ to them for thirty pieces of silver (Matt. 26:14).

THE LAST SUPPER

The day before His crucifixion, Jesus sat down to eat what would become known as the "Last Supper" with His disciples. During this meal, Jesus broke and gave His disciples bread to eat, symbolic of His Body which would be broken. He then gave them a cup with fruit of the vine, symbolic of His Blood which would be poured out for the remission of sins according to God's New Covenant with man (Matt. 26:26–29). Jesus told His disciples to do this in remembrance of Him (Luke 12:19). He then taught His disciples to be humble servants and to serve God by serving the least among men. Jesus did not want them to ever feel that they were lowering themselves by serving the needy. He demonstrated this teaching by washing the feet of His disciples. In those days sandals were worn, and it was customary to provide a guest with water to wash and comfort his feet. After having identified Judas as the one who would betray Him, Jesus told Judas to go and do that which he had planned (John 13:21).

THE WAY—THE TRUTH—THE LIFE

Jesus then commanded His disciples to love one another as He had loved them. By this, all men would know that they were His disciples (John 13:31–35). Jesus told them that where He was going, they could not go at that time, but not to worry because He would return for them at a later time. Jesus told them that in His Father's House (Heaven) there are many mansions, and that He would prepare a place for them (John 14:1–4). Thomas asked Jesus what is the "Way." Jesus told him that He is the Way, the Truth, and the Life, and that no one comes to the Father except through Him. Jesus then made it perfectly clear to His disciples that He and God the Father are One. Jesus told Thomas that He is the "Way" because it is only through Him that one can personally and consciously fellowship with His Heavenly Spirit known as the Father. Jesus said He is the "Truth" because He is the True Image of God in Word and in Person. Jesus said that His disciples are those that continue in His Word, which is the Word of God (John 17:8), and that these shall know the Truth and the Truth shall set them free (John 8:31–32). When one receives the Holy Ghost of God through faith in Jesus Christ and His Word, he receives the Love, Power, and Wisdom of God, and becomes free from the control of sin and false doctrine in his life. Jesus said He is the "Life," because it is through faith in Him that man receives God's Gift of Eternal Life (Rom. 6:23).

THE HOLY SPIRIT

After commanding His disciples to love each other and declaring His Oneness with God the Father, Jesus told them that the "Spirit of Truth" would come and live with and in those that love Him and obey His commandments (John 14:15–17). Jesus, the "Truth" of God, identified the Spirit of Truth as His Spirit and the Spirit of His Father (His Eternal Spirit Mind of Love). He told them that when they would receive the Holy Spirit, He and His Father would come and live in them and with them (John 14:23). Jesus told them that on that day, they would know that He was in His Father, and they were in Him, and He was in them (John 14:20). Jesus said that those that receive His Holy Ghost will be mentally conscious of His fellowship and will be led in the Will of His Heavenly Spirit. The Spirit of Truth comes into and teaches (John 14:26) those that call upon God in the Name of Jesus Christ. Jesus said that the Holy Spirit would speak, or relay His Words to them, which are the Words of God the Father (John 16:13–15). This illustrates the Oneness of God. God the Father is Jesus Christ's Invisible, Loving, Eternal, and Heavenly Spirit Mind of Love. Jesus Christ is the Image of God's Eternal Spirit Mind of Love in Word and in Person. The Holy Spirit is God's Ever-present, All-Knowing, and All-Powerful Spirit Body. As we learned, Jesus Christ is the "Truth" of God. Those that receive the Spirit of Truth receive the Mind (Divine Nature) of Jesus Christ, and become children (vessels or members) of God's Spirit Body. It is not through any worldly church or organization that one becomes a child of God. It is through the Spirit Blood of Jesus Christ.

THE TRUE VINE

As Jesus and His disciples went to the Mount of Olives, Jesus likened Himself to the True Vine of God, through Whom His disciples, likened to the branches of the vine, receive God's blessings, or the fruit of God's Holy Spirit. Jesus taught that apart from Him, one cannot receive God's blessings. He also lovingly warned that the branch that does not remain in Him is like a branch that withers and is thrown into the fire and burned (John 15:1–8). Jesus had earlier foretold, in His parable about the sower, that not everyone that heard and accepted God's Word would keep it. Some would abandon God's Word when tempted or persecuted, and others would depart from it in their pursuit of the cares, riches, and pleasures of this world. In both of these teachings, Jesus showed that being a true child of God is more than a spur-of-the-moment decision. It is a way of life in which one loves, fellowships with, is led by, and obeys His (God's) Holy Spirit dwelling in and with him.

GARDEN OF GETHSEMANE

After the Lord's Supper, Jesus and His disciples went into the Mount of Olives, unto a garden place called Gethsemane. Knowing that He soon would be arrested and suffer many things, Jesus took Peter, James, and John and told them that His soul was sorrowful, and asked them to stay awake with Him. Jesus then went forward a little, fell on His face, and prayed to His Father that if it were possible to let this suffering pass from Him, but if not, to let His Will be done (Matt. 26:39). Here Jesus showed that as the God Man, He experienced pain and suffering as do other human beings. As Jesus prayed, an angel from heaven appeared and strengthened Him (Luke 22:43).

NOTE

As we learned, Jesus knew and foretold that He would be crucified. By praying to His Heavenly Spirit, Jesus was teaching us (all mankind) how we are to pray when we are suffering and facing death. When we ask God for something, we should pray that if it is His Will, our request to be granted; but if not, His Will to be done. God through His Holy angels will then give us the strength to face each and every situation. All things turn out for the good for those that love God and do according to His Will.

BETRAYAL AND ARREST

Soon after these teachings, Judas, knowing the place where Jesus was, led the arresting officers of the chief priests and Pharisees to Jesus Christ. He betrayed and identified Jesus to them by giving Jesus a kiss. The officers then grabbed Jesus, at which time Simon Peter drew his sword and cut off an ear of one of the servants. Jesus told Simon Peter to put away his sword, as He touched and healed the ear of the servant (Luke 22:51). Jesus told Peter that if He chose to, He could call upon His Heavenly Spirit, and He would send thousands of angels to rescue Him, but instead He wanted to complete the Will of His Heavenly Spirit. Jesus asked the officers whom they wanted. They answered, Jesus of Nazareth. Jesus responded by identifying Himself as He. As Jesus spoke, the officers fell back on the ground from the Power of God in His Word. By doing this, Jesus proved to His disciples that He was in control. Jesus then told the officers to take Him and to leave His disciples alone, which is what they did.

JESUS IS SENTENCED

That evening the officers bound Jesus and took Him first to Annas, who sent Jesus to Caiaphas, his son-in-law (John 18:24). Caiaphas was the high priest at that time, and presided over the Jewish Sanhedrin, a counsel made up of elders drawn from among the chief priests and scribes. This entire group sought to have Jesus put to death. Caiaphas asked Jesus if He was the Christ (Sent One), the Son of God. Jesus not only affirmed this, but also told Caiaphas that he would see Him at the right hand of God's Power and coming on the clouds of heaven. The high priest then accused Jesus of blasphemy, which is speaking evil against God. Those present then sentenced Jesus to death, spat in His face, and punched Him (Matt. 26:63–68). We are told that they blindfolded Jesus, struck Him in the face, and taunted Him to prophesy by telling them who hit Him (Luke 22:64).

JESUS GOES BEFORE PILATE

In the morning, Jesus was officially sentenced to death by the entire council (Matt. 27:1). Due to the fact that the Sanhedrin could not execute a prisoner without permission from the Roman government, Jesus was taken and accused before Pilate, the Roman governor. Jesus told Pilate that His Kingdom was not of this present world, and that if it were, His servants would not have permitted Him to be delivered to the Jews. When Pilate asked Jesus if He were a King, Jesus declared that He was, and that the reason He was born and came into this world was to reveal God's "Truth." Jesus added that everyone that is of the Truth hears and listens to His Voice (John 18:36–37). Pilate found no fault with Jesus. Because Jesus was from Galilee, Pilate sent Him to Herod, who had jurisdiction over Galilee. Herod happened to be in Jerusalem at the time. Herod, who had John the Baptist beheaded, asked Jesus many questions, but Jesus did not answer him. Herod did not believe that Jesus was anyone special. He and his troops made fun of Jesus by dressing Him in a splendid robe before sending Him back to Pilate (Luke 23:6–11), who would be faced with sentencing Jesus Christ.

THE TRUTH

Notice Jesus said "My Kingdom," confirming His Oneness with God. When we pray "Thy Kingdom come," we are praying for Jesus to return to this world and set up God's Everlasting Kingdom. The Greek word for "born," which Jesus used when He said that He was born to reveal the "Truth," is the same word used to describe the water that was "born" or "had become" wine by Jesus at the wedding (John 2:9). When Christ, the Spirit Image (Soul) of God came into this world, He became Jesus Christ, the Physical Image of God. How could this have happened? The Greek word for "came," which Jesus used when He said that He was born and came into the world to reveal the Truth, means "to speak." What happened is this. God willed it in His Mind to become man. His Soul (Image of His Spirit Mind) then spoke the Word and became man by the Power of His Holy Spirit. After declaring that He was the "Truth" of God, in Word and in Person, Jesus was accused of blasphemy and sentenced to death.

MOCKED AND CONDEMNED

At the annual feast of Passover, it was a custom for Pilate to allow the crowd to pick one prisoner, whom he would then release unto them. Pilate tried to release Jesus after his wife informed him of a dream concerning Him, but the crowd which was persuaded by the chief priests and elders demanded that a murderer named Barabbas be released instead. Pilate then went into the judgment hall and asked Jesus where He was from. Jesus did not answer him. Pilate told Jesus that he had the power to crucify Him and the authority to release Him. Jesus responded by telling Pilate that he would not have had his authority, had it not been given to him from above (John 19:11). Jesus was then taken and scourged (whipped), which in those days was done with a leather whip with pieces of metal or bone on the end of the thongs. After having been whipped, Jesus was dressed in purple, the color of royalty, and a crown of thorns was placed on His Head. He was then presented to the Jews as their King. The crowd did not want Him to be released and shouted "Crucify Him" (Mark 15:13). Pilate yielded to the demands of the crowd by releasing Barabbas to them, and by handing Jesus over to the soldiers to be crucified.

SIMON OF CYRENE

After being mockingly hailed as King of the Jews, beaten, and spit upon, Jesus was put back into His own clothes and led away, carrying His own cross (Matt. 27:31). In those days, the one to be crucified was forced to carry the crossbeam to the execution site. Seeing that Jesus was weakened by the scourging and the beating that He had received, a man from Cyrene was compelled to carry the cross of Jesus behind Him to Golgotha, the execution site (Matt. 27:32).

JESUS IS CRUCIFIED

At approximately 9:00 A.M., Jesus was crucified along with two criminals, one to His right and one to His left. Over Jesus's Head was nailed a sign that read: "JESUS OF NAZARETH, THE KING OF THE JEWS" (John 19:19). Many, including the chief priests and scribes, mocked Jesus and told Him to save Himself if He was truly the Son of God, as He had declared (Matt. 27:43). While on the cross, Jesus taught and set the perfect example of how man is to forgive those that sin against them, by asking His Heavenly Spirit to forgive those that had crucified Him. The soldiers meanwhile drew lots (played straws) for His garments. One of the criminals that was crucified with Jesus told Him that if He were the Son of God, to save Himself and to save them also. The other criminal responded by telling this criminal that they were receiving their just reward, but that Jesus had not done anything wrong. This criminal then turned to Jesus, and asked Him to remember him when He entered into His Kingdom. Jesus looked at him, and told him that on that same day he would be with Him in Paradise (Luke 23:33–43).

FINAL HOURS ON THE CROSS

By noon, there was a darkness over all the land for three hours. This miraculous sign showed that Jesus was one with Yayweh God, Who said that He clothes the heavens with blackness (Is. 50:3). At about 3:00 in the afternoon Jesus cried out "My God, My God, why hast Thou forsaken Me?" (Matt. 27:46). Here Jesus showed and expressed the human pain and agony that He was enduring by quoting the words that King David used while in his agony (Ps. 22:1). As Jesus looked down and saw His mother and His disciple John, He told them to behold each other. Afterwards, John took her to his home and cared for her (John 19:26–27). Knowing that His earthly mission was ending, and knowing that He would be offered vinegar to drink, Jesus said that He was thirsty. The Old Testament prophecy that foretold this was thus fulfilled. Jesus then said, "It is Finished" (John 19:30). The Greek words translated as "commend" and "yielded up" could have been translated as "consign" and "gave over." No one could take Christ's life from Him, because as God, His Life is Eternal. Instead, Jesus Christ spoke the "Word" and delivered over His Life into the

Power of His Heavenly Spirit. The Body of Jesus Christ was dead, only in the likeness that a man's body without the spirit is dead. What really happened is that Jesus laid down His physical life when He "poured out His Soul unto death," as the prophet Isaiah foretold 700 years before the fact (Is. 53:12). Then, after three days and three nights, God's Soul re-entered the Body of Jesus Christ, and He rose from the dead as He had foretold.

TEMPLE VEIL SPLITS IN TWO

The moment Jesus yielded up His Spirit, the veil of the temple was split in two, from top to bottom, as the earth quaked (Matt. 27:53). As we learned, the veil of the temple was the curtain through which the high priest would pass before entering the Holy of Holies, where he would offer God the sacrificial blood for forgiveness of the Israelites' sins. This splitting of the temple veil marked the end of God's Old Covenant with man and the beginning of God's New Covenant with man. As we will learn, God's Holy Spirit would no longer dwell in temples made of hands, but in the minds and hearts of man.

BLOOD AND WATER

Because the Jewish Sabbath would begin at 6:00 P.M., and the Jews did not want the bodies of Jesus and the others to remain on the cross during this time, they requested to Pilate that their legs be broken. This was done in those days with a club to promote shock and a quick death. The legs of the two criminals were broken, but because Jesus was already physically dead, His legs were not broken. However, one of the soldiers pierced His side with a spear, and immediately came out blood and water (John 19:31–34). The Blood that Jesus Christ shed is the Everlasting Blood of God's New Covenant. The Living Water that poured from Christ's side is the Righteousness of God Who cleanses and clothes the souls of those that put their faith in the Shed Blood of Jesus Christ for the remission of their sins. The Holy Spirit clothes one's soul with the Righteous Nature of Jesus Christ, and gives Eternal Life to those that call upon God in the Name of Jesus Christ.

PLACED IN THE TOMB

Joseph, a disciple of Jesus from Arimathaea, asked Pilate for the Body of Jesus. After verifying that Jesus Christ was indeed dead, Pilate granted him permission. Joseph took the dead Body of Jesus and placed Him in a new tomb, which was cut in a rock. Nicodemus also came and brought with him an aromatic mixture of myrrh and aloes, which they applied to Jesus as they bound His dead Body in fine linen (John 19:38–40). A great stone was then rolled to the door of the tomb (Matt. 27:60). The chief priests, remembering that Jesus had said that He would arise after three days, asked Pilate to secure his tomb. Pilate told them to send their guard unit to secure Christ's tomb, which they did.

DAY OF BURIAL

The Sabbath to the Jew is both the seventh day of the week and any special feast or high day. Jesus was crucified the day before the high day called Passover (John 19:31). The Greek word "Paraskevi," translated as Friday, means the day of preparation for the Sabbath (Saturday or special feast day). Due to the fact that Saturday is the seventh day of the week, the weekly day of Friday is the normal day of preparation. However, the Paraskevi on which Jesus Christ was crucified and buried was not a normal Friday, because this Special Sabbath did not fall on Saturday. The Passover in this year fell three days before Sunday. The body of Jesus Christ lay in the tomb for three days and three nights, just as Jesus had foretold.

JESUS IS RISEN

Early Sunday morning, while it was still dark, Mary Magdalene and her friends came to the tomb of Jesus. The earth quaked as an angel of the Lord descended from heaven and rolled away the stone. He told Mary that "Jesus is Risen" and to go and tell the disciples (Matt. 28:2–7). Mary ran and told Peter and John, who entered the tomb and believed when they saw the linen cloths, that had been used to wrap the body of Jesus, lying there. After the disciples left, Mary remained at the tomb and wept. When Mary returned, she saw Jesus, and thought that He was the gardener until He called her by her name. Jesus told her not to touch Him because He had not yet ascended, and told her to go and tell the disciples that He was ascending to His Father and their Father, and to His God and their God (John 20:1–17). Jesus said this to let His disciples know that those that follow Him will also rise from the dead, and will enter into His Heavenly Kingdom of Love.

THE BODILY RESURRECTION OF JESUS

That same evening, all the apostles except Thomas were assembled behind closed doors, for fear of the Jews that had condemned Jesus. At this time Jesus appeared in their midst (John 20:19). At first they were frightened and thought that they were seeing a ghost. Jesus told them to see His Hands and His Feet, and to feel Him and see that, unlike a ghost, He had flesh and bones. He then asked them if they had anything to eat. They gave Jesus some broiled fish and honeycomb, and He ate it (Luke 23:37–43). When the apostles told Thomas that Jesus had appeared to them, he did not believe them. He said that unless he saw and put his finger in the nail-pierced hands of Jesus, and put his hand in His side, he would not believe. After eight days, Jesus again appeared to the apostles through locked doors. This time Thomas was there. So that he could believe, Jesus told him to bring his finger and see His Hands, and to bring his hand and see His Side. Thomas responded by saying, "My Lord and My God" (John 20:28).

JESUS BAPTIZES THE APOSTLES

When Jesus appeared before the apostles, they believed beyond a doubt that He was indeed the Christ, the Sent One from God. Jesus said for peace to be unto them, and as His Father hath sent Him, even so He sends them. Jesus then breathed on them and told them to receive the Holy Spirit (John 20:21–22). This is the Holy Spirit baptism that John the Baptist talked about when he said that he baptized with water, but One Greater would come Who would baptize with the Holy Spirit (Matt. 3:11). Jesus made it perfectly clear that His Breath is One with the Living Holy Spirit of God, Who enters and dwells with those that receive His Word. Those that keep their minds on God's Word are led by the Spirit of Jesus Christ and therefore do the Will of God's Heavenly Spirit Mind, known as God the Father.

APOSTLES ARE ENLIGHTENED

When Jesus breathed on His apostles, their minds were opened to understand the scriptures (Luke 24:45). Jesus reviewed with them the things He had told them before, and also the prophetic scriptures concerning Him that are found in the Old Testament books of Moses, of the prophets, and of the Psalms. Jesus showed them where it had been written that He would suffer, die, and then rise from the dead. It is important to remember the fact that unless one receives the Holy Spirit of God, he cannot know the things of God (I Cor. 2:11). As we learned, the Holy Spirit is the Living Spirit of God the Father, the Eternal Mind of God, and also the Living Spirit of God the Son, the True Image of God's Being (Heb. 1:3). Thus when one receives and yields to God's Holy Spirit, his mind becomes conscious of God's Will, and his soul becomes conformed to the Image of Jesus Christ, Who is One with, and always does the Perfect Will of God the Father (John 8:29). This person will desire to please God more than himself, and will dedicate his life to doing God's Will. It is through obedience to God that one's soul is conformed to the Image of Jesus Christ. This is the Will of God for every human being.

APOSTLES SENT TO PREACH

As we learned, Jesus said "Peace be unto you" before He breathed on His apostles (John 20:21), and sent them out to preach. When one receives God's Holy Spirit through faith in Jesus Christ, he receives a peace beyond all understanding (Phil. 4:7). No matter what the apostles would physically endure, they knew that it was nothing compared to the rewards that they would receive. They no longer feared death, knowing that as Jesus rose from the dead, they too would rise from the dead. Jesus said He was sending them as His Father sent Him. Let us understand this. One's word is carried by one's breath. Christ's Word was carried by the Living Breath of God known as the Holy Spirit. When one receives and shares God's Word with others, he is spreading God's Holy Spirit of Love. Those that hear and believe the Gospel of Jesus Christ, and then receive the Holy Spirit of God by asking (inviting) Jesus into their heart as their Lord and Savior, will be cleansed of their sins and will be saved from God's coming judgment upon this world (John 3:16). God's Holy Spirit comes in the Name of Jesus Christ. One can receive God's Holy Spirit only by believing God's Word and asking Jesus Christ into his heart. Jesus will spend eternity with those that will have chosen to love Him and will have put His (God's) Word in their hearts prior to His return.

THE DIVINITY OF JESUS CHRIST

Jesus told the eleven apostles to go to a certain mountain in Galilee and that He would appear to them there. There, Jesus told them that He was given all authority in heaven and on earth (Matt. 28:18). It is most important to understand the fact that God is, and has always been One, and that He has, and has always had complete authority over heaven and earth. In the above passage, Jesus was letting His apostles know that He would thereafter be the Fullness of God. When Jesus Christ returns to this earth, He is returning as King of kings and Lord of lords (Rev. 19:16). Christ willingly chose to limit his authority and become like a man, until He, in the Person of Jesus Christ, could establish God's New Covenant (Agreement) with man in His Shed Blood. God in, as, and through the Person of Jesus Christ chose to unite and to purify unto Himself (in His Name) a people zealous of good works (Tit. 2:14). This is God's Master Plan.

FINAL INSTRUCTIONS

Jesus instructed his disciples to remain in Jerusalem until they would be clothed with Power from on high (Luke 24:49). After the convicting Power of God's Holy Spirit would descend, Jesus told His disciples that they would be "His Witnesses" (not Jehovah's Witnesses) beginning in Jerusalem to the ends of the earth (Acts 1:8). After saying these final words from the Mount of Olives, Jesus was taken up to heaven in a cloud before their very eyes. As they watched, two angels appeared to them and told them that Jesus would return in the same manner in which He ascended (Acts 1:8–11). As we will learn, Jesus will soon return to the Mount of Olives as the two angels promised.

PART VI

THE CHURCH AGE

THE CHURCH AGE

PENTECOST

After Jesus ascended into heaven, His disciples gathered in Jerusalem to await the descent of the Holy Spirit, as Jesus had commanded them. As they were gathered, Matthias was chosen as the twelfth apostle to replace Judas Iscariot, who had committed suicide after betraying Jesus. Many Jews from various nations were in Jerusalem at this time for Pentecost, or the Feast of Harvest, in which they celebrated the early spring and the major fall harvest. It was on the day of Pentecost, fifty days after Jesus had risen from the dead, that God's Holy Spirit, as a mighty breath from heaven, descended, and filled the whole house where the disciples were gathered. After being filled with the Holy Spirit, the disciples began to speak in the different languages which the Holy Spirit gave them to speak (Acts 2:1–4). When word of this spread, multitudes in Jerusalem came to see for themselves what had happened. They that came were amazed when they found the disciples giving their testimonies about the things they had witnessed concerning Jesus Christ, in each of their various languages.

JEWS AND JESUS

It is important to note that the order of the Jewish feasts, that God ordained in the Old Testament, were and are going to be fulfilled in Jesus Christ. For instance: Jesus Christ was crucified as the Sacrificial Passover Lamb; He was buried on the Feast of Unleavened Bread; He was resurrected on the Feast of First-Fruits; and the Holy Spirit descended on the Feast of Harvest or Pentecost. From the day of Pentecost until this very day, we have two kinds of Jews: the "born-again" Jews are those who have heard and believed the Gospel of Jesus Christ, and have received God's

Holy Spirit in their minds and hearts; the Orthodox Jews are those that continue to observe the rituals and the traditions of Old Testament Judaism, and have either rejected or neglected to believe that Jesus Christ is the "Sent One" described in their Old Testament Scriptures. The born-again Jews, as all born-again believers, are expecting the Lord Jesus Christ to return to Jerusalem and set up God's Kingdom on earth. The Orthodox Jews are expecting a different Messiah to come to Jerusalem and set up God's Everlasting Kingdom.

CHURCH AGE BEGINS

The Day of Pentecost marks the official beginning of the Church Age. The twelve apostles of Jesus, along with over one hundred of His Jewish disciples that were infilled with God's Holy Spirit on the day of Pentecost (Acts 1:15), are the first members of the Body of Jesus Christ, known as His Church. As we learned, Jesus had told His disciples that when the Holy Spirit would come, they would receive Power from on high, and would be His witnesses beginning in Jerusalem to the uttermost parts of the earth. This came to pass the moment that Christ's disciples were filled with the Holy Spirit. At this time, the Spirit of Jesus Christ entered into His disciples, as He had promised (Matt. 28:20), and they received the power to proclaim His Gospel in languages that they did not previously know. It is presently God's Will that His children (the body of born-again believers), known collectively as His "Church," offer Eternal Life to all people of all nations through faith in the Name of His Living Son (True Image), Jesus Christ (John 20:31). It is most important to remember that when mankind came together without the Holy Spirit to build the tower of Babel as a monument to themselves, God confounded their languages. The fact that God now empowered His disciples to talk various languages proves that He wants and is establishing His Kingdom in the Name of Jesus Christ, and that it is His Will that all nations hear and believe his Gospel, the Gospel of Jesus Christ.

BEGINNING IN JERUSALEM

Jesus commanded His disciples to be His Witnesses beginning in Jerusalem. It is here that King David set up his throne after uniting the ten tribes of Israel. David was from the tribe of Judah,

from which the members of David's kingdom got the name "Jews."
When the Tabernacle of God was moved to Jerusalem, it became
the center of worship for the Jews. It is there that King Solomon,
David's son, had God's Temple built according to God's intricate
details. God told David and the prophets that His Sent One—the
Messiah—the Christ would come through the lineage of David,
and would establish and rule God's Everlasting Kingdom from
Jerusalem (Is. 9:7).

JEWISH HISTORY

After the death of King Solomon, the Jews fled and were
taken captive to other nations. Their kingdom was first captured
and divided by the Assyrians, and then by the Babylonians, by the
Greeks, and by the Romans. This is how and why in the days of
Jesus, many Jews lived outside the Promised Land and spoke
various languages. When the Jewish Messiah (Jesus Christ) came,
the majority of Jews rejected Him because they were expecting
their Messiah to immediately overthrow the Roman government,
and to re-establish and rule over the Davidic kingdom. As we
learned, the Word of God was not in their hearts. Therefore, they
did not know that He would first appear as a "Lamb to Slaughter."
Prior to His ascension, Jesus told His disciples to be His witnesses
beginning in Jerusalem, in order for the Jews and all the world to
know that He is the Sent One of God, of Whom the Old Testament
Scriptures testify. By looking at the hundred-plus prophecies that
Jesus Christ fulfilled on and during His first appearance, man can
have peace in knowing that Jesus Christ will soon return as King of
kings, and will rule this earth from Jerusalem as the prophets
foretold. When God's Spirit of Love replaces Satan's evil spirit, this
earth will be a glorious place to live. Jerusalem is where the
Church Age began, and Jerusalem is where this present Church
Age will soon come to an end.

PETER'S SERMON

On the day of Pentecost, as the crowds of devout Jews were
gathered in amazement around the disciples, Peter stood up and
proclaimed to them that Jesus, Whom they crucified and Who
rose from the dead, was and is their Lord and their Messiah. He
told them that God (the Eternal Spirit Mind of Love) sent Christ

(His Soul or True Image) to them and did many miracles through Him in their presence, knowing that they would have Him crucified. Peter showed them by reciting from the Holy Scriptures that Jesus Christ is the Lord of Whom the prophet Joel spoke. Joel foretold that everyone must call upon Jesus Christ in order to be saved from the "Day of the Lord," which is God's soon to come period of judgment upon this earth, upon Satan the devil, and upon Satan's followers. Peter continued by showing them through God's Word that Jesus is the Lord that David called "My Lord," and is also their Messiah, Who David said would come and rule the nations from Jerusalem.

DAVID'S LORD

Peter told the Jews that David had said that he foresaw Him (Jesus Christ), and that Christ was at his right hand so that he should not be shaken. In other words, Jesus Christ, as David's Lord, was there to sustain him. David, talking about Jesus Christ, said the Presence of the Lord filled his heart with joy, made his tongue rejoice, and allowed his flesh to dwell in hope. This is due to the fact that he knew that the Soul of Jesus Christ would not be abandoned in Hades, nor would His Body see corruption in the grave (Acts 2:25–27). Peter told them that David, being a prophet, was told by God and knew that God would raise up Jesus Christ, to which they were all witnesses.

NOTE

It is important to note that the Presence of Jesus Christ, as David mentioned, fills one's heart with joy, makes one's tongue rejoice, and allows one to physically dwell in hope. When one's soul is driven by the Love of God, his mind dwells in peace and joy, and is full of loving thoughts. This person will express and spread God's Love by sharing the Gospel of Jesus Christ, and by helping those in need. A child of God will both live and die in peace, knowing that his eternal destiny is in God's Hand.

GOD'S RIGHT HAND

Peter told the crowd that Jesus Christ, from the right hand of God, shed forth the Holy Spirit, which they were both seeing and hearing. For Jesus to be at the right hand of God signifies that Jesus Christ is on the Throne of God's Power and directs the Holy Spirit to reach out and to do God's Will (Acts 2:33). As you can see, it is Jesus Christ Who expresses the Will of His Eternal Spirit Mind, known as God the Father, and directs the Holy Spirit. The Holy Spirit is the Spirit Body of God that makes manifest the Will of God, as directed by the Words of Jesus Christ. Peter ended his sermon by stating, for the whole house of Israel to know, that God made Jesus, Whom they crucified, both Lord and Christ. The Greek word translated as "made," which Peter used when he said that God made Jesus Christ both Lord and Christ (Acts 2:36), means to give, to endow, or to appoint an already existing thing or person with a certain quality. When Christ, as the Soul of God, spoke the Word to be made as a man so that He could shed His Blood for the forgiveness of man's sin, God's Will was fulfilled through the Power of the Holy Spirit. Being One God, Jesus Christ always expresses the Will of His Eternal Mind, and His Holy Spirit Body always brings His Word to pass.

JESUS THE GOD-MAN

The prophet David foretold in the 110th Psalm, 1,000 years prior to Peter's speech: "The LORD (referring to Yayweh God) said to my Lord (referring to Jesus Christ), "Sit Thou on My Right Hand until I make Thy foes Thy footstool." How can Yayweh God talk to the Lord Jesus Christ if the LORD God is One? The answer to this question is, Yayweh God can talk to the Lord Jesus in the same likeness that the rich fool talked to his soul, and in the same likeness as our mind speaks to our soul. Everything we do is a result of mind to soul conversation. This conversation between mind and soul is internal, and is only outwardly expressed when the soul directs the body to speak or act accordingly. When man was first created, God's Eternal Spirit was: Spirit Mind, Spirit Soul, and Spirit Body. When God chose to send His Eternal Soul into the world, God's Eternal Soul assumed the role of God's Son. God's Eternal Spirit Mind remained in heaven and assumed the role of God the Father (Heb. 1:5). God's Spirit Body is and always has been everywhere (Ps. 139:7) to make manifest God's Spoken Word. When Christ, the Soul of God, spoke the Word (Will) of God to become man, He chose to Personally and temporarily lower Himself from His Heavenly Glory in order to draw all creation unto Himself. Christ in the form of God emptied Himself, took on the appearance of a servant, was transformed into the likeness of man (Phil. 2:7), and humbly shed His Spotless Blood on the cross for the forgiveness of man's sin. Even though Jesus received a human body through the lineage of David, He was perfect. In order to understand this, consider the following. God declared that the life of all flesh is in the Blood thereof (Lev. 17:14). Jesus Christ did not receive life from fleshly blood (John 1:13). His Life was and is from Above (John 8:23).

BLOOD

In order to understand the True Gospel of Jesus Christ, one must consider the significance of blood. Webster's dictionary defines blood as "the essence of life." It is the blood that carries and supplies oxygen throughout the body. God told Moses 3,500 years ago that the life of all flesh is in the blood, and that it is the sacrificial blood, which is placed on the altar, that makes an atonement (a covering) for the sins of one's soul (Lev. 17:11). God also told us that Adam's sin infected the human race. Now, almost 6,000 years later, medical scientists are reporting that man inherits personality traits, addictions, and disease from their family blood line. Due to the fact that the life in Adam's blood became tainted when he chose to sin, he could not pass on a perfect nature to his descendants, the human race. Man's mind and soul turned from being Godward to being selfward. Man began to trust in himself instead of looking towards and trusting in God. The goal of man's life was no longer to please God and to love one's fellowman, but to work and to satisfy his flesh and the selfish desires of his corrupt mind (Eph. 2:3). Man switched from the path that leads to eternal life to the path that leads to death.

BLOOD SACRIFICE

After Adam sinned, God instituted animal sacrifice as a way through which man could receive a temporary forgiveness of his sins. As we learned from the story of Cain and Abel (Gen. 4), only a blood sacrifice was acceptable to God for an atonement for sin. Under God's Old Covenant, the lambs required for sacrifice were the firstborn of the flock. These animals meant a lot to the families that offered them. For one to watch the life pour out of their animals, after they themselves slashed their necks, in exchange for the forgiveness of their sins and their reconciliation with God, made them realize the seriousness of sin. The life of these spotless animals was the ransom (the payment) necessary for one's family to be redeemed (delivered) from the wages of sin, which is death (Rom. 6:23).

OLD COVENANT BLOOD SACRIFICE

According to God's Old Covenant, man could receive God's forgiveness for his sins only through the high priest. The high priest would go into the Holy of Holies and offer the LORD God the blood of the sacrifice by burning the blood upon the altar. It would then go up to God in smoke in exchange for the pardon of sin. This offering of life was instituted to prepare mankind for God's future offer of Eternal Life through faith in the Sacrificial Blood of Jesus Christ. Animal sacrifice through a high priest was a shadow of the future time in which Jesus Christ would enter into the real Holy of Holies (the Presence of His Heavenly Spirit) with His Own Blood, and would obtain eternal redemption for man (Heb. 9:12). Even though God never received pleasure in animal sacrifice (Heb. 10:6), it was necessary in order to prepare mankind for His Ultimate Sacrifice. By learning that only the spotless blood of a firstborn could purge one's mind, or spirit conscience, man can begin to understand and appreciate why God came into this world as a man. God took on a Body with Blood in order to offer Himself for the remission of man's sin. By learning that only the high priest could enter into God's Presence, and only with a blood sacrifice could he receive God's blessings and mercy, we can now understand the fact that man can receive God's blessings and forgiveness only through Jesus Christ. He is man's present-day High Priest.

NOTE

Past and present false religious teachings have led many to believe that salvation and eternal life are available only through membership in certain religious institutions. This was done to control man. The Truth is that no church, no religion, no one but Jesus Christ can grant Eternal Life. Anyone that hears and believes the Gospel of Jesus Christ can enter into the Presence of God by personally inviting God in the Name of Jesus Christ (which is the Name of the Father and of the Son and of the Holy Spirit) into his heart. Those that keep Jesus Christ and His Word in their hearts until the end will inherit eternal life. This is the Promise of God's New Covenant, in which man is commanded not to address any religious leader on this earth as "Father." Many through tradition, intimidation, and lack of Biblical knowledge are being led by man instead of by God's Holy Spirit.

GOD'S NEW COVENANT

Jesus Christ did not come into this world to judge man, but rather to save him from the second death. Those that do not believe in Jesus Christ as the Only Begotten Son (True Image) of God will be sentenced because they chose to live in the darkness of this world instead of the "Light" of God. Those that fall in this group hate God's Light (Truth) because He, Jesus Christ, exposes their sin (John 3:17–20). Jesus referred to Himself as the "Son of Man" because He came into this world to give Himself for man. Faith in the Power of His Shed Blood is man's "Way" to clothe his soul in the Righteousness of God. God's New Covenant (Agreement) with man is as follows. Those that hear the Gospel of Jesus Christ, believe that Jesus is the Son (True Image) of God, believe He shed His Blood to cleanse them of their sin, and then ask and receive God (in the Name of Jesus Christ) into their hearts, will have their spirit renewed. In this "born-again" experience, one's mind receives the Living and Righteous Nature of Jesus Christ. God's Spirit of Righteousness then works to transform this person's soul into the Image of Jesus Christ. Those that are truly born again receive the Holy Spirit Righteousness of Jesus Christ, and will pass from physical death into eternal life as did Jesus. When one receives and is led by the Spirit of Jesus Christ, he or she becomes a member of the Body of Jesus Christ, known as His Church. God is presently working through these, His earthly vessels, to gather together those that will spend eternity with Him.

THE RESTORATION OF MAN

As we learned, man was given a free thinking mind. The LORD told man that He set before him two paths, the Way of Life and the way of death (Jer. 21:8). When man switched paths, God did not stop loving him, just as a loving father does not stop loving his child when he or she disobeys him. It is the disobedience that is hated and not the child. If the child repents and returns with love, he is received with love. It is up to the child. If a parent tells his child not to step in the path of a speeding automobile, and the child disobeys and is killed, one cannot blame the parent. In the same likeness, one cannot blame God for the disobedience that is destroying this world and the souls of many. It is God's Will that all turn from their evil ways and turn to Him, in the Name of Jesus Christ, so that He can grant them Eternal Life in His Kingdom. In the parable of the prodigal son, God taught man that His arms are ready to embrace those that repent and return to Him. Looking down and seeing that man was headed for destruction, God, in His Love for man, sent His Soul as a servant into this world, in the Person of Jesus Christ, to save mankind. God declares in His Word that we like sheep were going astray, and Jesus, as the Shepherd and Bishop (Guardian) of our souls, has returned us to the Way of Life (I Pet. 2:25). One is led onto the Path of Righteousness when the Living Spirit of God is invited and enters into one's mind, and works in him the desire to do God's Will.

NOTE

In the Old Testament times, the Eternal Spirit of Jesus Christ dwelt in the innermost tent of the Tabernacle called the Holy of Holies. From the day of Pentecost until this present day, the Spirit of Jesus Christ comes and dwells in the minds and hearts of those that ask Him into their hearts. It is the Spirit of "Truth" (Jesus Christ) Who makes God known to man. Those that think that they have to go to a physical church to be in the Presence of God are deceived. This is due to the fact that the Holy Spirit no longer lives in temples made by hands, but in the minds and hearts of born-again believers, who are the temple of God (I Cor. 6:19). The Church is called the "Body" of Christ (Col. 1:18) because it has many members. The commission of the church is to spread the Love of God through the Gospel of Jesus Christ. Each member, in various ways, works to accomplish this. Just as a body has different members with different functions, the church also has many members with different functions, each of which benefits the Body of Christ as a whole.

REPENT AND BE BAPTIZED

Man is justified (accounted as righteous) by Grace (God's Mercy) when he is baptized (cleansed of his sin) by the Holy Spirit. The Holy Spirit is God's Free Gift to man for believing and trusting that He, in the Person of Jesus Christ, came into this world and shed His Blood for our sin. One does not have to work for, pay for, or go through a man-made ritual to receive God's Holy Spirit. God's Holy Spirit comes freely to those that receive faith in Jesus Christ after hearing His Gospel, and then invite God in the Name of Jesus Christ into their hearts. After Peter preached the Gospel of Jesus Christ to the Jews gathered in Jerusalem, many believed that Jesus was the Lord and that He shed His Blood for their sins, and wanted to be saved by receiving God's Free Gift of the Holy Spirit. Peter told these believing Jews to repent and be baptized in the Name of Jesus Christ, which as we learned is the Name of God the Father, God the Son, and God the Holy Spirit. Unlike the water baptism of John, these early believers and all those that confess their faith in Jesus Christ, during this Age of Grace, are baptized by God's Holy Spirit. In order to receive God's Holy Spirit, one must publicly confess his faith in Jesus Christ with his mouth and believe that He rose from the dead by the Power of God (Rom. 10:9). Jesus Christ said that He would confess before (or in the Presence of) His Heavenly Spirit, those that confess Him before men (Matt. 10:32). On that first day of Pentecost, 3,000 devout Jews received the baptism of the Holy Ghost after hearing the Gospel of Jesus Christ (Acts 2:41).

TO THE JEW FIRST

For the first twelve years, the Church of Jesus Christ was made up of Jews, who preached the Gospel of Jesus Christ to other Jews. After all, what did the Gentiles (non-Jews) know about Yayweh God, Moses, and the prophets? It would take time for the Gentiles to learn about and to understand God's promise to send His Sent One into this world, through the seed of Abraham, to bless all nations. At that time, only the Jews had and could refer to the hundreds of Old Testament Scriptures that foretold that Jesus Christ would come as a "Lamb to Slaughter," would be crucified, would rise from the dead, and would return again, as King of kings and Lord of lords, to rule God's Earthly Kingdom from Jerusalem.

It was in Jerusalem that Jesus Christ officially began His Church, which grew as His disciples entered the synagogues outside Jerusalem, and gave their eye-witness accounts of Jesus Christ and of His resurrection from the dead.

GENTILES INCLUDED

The Church of Jesus Christ began to officially accept Gentiles as members after God showed the apostle Peter in a vision that He is no respecter of persons, and that He accepts all who fear and follow Him (Acts 10:34–35). As Peter shared the Gospel of Jesus Christ in Caesarea with the Gentile Cornelius and his household, the Holy Spirit fell on all those hearing God's Word. The Jews with Peter were amazed when these Gentiles received the Holy Spirit and began to talk in tongues and magnify God. Peter then commanded them to be baptized in water. He wanted everyone to see and to know that the Good News (Gospel) of Jesus Christ was God's Way of Salvation for all mankind. When Peter returned to Jerusalem, he was criticized for going into a Gentile home and eating with them. After Peter explained his vision to them, they praised God for granting even the non-Jews repentance unto life (Acts 11:18). It is through Jesus Christ, who came into this world through the seed of Abraham, that all people of all nations can receive God's Blessing of Eternal Life.

CHURCH UNITY

Many miracles were performed through the apostles (Acts 2:43), including healings in the Name of Jesus Christ. The church grew, as many witnessed the Power of God's Holy Spirit. The early church was united both spiritually and materially, and there were no needy among them. This is because all that believed were together and had all things in common (Acts 2:45). Nobody owned anything personally but shared everything as a family. Their hearts were pure because they were dedicated to Jesus Christ. They desired to share the Gospel of Jesus Christ with others, so that they too could receive His Holy Spirit and spend eternity with Him in God's Glorious Kingdom. The early church was not living for the temporary pleasures and luxuries of this world, but was working to spread the Gospel of Jesus Christ. They understood that God, through them, was uniting and purifying unto Himself, in the Name of Jesus Christ, a people zealous of good works (Titus 2:14). These folks, as all true born-again believers, were living in the hope of Christ's return.

CHURCH IS PERSECUTED

Jesus Christ told His disciples that they, as He, would be both hated and persecuted. The same religious leaders that had Jesus Christ crucified for fear of losing their positions and power, now began to persecute the disciples of Jesus Christ. This persecution began with the arrest and the beating of Peter and John for preaching the Gospel of Jesus Christ (Acts 5:40). Later Stephen was stoned to death. Being in the Spirit of Jesus Christ, Stephen asked God to forgive those that stoned him before he died (Acts 7:58–60). Next James was killed by the sword (Acts 12:1). This did not stop the disciples of Jesus Christ, because they were warned and knew that those that share in Christ's suffering will also share in His coming Glory (I Pet. 4:11). Being a Christian does not guarantee a present life of health, wealth, and joy as many falsely teach. Christ and His disciples suffered tragic and agonizing deaths. What true Christianity does offer is a peace beyond all understanding. God's Peace results from knowing, without a doubt, that no matter what one is presently facing, there is a glorious future just ahead. The early disciples entrusted their lives to Jesus Christ, even if it was His Will that they suffer temporarily for the Glory of God (I Pet. 5:6). They understood that even if they were physically killed, being absent from the body would mean being present with the Lord (II Cor. 5:8).

SAUL OF TARSUS

Saul, a Roman officer who was also a Pharisee, was ravaging the early church, which as we learned is the body of Christ's Holy Spirit-filled believers. He and his officers were entering the homes of these early believers and were dragging them, both men and women, to prison (Acts 8:3). After receiving authority from the high priest, Saul set out to persecute the church in Damascus. (It is important to note that it was the Jews of Judaism that were heading up this persecution against the Jewish believers in Jesus Christ.) On the way, Saul fell to the ground when Light from heaven shone around him. He then heard a voice from heaven ask him, "Saul, why persecuteth thou Me?" (Acts 22:7). When Saul asked who it was that was speaking, Jesus Christ said it was He, and that he should arise and go into the city. When Saul arose and opened his eyes, he was blind. Saul and those with him proceeded to Damascus and waited there three days, after which Ananias, a disciple of Jesus Christ, came and put his hand on Saul, and he received his sight. Ananias told Saul that the Lord told him that he, Saul, was a chosen vessel to carry the Name of Jesus Christ to the Gentiles, to kings, and to the children of Israel. Saul immediately began to preach the Gospel of Jesus Christ in the synagogues. The born-again Jews, who had feared Saul, were amazed that he had become one of them. The Jews of Judaism on the other hand were angered, and plotted to kill Saul. Saul, known mainly by his Roman name of Paul, not only became a great missionary of the early church, but also wrote thirteen of the Epistles found in the New Testament.

NOTE

Notice that Jesus asked Saul why he was persecuting Him. When one persecutes a Holy Spirit-filled Christian, he is persecuting Jesus Christ. This is because Jesus Christ through the Holy Spirit lives inside His members, which make up His Body known as His Church. Followers of Jesus Christ became known as Christians. One is a true Christian only if he has been "born again" by receiving Christ's Spirit of Truth into his heart. God's Holy Spirit answers and comes into the hearts of only those that receive Him in the Name of Jesus Christ. Those professing Christians that deny the fact that Jesus Christ is the "Son" (the True Image) of, and "One" with God's Invisible Holy Spirit, are not truly born again, and are therefore not being led by God's Holy Spirit. These folks know "of" Jesus, but they do not know Jesus Christ, because His Spirit, which is the Holy Spirit of God, is not in them. As we learned, one becomes a true child of God when God's Holy Spirit dwells in them and leads their life.

THE LOCAL CHURCH

The universal church of Jesus Christ, as we learned, is the entire body of believers that have received and are abiding in God's Holy Spirit. In addition to the universal church of Jesus

Christ, local gatherings of believers known as churches were formed and became a part of the universal church of Jesus Christ. When Paul, who was a Jew, went into various cities, he would enter the synagogues on the Sabbath day and preach the Gospel of Jesus Christ. Those that believed the Gospel and received the Holy Spirit would then gather together in various homes and have church (Col. 4:15). These local churches were independent gatherings that were pure in heart. The members were dedicated to spreading the Gospel of Jesus Christ, taking care of the needs of all their members, and reaching out to others in the Spirit of Love, while waiting for the blessed hope of the return of their Lord and Savior Jesus Christ (Titus 2:13).

NOTE

The purity and love that existed in the early church is almost beyond imagination. Local churches were groups of people who gave all they had, and came together as one big family in which everyone was equal. The doctors, the carpenters, the farmers, etc. did not work for personal gain, but rather for the benefit of Jesus Christ, alive in His earthly body of believers. The early Church spread God's Love through the Gospel of Jesus Christ and through their good deeds. These born-again believers were more concerned with the future Kingdom of God than with the temporary things of this world. Jesus Christ was the center of their pastime conversation, much like sports and gossip are today.

JESUS THE JEW

It is most important to understand that God chose the Jewish people through whom He brought salvation to the world (John 4:22). God, through His Word, made His covenant with Abraham and his descendants, which became the Jewish race and the nation of Israel. The "Word" of God then revealed Himself in the Person of Jesus Christ, the Son of God, the Jewish Messiah, Who is over all, God Blessed forever (Rom. 9:4–5). Jesus Christ came into this world as a Jew to fulfill God's Promise to Abraham, which stated that all the nations of the earth would be blessed through his seed. As we learned, Jesus Christ was born into this world by the Virgin Mary, a Jewess, a descendant of Abraham. God, in the Person and in the Name of Jesus Christ, began to establish His Kingdom with the Jew first, and then with the Gentiles, which include all people of all nations. All those who receive the Holy Spirit of Jesus Christ become children of God and heirs to His coming Kingdom. All born-again children of God, regardless of color, race, or nationality, are "One" in the Blood and in the Spirit of Jesus Christ (Col. 13:10–11), and shall all be like Him when he returns (I John 3:2).

ONE WORLD UNDER JESUS CHRIST

Jesus Christ's Heavenly Spirit Mind, known as God the Father, is neither white nor black, Jew nor Gentile; He is the Eternal Spirit of Love. All who receive the Holy Spirit are newly created beings, whose thinking is being renewed by the Living Spirit of their Creator, Jesus Christ (Col. 3:9). God tells us in His Word that it is by the mind that one can serve God (Rom. 7:25). Those that receive the Holy Spirit of God receive the Righteousness of Jesus Christ in their minds. Afterwards they desire to do Christ's Will, which is the Will of His Heavenly Spirit known as the Father. This is why Jesus said "My Father and your Father" to His disciples (John 20:17). When one's mind partakes of the Divine Nature of Jesus Christ, his soul, which is the true image of his mind, conforms to the Image of Jesus Christ. Jesus as a man always did what was pleasing to His Heavenly Spirit of Love (John 8:29). This is why God's Will is to head up all things in Jesus Christ, the True Image of His Essence, in both heaven and upon earth (Eph. 1:8–10).

BORN AGAIN

Those that receive God's Holy Spirit are "born again." They are new creatures in Jesus Christ. Old things are passed away and all things are become new (II Cor. 5:17). Jesus said that unless one is born again, he cannot enter into the Kingdom of God (John 3:3). This, as we learned, happens when one receives the Divine Nature of Jesus Christ through God's Holy Spirit. One becomes a new creature because he turns from his old ways. The Living Spirit of God gives him the Mind of Christ. A truly born-again person is no longer driven by the lustful spirit of this present world, but is now driven and led by the Spirit of Jesus Christ living inside him. His heart changes from wanting to do things for personal satisfaction and glorification, to wanting to do things for the Glory of

Jesus Christ. According to God's Word, personal accomplishments are called dead works if they are not done in the Spirit of Love, and for the Glory of Jesus Christ. Jesus Christ came into this world to save mankind. Those that receive His Spirit will also desire and work to save their fellowman from God's coming Judgment upon this world. One can do this only by sharing the Good News, or Gospel of Jesus Christ during this soon to end Age of Grace. There is no other way. Jesus Christ, the Only True Image of God's Invisible Spirit of Love, said that in order to enter the Kingdom of God "Ye must be born again" (John 3:7). Those that say that one should not share the Gospel of Jesus Christ with others, but should keep his faith to himself, do not have the Spirit of Truth in their hearts, and need to be "born again" in order to inherit Eternal Life in God's coming Kingdom. Reaching out to others in the Name of Jesus Christ is both God's Will and God's Command.

WAY TO SALVATION

The fact that sin entered the human race does not mean that man became outright evil, but rather that man lost favor with God. Many people who are not "born again" do by nature many good and loving things (Rom. 2:14). This however cannot cause one to be saved. All of man's rightousenesses are as filthy rags unto God (Is. 64:6). The LORD God declared that He Alone is man's Savior and Redeemer (Is. 49:26). He revealed Himself in Jesus Christ, the Savior (John 4:42). Jesus Christ is the only Way of Salvation (Acts 4:12). There is no other name under Heaven whereby one can be saved. Those that think they can save themselves by abstaining from evil lusts, or by doing good deeds are deceived. These are the results of being "born again," but they are not the cause. As we learned, the remission of sins is possible only through faith in the Shed Blood of Jesus Christ (Heb. 10:14). One is saved by God's Free Gift of Grace through the Faith he receives from the Holy Spirit (Eph. 2:8). In order for one to receive "Faith," he must first hear the Gospel of Jesus Christ. This is because Faith comes by hearing the Word of God (Rom. 10:17). This is why Jesus Christ commanded His followers to preach the Gospel as they go out into the world in their everyday lives. True disciples teach, build, and comfort those around them by sharing God's Word and Love with others. Faith is a Gift from God for the purpose of enlightening others.

ONE NAME, ONE BLOOD, ONE SPIRIT

When Jesus Christ, the Eternal Soul (Image) of God's Eternal Spirit of Love, became man, His Nature (unlike Adam's) remained Holy because Jesus Christ did not sin. Jesus proved by His Bodily resurrection that Satan and death cannot rightfully accuse, claim, or hold a Righteous soul in Hades. Those that willfully sin are of the devil (John 3:8). Due to the fact that Jesus Christ did not sin, Satan the accuser, could not lay any claim to His Soul. When Jesus Christ ascended into the Presence of His Heavenly Spirit, He poured down His Divine Nature through the Holy Spirit on the day of Pentecost. From that day, until the end of this Age, those that hear and believe the Gospel of Jesus Christ, and receive the baptism of the Holy Spirit, are spiritually cleansed of all their sin. They will be justified to enter into God's Kingdom through the Living Righteousness of Jesus Christ in them. All God's children are united in the Name and by the Spirit of Jesus Christ, Who is the Holy Spirit of God. Those that are led by the Righteousness of Jesus Christ, while on this earth, will enter into God's Eternal Kingdom. At the end of this Age of Grace, there will be only two groups of people: those united under Jesus Christ who will be on one side, and everyone else who will be on the other side. Those on Christ's side will have their names written in God's Book of Life, and will rule and reign with Jesus Christ for all eternity. Those whose names are not written in the Book of Life will be judged and eternally separated from Jesus Christ and His followers (Rev. 21:27).

POWER IN HIS BLOOD

When Adam sinned, Satan's sinful nature entered the blood of man and corrupted his perfect nature. In Old Testament times, the high priest would offer God the nature of a spotless animal in exchange for the forgiveness of man's sins. He would do this by burning its blood upon the altar. In the same likeness, God, through Jesus Christ, man's High Priest, placed His Shed Blood on Heaven's Altar, and offers His Perfect Nature to all those that partake of His Shed Blood through faith. Jesus, during the Last Supper, taught His apostles how to partake of the "Lord's Supper" (also known as Holy Communion), and commanded them to do this often in remembrance of Him. To better visualize this, it is important to know that the Israelites made bread with flour and water, and without yeast. It was made in the form of a cake, about half an inch thick, and was broken—not cut. At the Last Supper, Jesus took a loaf (cake) of bread, broke it, and gave a piece to His apostles to eat, saying: "This is My Body which is given for you: This do in remembrance of Me" (Luke 22:19). After they ate it, Jesus took a cup of grape juice and told His apostles to all drink of it, "for this is My Blood of the New Testament (Covenant) which is shed for many for the remission of sins" (Matt. 26:28). The early church would meet in their homes and would partake of the "Lord's Supper." From that day until this present day, believers of Jesus Christ partake of the Lord's Supper in homes, hospitals, churches, etc. around the world, as the Lord Jesus commanded.

RESULT OF SALVATION

There is no greater love that one can have than to lay down his life for his friends (John 15:13). This is what Jesus did, so that through faith in His Shed Blood, all could receive God's Mercy and be eternal members of His family. Through the Knowledge and the Righteousness of Jesus Christ, God has given us the divine power necessary to know and to abstain from the worldly lusts that destroy men's lives (II Pet. 1:4). Diligence, virtue, knowledge, self-control, patience, godliness, kindness, and Godly Love are characteristic qualities one receives when he partakes of Christ's Divine Nature. As we learned, those that are born again no longer live to make a name for themselves, but to glorify the Name of Jesus Christ. They turn from doing dead works to doing good works (Eph. 2:10). Good works are things said and done to spread the Gospel of Jesus Christ and the Love of His Heavenly Spirit.

THE ROYAL PRIESTHOOD

Jesus Christ said "Ye must be born again" (John 3:7). One is born again after asking God in the Name of Jesus Christ to come into his heart (John 14:26). Jesus, the Image of the Invisible God, declared that God would give the Holy Spirit to those that ask Him (Luke 11:13). Those that receive God's Holy Spirit become members of God's Royal Priesthood (I Pet. 2:9). When a child of God shares the Gospel of Jesus Christ with two or more that are gathered together in the Name of Jesus Christ, Jesus is in their midst (Matt. 18:20). The Holy Spirit always accompanies the Name, the Gospel, and the Blood of Jesus Christ. As a member of the Body of Jesus Christ, we are the vessels and instruments through which God is presently establishing His Kingdom. Every believer is a temple of God (I Cor. 3:16), and can hold church wherever and whenever he is led by the Holy Spirit to share the Good News of Jesus Christ. No matter what a person is presently going through, Jesus Christ can give him Peace. During their daily lives, born-again believers find opportunities to comfort the sick, the needy, the lost, and the dying. They also admonish in love those that are not living according to God's Will. Everyone that hears and receives Jesus as his Lord and Savior while on this earth is immediately blessed with the Peace and the Love of God, that can come only when one meets his Creator, Jesus Christ. Many people, for whatever reason, will never step into a local church. Unless a loving, born-again believer takes the time to share the Gospel of Jesus Christ with these folks, they will never be born again and inherit God's Eternal Kingdom of Love, Peace, Health, and Joy. Every Christian can reach someone that would otherwise remain lost. This is why Jesus Christ commanded His followers, later known as Christians, to go out into the world and be witnesses unto Him. This is what pleases God and all of heaven, and not self-righteous ceremonies and rituals.

UNDERSTANDING OURSELVES

Only our Creator, Jesus Christ, can enable and has enabled us to understand ourselves through His Word. Jesus said that it is what comes out of a man that defiles or makes him unrighteous. He said that evil thoughts, pride, and sinful acts come out of the heart of man (Mark 7:20–23). The Lord also told us that what comes out of one's mouth comes forth from the heart, and is what defiles him (Matt. 15:18). From these revelations, we know that the way one thinks, talks, and acts depends upon the nature of one's heart, which is the sum total of the deep thoughts and desires that clothe one's soul. Those that receive the Divine Nature of Jesus Christ receive the Love of God in their heart, and their souls become clothed in the Righteousness of God. This group of people desire to do, and do what is pleasing to God from a pure heart (Phil. 2:13). Their thoughts, words, and actions are born out of (arise out of) their love for God and for their fellowman (I. Cor. 16:14).

GOD'S GIFT OF RIGHTEOUSNESS

When man was first created in the image and after the likeness of God, his body, soul, and spirit were in perfect agreement and harmony. This is because man was created in the Image of Jesus Christ. When man sinned, man's perfect nature became spotted with Satan's sinful nature, which looks selfward instead of Godward. Due to this, it was appointed for man to physically die, and to then face judgment (Heb. 9:27). By providing Himself, through Jesus Christ, as man's Perfect Sacrifice, God provided the "Way" through which man could replace his sinful nature with the Righteousness of Jesus Christ. In the latter days of this Age, the dead and living bodies of those whose souls have been clothed in the Righteousness of Jesus Christ will be transformed into new, glorious, eternal, and sin-free bodies. These folks will enjoy Everlasting Happiness in the Kingdom of Jesus Christ. Those that have not received the Righteousness of God, through Jesus Christ, will face the second death, which is eternal separation from Jesus Christ. These souls will be eternally lost in the darkness and torments of hell. Man's righteousnesses, as we learned, are as filthy rags unto God (Is. 64:6). God's Gift of Righteousness is available only through Jesus Christ (Rom. 5:17). Those that are too proud to humble themselves and ask Jesus Christ into their heart while on this earth will bow to Him on judgment day, but it will be too late. Those that believe that Jesus Christ is for losers and for the weak-minded are turning their backs on God, and will not be able to blame anyone but themselves for their eternal destiny.

FLESH WARS AGAINST SOUL

Man is not totally freed from the lusts of his flesh until the time that he receives his new glorified body. This is why man's present body cannot inherit the Kingdom of God (I Cor. 15:50). When one receives the Righteousness of Jesus Christ, his soul is clothed with the Righteousness of God, but his body is still plagued with fleshly lusts which war against the soul (I Pet. 2:11). One should understand the fact that when he or she accepts God's

Free Gift of Righteousness through Faith in Jesus Christ, this does not mean that their strugglers with sin are over. Man's spiritual battles will continue until he dies, or until the Rapture, whichever comes first. By yielding to the Holy Spirit within one's heart, one is given the Love, the Power, and the Wisdom of God. Only then can one overcome the desires and deceptions of this present world. Jesus said that he that overcomes will not be blotted out of the Book of Life (Rev. 3:5).

SAVED?

Jesus Christ illustrated in His parable of the sower (Luke 8) that all who accept the Gospel of Jesus Christ will not necessarily inherit the Kingdom of God. Some allow the devil to take God's Word out of their hearts before they can believe it and be saved. This group allows others to discourage and to turn them away from Jesus Christ. Some receive God's Word, but when they are tempted or persecuted, they turn away from Jesus Christ. Others get so caught up with the cares, riches, and pleasures of this life that they dedicate their life to these, instead of spreading the Love of God through the Gospel of Jesus Christ, which is Christ's Command to each of His followers. The above groups of people began the race, but they did not endure, and will therefore not receive the prize. Jesus Christ said those that endure to the end shall be saved (Matt. 24:13). Jesus Christ described the saved as those that hear, keep, and out of a pure heart share God's Word with others, so that they too can inherit Eternal Life in the Presence of Jesus Christ and His Heavenly Spirit of Love.

YOU CAN'T FOOL GOD

As we learned, Faith in the Shed Blood of Jesus Christ is the only way to receive the Righteousness of God. Those that proclaim to be "born-again" Christians, and live like the devil, are not abiding in God's Spirit of "Truth." These are hearers only, and not doers of the Word, and are deceiving themselves (James 1:22), because Faith without works is dead (James 2:20). One can go to church and profess to be a Christian, and be rotten and full of evil on the inside. This is why God made it clear that He does not judge a person from his outward appearance, but instead by looking upon his heart. Jesus said those that endure in the Faith

and overcome the world will be saved. In order to overcome this
world, one must put God first in one's heart, the result of which
will be righteous thoughts, words, and actions. When one's heart
is righteous, he will desire to please God before pleasing himself.
This includes turning and abstaining from every form of wicked-
ness (I Thess. 5:22), and turning towards and doing what is
pleasing to God. This is God's Will for each member of His
Coming Kingdom. Remember, God in His Master Plan is purifying
unto Himself, in the Name of Jesus Christ, a people zealous of
good works (Titus 2:14), who set forth the virtues of Jesus Christ
(I Pet. 2:9). This can be done only by living and working in God's
Spirit of Love.

GOD'S WARNING ABOUT SIN

The Eyes of the Lord are on the righteous and His Ears hear
their prayers, but the Face (Countenance) of the Lord is against
those doing evil (I Pet. 3:12). God declares in His Word that where
sin is being willfully committed, after the knowledge of the
"Truth" has been received, there no longer remains a sacrifice for
sin (Heb. 10:26). Those that willfully sin, trample upon Christ,
profane His Blood by which they were sanctified, and insult the
Holy Spirit (Heb. 10:29) will definitely have their name blotted
out of the Book of Life, and will be cast into outer darkness. Do
not be deceived! Knowing God's "Truth" through and in Jesus
Christ comes with much personal responsibility. This is why Jesus
Christ told His disciples to take up their cross and follow Him
(Mark 10:21). Those that have received Christ are to recall the
former days when they were first enlightened. This is how one is
to endure until the end, so that he may do the Will of God and
keep his soul. The relatively few years of persecution, suffering,
and sacrificing of one's self while on this earth are a small price to
pay for eternal happiness, beyond human imagination.

ABOMINATIONS TO GOD

Those that have not been "born again" do not have the Mind
of Christ, and are therefore confused about what is really moral or
immoral. This is due to the fact that many things that are socially
accepted are abominations to God. The apostle Paul, out of love,
identified those that would lose their souls if they did not repent

(turn from their sinful ways) and receive the baptism of God's Holy Spirit. This group includes fornicators (those participating in sex out of wedlock), idolaters (those worshipping false gods), adulterers (those having extramarital sex), men acting like women, homosexuals, thieves, coveters (the greedy), drunkards, those that slander and call another bad names, and those that seize the property of others (I Cor. 6:9–10). In addition to these, the apostle John listed cowards (those that reject Jesus due to fear of persecution or social acceptance), unbelievers, the polluted, murderers, sorcerers (users of drugs and magical arts), liars (Jesus said that anyone who says that they love Him and hate their brother is a liar), and everyone that loves and practices falsehood (the deceitful and hypocrites) (Rev. 21:8, 22:15). These sinners are lovingly warned that their sin will cost them their soul, unless they turn from their sinful ways and receive God's Gift of Righteousness through Faith in the Shed Blood of Jesus Christ. Those that are truly "born again" will overcome the world and will inherit Eternal Life. They will put and keep God's Word in their minds and hearts, and will not use the Name of Jesus Christ in vain, as so many are presently doing.

OVERCOMING EVIL

God warns man through His Word that he is in a spiritual battle (Eph. 6:12), and that Satan and those that he controls are out to destroy him. As we learned, Paul was controlled by Satan's spirit, until the Brightness of Jesus Christ appeared to him on his way to Damascus. When he received the Spirit of Jesus Christ in his mind and soul, he became a new creature. His hatred for Christ and His Church was turned to love, as the Brightness of God cleansed his mind and soul from its former nature. The Righteousness of Jesus Christ will allow one to see, to hate, and to overcome the former evil desires that were once infecting and controlling his very life. If one sincerely wants to turn away from his sinful desires and addictions, one must confess with his mouth his faith in Jesus Christ and the merits of His Shed Blood, and then ask God in the Name of Jesus Christ to come and live in his heart as Lord and Savior. If one prays this, and sincerely means it, he will be "born again," as the Holy Spirit of God cleanses his soul and fills him with the Righteousness of Jesus Christ. Every born-again believer has the Power of God necessary to overcome the

devil and his demons in this present world. This is due to the fact
that God in them, is Greater than the devil who is in the world (I
John 4:4). Jesus Christ proved this through His bodily resurrection
from the dead. Those that receive and walk in the Life Giving
Spirit of Jesus Christ will also pass from death unto eternal life,
and will receive new glorified bodies.

ARMED WITH GOD'S WORD

God's children know that there is a devil, and that he and his
demons desire to get them off God's Path. For this reason they
stand firmly on God's Word. When the devil tried to get Jesus to
sin, Jesus responded by saying that it is written, and by then
quoting Scripture. The earthly life of Jesus Christ is man's
example of how we are to live (I Pet. 2:21). By living in His Spirit,
one will overcome the evil spirits of this world. These spirits are
working hard to seduce man's mind and to control his soul
through fleshly pride, pleasure, lusts, and false doctrines. This is
why one is to study, to know, and to use God's Word to overcome
the lies of the devil, whose promises of love, joy, and peace are only
lies that lead to destruction. Jesus said that man cannot live by
bread alone (Luke 4:4). Man must feed not only his body but also
his mind in order to nourish and strengthen his soul. God's Word,
the Holy Bible, is the Spiritual Food necessary to learn, grow, mature,
endure, and overcome Satan and his followers. This is why the devil
is trying ever so hard to have the Holy Bible banned from the face
of the earth. Satan knows that the Word of God enlightens man,
and enables him to know that what is legally and socially accepted
is, in many cases, an abomination to God. God's Word instructs
man not to keep company with those that cause them to leave the
Presence of God (I Cor. 5:10). This group includes those that
refuse to turn from their sinful ways and accept Jesus Christ. These
vessels of Satan promote immoral sex, drunkenness, theft, gossip,
and the usage of unprescribed drugs (I Cor. 15:33), and spread
Satan's spirit of pride, greed, jealousy, lust, and hate towards Jesus
Christ and one's fellowman.

DOERS OF THE WORD

God's children are commanded to be doers of the Word of
God and not hearers only (James 1:22). Being a doer requires

action. Only God's Truth can prevent one from being spiritually seduced by Satan's worldly spirit, and can set one free from the bonds of sin that presently have a hold on one's life. One must remember that the Word of God is accompanied with the Brightness and Power of Jesus Christ. When God's Word enters one's mind and heart, the devil must turn or burn. When one becomes lax in doing or meditating on God's Word, his fleshly nature will rise up and war against his soul. The only way to keep one's body under subjection is to hate and refuse to dwell on evil thoughts, and to keep one's mind on Jesus Christ and His Promises. This is why Christians are to pray without ceasing (I Thess. 5:17). If one falls, he must get up, ask Jesus to forgive him, and get back on the right path by meditating on God's Word. Man is not supposed to keep God's Word unto himself. When family and friends are gathered together, they are to talk about God's Word and encourage each other, especially as the time of Christ's return draws near (Heb. 10:25). Satan's spirit has deceived many into believing that it is not proper to talk about Jesus Christ. For this reason they talk about sports, their homes, their cars, their businesses, etc. Jesus Christ foretold that He will be ashamed of those that were ashamed of Him (Luke 9:26). True Christians realize that they are in a spiritual battle, and watch for opportunities to share God's Word with others. No matter what one is faced with, whether sickness, disease, fear of the future, or physical death, a true Christian will ask God in the Name of Jesus Christ to remove that evil from him, but if not, to let His Will be done. Then the Spirit of God will fill the hearts of those involved, and will give them the strength to endure. This is how Jesus Christ taught man to pray in the Garden of Gethsemane (Matt. 26:39).

JESUS CHRIST WINS

One can summarize the message of God's Word in the following statement: "Jesus Christ Wins." Those that overcome this world are those that believe that Jesus Christ is the Son (True Image) of God's Heavenly Spirit of Love, trust in the merits of His Shed Blood, and keep God's Commandments (I John 5:2–5). As we learned, Jesus summarized God's Commandments as love God, and love your fellow man. One can love God only by loving His Word and True Image, Jesus Christ. In order to love one's fellow-man, one must drop his personal prejudices and hatred towards

others. One can and should hate the evil spirits that are controlling so many people today, but should not hate the people
themselves. Instead, one is to love and pray for his fellowman. God
declares in His Word that everything works together for good to
them that love Him, and live according to His Will (Rom. 8:28).
Knowing that God is Love, we can understand why He wanted
man to do all that he does in His Spirit of Love (I Cor. 16:14). Man
is not to seek revenge on those that persecute him. Jesus said
"Vengeance is mine" (Rom. 12:19). Jesus will soon return and
reward the righteous with righteousness, and the evil with evil. No
matter what they must suffer, true born-again Christians have an
inner peace in knowing that their eternal soul is in the Hand of
God.

THE TRUE GOD

Approximately twenty years after the Church of Jesus Christ
officially began, the apostle Paul went to Athens, Greece, to
preach the Gospel of Jesus Christ. There he found the city full of
idols, including an altar dedicated to the unknown God. Paul
entered the synagogue there, and introduced the Jews there to
their unknown God, the Lord of heaven and earth, Jesus Christ
(Acts 17:16–25). Notice that the apostles always entered the
synagogues, and preached to the Jews first, as the Lord commanded. After all, God's Word was given to mankind through the
Jews. The Jewish apostles entered the Jewish synagogues and
pointed to the over one hundred Jewish Scriptures, which clearly
identified Jesus Christ as the Messiah, the Sent One of God. God
said that man would know that He is the Only True God by the
fulfillment of His Word (Ex. 8:10). Only God can write history
before it takes place, and that is exactly what God did. There is no
other faith in the world that has a history book of the future. In
the following section of this book, we will look at both the fulfilled
and the future prophecies contained in God's Word.

PART VII

PROPHECY

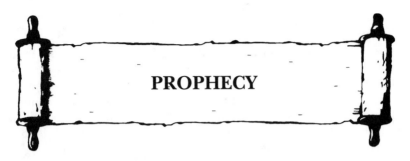

PROPHECY

BIBLE PROPHECY

Unlike false gods that neither speak, see, hear, smell, touch, walk, nor breathe (Ps. 115:4–7), the LORD God told the Israelites that He is God and that there is none like Him. The LORD God told them that He could tell them the end from the beginning, and from ancient times the things that are not yet (Is. 46:9). Bible prophecy is the recorded history of future events. As we will now learn, past, present, and future prophecies have been, and are being fulfilled exactly as God said they would. The early prophets heard God's Voice, and they spoke as they were moved by God's Holy Spirit (II Pet. 1:21). Those that want proof of the accuracy of God's Word will be well pleased. We will begin by looking at the early Old Testament Scriptures, which foretold in detail the birth, the earthly mission, the death, the resurrection, and the future glory of Jesus Christ. These prophecies contained such intricate details that critics claimed they were written after the fact. This lie was put to rest when exact copies of the Holy Bible's present Old Testament Scriptures were found along with the Dead Sea scrolls, and through carbon dating are said to have existed 250 years before the birth of Jesus Christ.

FULFILLED PROPHECIES

There are over one hundred Old Testament prophecies that not only foretold the coming of Jesus Christ, but also gave detailed accounts of His life and death. By looking at these fulfilled prophecies, one can have complete faith that the hundreds of future prophecies, which describe the events preceding and following the soon return of Jesus Christ to this earth, will also be fulfilled. God, through His Word, foretold: that Jesus would come from a seed of a woman, 1,450 years before the fact (Gen. 3:5);

169

that Jesus would be born in Bethlehem, 731 years before the fact (Mic. 5:2); that Jesus would be born of a virgin, 700 years before the fact (Is. 7:14); that Jesus would ride into Jerusalem on a donkey, 500 years before the fact (Zec. 9:9); that Jesus would enter Jerusalem through the Eastern Gate at the exact time that He did, 550 years before the fact (Dan. 9:24–27); that Jesus would be rejected by his own people, 700 years before the fact (Is. 53:1); that Jesus would be betrayed for 30 pieces of silver, 500 years before the fact (Zec. 11:12); that Jesus would be tried and condemned, 700 years before the fact (Is. 53:8); that Jesus would be beat and spat upon, 700 years before the fact (Is. 50:6); that Jesus would be crucified, 1,000 years before the fact (Ps. 22:14); that Jesus would be given vinegar to drink, 1,000 years before the fact (Ps. 69:21); that Jesus would be pierced in His side, 500 years before the fact (Zec. 12:10); that Jesus would die as man's Sacrifice, 700 years before the fact (Is. 53:5); that Jesus would rise from the dead, 1,000 years before the fact (Ps. 16:10); and that Jesus would sit in the Throne of God's Power and Authority, 1,000 years before the fact (Ps. 110:1). These are just a few of the hundred-plus fulfilled prophecies that prove beyond a doubt that God's Word is Truth.

MAN'S SOUL AFTER DEATH

It is important that we study the plight of man's soul before we continue. Jesus Christ proved by His resurrection that Satan the devil no longer possesses the keys to hell (hades) and death. Satan can no longer hold a righteous soul prisoner in this place of disembodied spirits called hades. When one receives and abides in the Spirit of Jesus Christ, his soul becomes clothed in the Righteousness of God. At the time of one's physical death, his soul leaves his body. If one's soul (true spirit image) is clothed in the Righteousness of God, one will immediately enter the Heavenly Presence of his Master, Jesus Christ. This is why the apostles did not renounce their faith as they faced their cruel and agonizing deaths. They knew that being absent from their bodies would mean being present with the Lord (II Cor. 5:8). The unrighteous souls, those that rejected or neglected the opportunity to be "born again" by receiving the Divine Nature of Jesus Christ into their minds and hearts before their physical death, will spend eternity in hell with their master, Satan the devil. Every human being, either knowingly or unknowingly, will choose to serve one of these two masters while on this earth. At the time of one's physical death, his soul will spend eternity with him whom they were serving, either the "Truth" of God—Jesus Christ, or Satan the devil.

HADES

When Jesus Christ physically died on the cross, His Soul went to Hades. Hades, as we learned, was the temporary holding place for all souls. As Jesus Christ revealed to us in the story of Lazarus and the rich man (Luke 16:20), Hades was separated into two compartments. One side was a place of comfort known as Paradise. This is the place where the soul of the thief on the cross went after he died. Why? Because this thief turned to Jesus Christ and asked Him to remember him when He would come into His Kingdom. The other side of Hades, which still exists today, is a place of torment. This is where the souls of those that did not receive the Spirit of God's Word, which is the Eternal Spirit of Jesus Christ, in their minds and hearts are presently dwelling. In His teaching about Lazarus and the rich man, Jesus Christ made it clear that one's soul does not sleep after death as some believe. Jesus wanted mankind to know that their souls are eternal, and will spend eternity either in Perfect Peace, Health, and Happiness in His (God's) Kingdom, or in eternal torment in Satan's kingdom.

THE FIRSTFRUITS

Even though Satan could not touch the souls of those Old Testament believers that received God's Word into their hearts, and obeyed God by offering Him the blood of a spotless animal sacrifice for the forgiveness of their sins, Satan could still accuse them of being sinners before God. This was due to the fact that an animal sacrifice could only cover, but could not cleanse away all of man's sin (Heb. 10:4–5). Only God's Perfect Blood, shed by Jesus Christ, can wash away all of man's sin. When Jesus Christ poured out His Soul (the Eternal Soul of God) in His Shed Blood, as the prophet Isaiah foretold (Is. 53:12), God's Soul (True Image) went to Hades, which as we learned has two compartments. After entering and proclaiming Himself as the Son (Soul or True

Image) of the Living God, those on the unrighteous side were put to shame for not receiving Him, as the "Word" of God, into their minds and hearts. Abraham and those that received God's "Word" (the Eternal Spirit of Jesus Christ) rejoiced. Now, through faith in His Shed Blood for the forgiveness of their sins, they were clothed in the Righteousness of God's Holy Spirit. Afterwards, Satan the accuser (Rev. 12:10) could no longer accuse them of being sinful. Therefore he could no longer claim them as his children, and keep them in his custody in Hades. Jesus Christ thus took the keys (the authority) over Hades and death away from Satan, and led all the righteous souls with Him into Heaven (Eph. 4:8). On the way up, the Soul of Jesus Christ re-entered His Physical Body, which was then transformed into a New Glorified Body. Some of those that followed Jesus Christ out of their graves were seen walking on the streets of Jerusalem (Matt. 27:53). This happened on the Jewish feast of "First Fruits" (Lev. 23:10–11), which became known as Resurrection Sunday. Jesus Christ is the First Fruit from among the dead (I Cor. 15:20). The apostle Paul noted that just as Jesus Christ rose bodily from the grave, so shall all His followers when He returns (I Cor. 15:23). Presently, the souls of all "born-again" believers that physically die are welcomed into God's Kingdom by Jesus Christ.

FIRST RESURRECTION—PART 2

In the second part of the first resurrection, known as the "Rapture," all the righteous souls in Heaven will return to their former bodies. Their bodies will then, along with the bodies of all living "born-again" believers, be transformed into new glorified bodies, as they are drawn up together into the air to meet their Master, Jesus Christ (I Thess. 4:16–17). When one is "born again," through faith in the Shed Blood of Jesus Christ, he partakes of the Divine Nature of Jesus Christ, and becomes One Spirit Blood with Him. These, God's true children, will be removed from this earth in the coming Rapture. God's Wrath will then be unleashed on an unrepentant and evil world. Let us now consider the prophesied events that have led, and are leading us to this period of Divine cleansing, which will usher in the Kingdom of God upon this earth.

TIME OF THE GENTILES

As we learned, after the Jews (as a whole) rejected their Messiah—Jesus Christ, God's Kingdom was opened to all humanity. Jesus Christ foretold this in one of His parables (Matt. 22:1–14). In this parable a King (God) sent His servants (the prophets) to call those that were invited to the wedding feast (the Kingdom) of His Son (Jesus Christ). The guests (the Jews), being more concerned with their personal matters, did not come. The King then destroyed their city, and sent his servants to invite as many others (Gentiles or non-Jews) as they could find. Those that came clothed in God's Righteousness were welcomed to the wedding feast. Since the time in which the Jews (the majority of them, but not all) rejected Jesus Christ, people of all nations and without any discrimination have been invited to enter into God's Kingdom through the Good News, the Gospel of Jesus Christ. Anyone that hears and believes God's Word and invites Jesus Christ into his heart during this present Age of Grace, will be cleansed of his sin and will receive the Divine Nature of Jesus Christ. Due to the fact that the wedding feast (the Kingdom) of Jesus Christ is rapidly approaching, God's invitation to enter in is nearing an end.

JERUSALEM IN PROPHECY

Before Jesus Christ came into this world, the angel Gabriel announced that Jesus Christ would sit on the throne of David (Jerusalem), and reign over the house of Jacob forever (Luke 1:32–33). While Jesus was on this earth, Israel was part of the Roman Empire. When the disciples asked Jesus when He would restore the Kingdom to Israel, He told them it was not for them to know (Acts 1:6–7). Jesus then proceeded to tell them about future events. He told them that the temple in Jerusalem would be destroyed, that the Jews would be led away captive into all nations, and that Jerusalem would be trodden down of the Gentiles until the times of the Gentiles be fulfilled (Luke 21:24). In other words, Jesus told them that Jerusalem would be captured, and the Jews would be forced to live in other nations until just prior to His return, at which time they would re-gather as a nation and control Jerusalem once again. Just forty years later, in 70 A.D., the Romans marched into Jerusalem, destroyed the temple, and took control of the city. Later the Romans mockingly imposed the name Syria-Palestina on the area, reminding the Jews of their battles with the Philistines. From that time until 1967, Jerusalem was controlled by the Gentiles, as the Gospel of Jesus Christ was preached across the world to all people. As Jesus prophesied, God's offer to enter into the Kingdom of Jesus Christ (the True Image of God's Invisible Spirit) is nearing its end. The greatest proof of this and of all Bible prophecy was the re-gathering of Israel as a nation in 1948, and the Jews regaining control of Jerusalem in 1967. In order for Jesus Christ to return and reign from the throne of David, there had to be a nation of Israel with its capital at Jerusalem, and this just happened in our generation.

THE YEAR 2000 A.D.

Both the Jewish rabbis before the time of Christ, and also the early Church taught that the Messiah (the Christ or Sent One of God) would come around the year 2000 A.D. In order to understand this, we must look at God's Word. In the story of creation, God worked six days and rested on the seventh day, or the sabbath (Gen. 2:2). God did not rest because He was tired, but rather to let man know that the seventh day is special to Him. To magnify the importance of the sabbath day, God told the Israelites that they could work six days, but not on the seventh (Ex. 31:15). During the Exodus, the Israelites were allowed to gather manna for six days, but on the seventh day, there would be no manna (Ex. 16:4–5). This is why they gathered twice as much manna on the sixth day. Once in the Promised Land, God told the Israelites that they could till the land and plant their crops for six years, but not on the seventh, in which they were commanded to allow the land to rest (Lev. 25:4). By considering that one day is as one thousand years to God (Ps. 90:4), the early Jewish rabbis, as well as the early Church, taught that the Christ would come and rule this earth during the seventh millennium, or after 6,000 years from the time of Adam. By considering that the time from Adam to Abraham was approximately 2,000 years, 4000 B.C.–2000 B.C., that the time from Abraham to Jesus Christ was approximately 2,000 years, 2000 B.C.–1 A.D., and that the time from Jesus Christ to the year 2000 A.D. is 2,000 years, they concluded and taught that the Christ would come and rule this earth for 1,000 years, beginning in the year 2000 A.D. From the signs that He has given us, Jesus Christ

said that we would know when the time was near, even at the door
(Matt. 24:33). Experts have determined that our present calendar
is off only by a few years. With this in mind we know without a
doubt that God's Kingdom of Love, Peace, Health, Joy, and Rest
will soon come upon this earth, for those that have received and
are abiding in the Spirit of Jesus Christ. Unfortunately, there will
be trials and tribulations which this generation of believers will
have to face, before the beginning of this glorious 1,000-year
period known as the "Millennium Age."

BIRTH PANGS

In conjunction with the re-gathering and the re-establishment
of Israel as a nation, Jesus mentioned certain signs that must come
to pass (be born) prior to His return (Matt. 24:6). Jesus likened
these signs to the birth pangs that a woman goes through during
her pregnancy. The closer she gets to delivery, the number and
the intensity of her pangs increase, until she delivers her baby. In
the same likeness, human suffering will increase until mankind is
freed from the evil works of Satan and his followers. Let us now
look at some of these increasing signs that Jesus mentioned.

INCREASING SIGNS

Jesus said to watch for an increase in ethnic wars (Matt. 24:6).
In this century alone, millions upon millions have been killed in
wars. Every time you turn around there is a new war. Jesus said to
watch for an increase in famine. There is great famine in the world
today. The number of people that are presently starving is
enormous. Jesus said to watch for an increase in pestilences or
diseases. We live in a disease-ridden world in which AIDS, cancer,
venereal diseases, and other viruses are spreading at alarming
rates. Jesus said to watch for an increase in earthquakes in various
places. In this century, major earthquakes have devastated many
parts of the world. Sizematologists are predicting that more and
greater earthquakes will hit various major cities across the world.
This could lead to the collapse of the world economy, at which
time all the currencies of the world will become worthless.

DAYS OF NOAH

Jesus said that the days preceding His return would be like the days of Noah (Matt. 24:37). In those days, before the flood, something very strange and frightening happened. Angels were taking on and possessing bodies of men, and were marrying the daughters of men (Gen. 6:2). We know these were among God's disobedient angels that chose to serve Satan, and to rebel against God. In addition to this, the children being born from these marriages were very violent. When the Lord saw the wicked actions of men increasing upon the earth, and saw that everyone's heart was full of evil imaginations, He was forced to send the flood and destroy all evil humanity except for Noah, who found Grace in God's Eyes. It was through Noah and his family that the human race was allowed to continue. Jesus said that just before He returns, men's hearts would be filled with violence and evil imaginations, as in the days of Noah. This is certainly a picture of the times in which we now live. Hateful and violent criminal acts are becoming commonplace in this high pressure and evil-filled world. With nuclear weapons now in the hands of terrorists, we are indeed headed for perilous (dangerous) times (II Tim. 3:1–7).

DAYS OF LOT

Jesus said the days preceding His return would also be like the days of Lot. People at that time were eating, drinking, buying, selling, planting, and building (Luke 17:28). They were so involved with the cares and the pleasures of this world that they put God out of their minds. It was a time of moral decay, with homosexuality being the earmark of the day. Today homosexuality is on the rise just as Jesus Christ foretold. According to God's Word, homosexuality is an abomination (Rom. 1:26–27). It is unacceptable in God's eyes regardless of what society says. Those that receive God's Holy Spirit in the Name of Jesus Christ receive the Righteous Nature of Jesus Christ, and will turn away from and abstain from this sin. Lot warned his sons-in-law to flee Sodom, but they would not listen. After Lot left the city with his wife and daughters, God rained fire and brimstone from heaven and destroyed the entire city (Luke 17:29). This is a picture of the Wrath of God that will befall this earth after God's children (the Body of Christ, known as His Church) are removed from this earth in the

"Rapture." Christ's Church is not a worldly establishment, but rather a Spiritual establishment. One can join only by calling upon God in the Name of Jesus Christ and receiving His Holy Spirit.

ANTI-SEMITISM

After mentioning the increasing signs that we are to watch for, Jesus Christ continued by telling His disciples that they, the nation of Israel, would be hated by all nations for His Name's sake (Matt. 24:9). Hatred towards the Jews is called anti-Semitism, and it is growing at an alarming rate throughout the world, just as Jesus Christ foretold. One must never forget that God chose to bless the entire world through Israel and the Jewish people. Many people hate the Jews for a reason that is unknown to them. This worldly spirit of anti-Semitism stems from the fact that the Holy Bible and God's True Image, Jesus Christ, were revealed to mankind through the Jewish race. This is why Satan is trying desperately to destroy the Holy Bible and the Jews. As we will learn, those that hate the Jews will be destroyed when Jesus Christ returns to this earth to rule and reign. God told mankind through the prophet Ezekiel, 2,600 years ago, that He would gather the Jews out from all countries and bring them to their land (Ezek. 36:24). God said that by this we would know that His Word is Truth, and what He speaks will come to pass (Ezek. 37:11–14). Not only has Israel become a nation, but also every sign that Jesus Christ mentioned is increasing in frequency and in intensity.

FALSE PROPHETS

Jesus Christ warned His disciples that many false prophets would arise and deceive many (Matt. 24:11). The apostle Paul, under the inspiration of the Holy Spirit, said that in the latter days, many would depart from the Faith and give heed to seducing spirits (I Tim. 4:1). The apostle John described and categorized all teachings that deny the fact that Jesus Christ is the Son (True Image) of God's Heavenly Spirit, as having the spirit of antichrist. **STOP NOW!** Ask yourself if your present religion denies this Truth. If it does, get out. Antichrist means against Christ. Even though there are many religions in the world today, at the end of this Age, every human being that ever lived will be on one of only two sides. Those on the winning side will be those that will have received God's Holy Spirit, in the Name of Jesus Christ, into their minds and hearts. Those on the losing side will be those that will have failed to receive God's Holy Spirit, by either neglecting or rejecting Jesus Christ as their Lord and Savior. This group will be eternally lost in darkness as they are separated from Jesus Christ, the Light of the world (John 8:12). No one can, or ever will be able to accuse God of being unfair. God first sent his Soul (The True Image of His Mind) into this world as His "Word" to talk to and to lead man. God then sent His Soul (The True Image of His Mind) into this world as His Son, so that He through Jesus Christ, could bring man unto Himself through His Shed Blood. How? To those that accept God's Sacrifice, and follow Him in the name of Jesus Christ, He imparts His Holy Spirit. These "born-again" believers become "One Blood" when they receive the Righteous Nature of Jesus Christ (the "Spirit of Truth") into their minds and hearts. Yes, during this present Age of Grace, God has promised to have Mercy on, and to forgive the sins of those that believe in the Shed Blood of Jesus Christ for the forgiveness of their sins (Heb. 10:14). Jesus Christ's Sacrifice became the last, and only Acceptable Sacrifice, because He Alone is Perfect. God's New Covenant (Agreement) with man was and is established in the Shed Blood of Jesus Christ (I Cor. 11:25). Those that believe and confess with their mouth that Jesus Christ is the Son (the True Image) of God, and that He shed His Blood for the forgiveness of their sins, will receive His Holy Spirit when they invite Him into their heart as their Lord and Savior. The Living Water (the Holy Spirit of God) in one's mind and heart is God's Free Gift to all people for accepting and believing in His Sacrificial Blood offering, which He made through Jesus Christ, for the forgiveness of their sin. There is no other Way to enter into God's Eternal Kingdom. Due to the fact that Jesus Christ is the True Image of God's Heavenly Spirit, those that reject Him and His Sacrifice are rejecting God and His Way of salvation. These will be able to blame only themselves for their eternal destiny.

U.F.O.S, TORNADOES, HURRICANES

U.F.O. sightings have not only been reported, but have also been scientifically confirmed. Jesus Christ said that preceding his return, there would be signs in the sun, moon, and stars. He foretold that these signs would cause a coming together of nations in confusion, as the seas and the waves roar, and men fear as the powers of heaven are shaken (Luke 21:25–26). With the growing number of U.F.O.'s, tornadoes, and hurricanes, we can be sure that something is going on in the heavens. It is important to note that the whirlwind descriptions given for the way U.F.O.'s travel are identical to the description of the chariot of fire that picked up Elijah and went like a whirlwind into heaven (II King. 2:11). God reveals in his Word that Satan has the ability to travel to this earth and walk around on it (Job 1:7). God's Word also reveals the fact that angels can assume human form (Luke 1:26) and, as in the days of Noah, interact with human beings (Heb. 13:2). Jesus Christ is reminding man about these things so that man does not get deceived. As the time of Christ's return draws near, mankind will witness more frequent and intense supernatural occurrences. Satan and his angels will bring these on in their attempt to unite and destroy mankind.

NEW AGE MOVEMENTS

With the increasing fear of U.F.O.'s, nuclear war, crime, violence, natural disasters, health epidemics, racial unrest, and financial collapse, Satan is bringing mankind together in fear, as Jesus Christ foretold. Many are being deceived by the false prophets of the New Age, who are being controlled by Satan's spirit of antichrist. These workers of iniquity have deceived, and are deceiving many into believing that if mankind comes together in mind, they will be able to bring on a New Age Utopia. As we learned, Satan has always wanted to be like God (Is. 14:13–14). We also learned that those that receive God's Holy Spirit in the Name of Jesus Christ receive the Mind of Christ (I Cor. 2:16). Satan, the imitator, is trying to destroy mankind by bringing man together in the name of humanity, instead of in the Name of Jesus Christ. Remember, Satan's spirit of "antichrist" is against Christ and His creation. Satan is a murderer (John 8:44). He does not want man to come together in the Mind of Christ and be saved. His desire is to lead as many souls to hell with him as possible. Do not be deceived! Those that do not accept Jesus Christ (God's True Image) into their hearts will be barred from His (God's) Kingdom. The New Age believers, many unknowingly, are children of the devil. They are telling God that they do not need Him, and are shaking their fists in His Face. In the spirit of antichrist, they refuse to acknowledge their Creator, Jesus Christ (Col. 1:16). Never forget, Satan and the angels that followed him fell when they tried to rise up and be like God. Humanity failed when man came together at the tower of Babel and tried to reach heaven by his own efforts (Gen. 11:4). The New Agers will also fail, because Jesus Christ is the only "Way" through which anyone can enter into the Kingdom of God.

NOTE

If you are involved in a New Age religion, get out. To become a child of God, confess with your mouth your faith in Jesus Christ as the Son (True Image) of God, and your faith in His Shed Blood for the forgiveness of your sins. Then ask God in the Name of Jesus Christ to come into your heart. Afterwards, put God's Written Word into your minds and hearts, and allow God's Spirit to teach you. God's children are those being led by God's Holy Spirit (Rom. 8:9). Gather together and talk about Christ's return with family and friends. God wants us to encourage one another (Heb. 3:13). Jesus Christ promised that where two or three are gathered together in His Name, He will be there (Matt. 18:20). The first, pure, and unadulterated local churches were people and family members gathering together at their homes to talk about Jesus Christ. From the day of Pentecost, the Holy Spirit began to dwell in the minds and hearts of God's children. Those that believe that God dwells in buildings of brick and stone, and that they must go there to be with Him, do not know God because they do not know His Word. Jesus Christ told man not to be like the Pharisees, who pray to the seen, but rather to enter into their closet and pray (Matt. 6:6). The truth is that God is always with, and leading those that have His Word in their minds and hearts. If you go to a local church, go to a Bible-teaching church. Avoid any church that calls its priest "Father," or which denies the fact that Jesus Christ is God.

DANIEL & REVELATION

As Jesus Christ continued to describe the latter days preceding His return, He pointed to the Old Testament scriptures written by Daniel the prophet (Matt. 24:15). Daniel's God-given vision of future events leading to the return of Jesus Christ are recorded in the Old Testament Book of Daniel. After recording his vision, Daniel was told by God that his book would not be understood until the latter days (Dan. 12:4). Jesus pointed to the book of Daniel to let His disciples know that these scriptures describe the latter days prior to His return to this earth. While the apostle John was in exile on the island of Patmos, Jesus Christ, through His angel, commanded John to write down what He would show him (Rev. 1:11). John's Christ-given vision of end time events is recorded in the final book of the Holy Bible, the book of "Revelation." In His closing statements, Jesus Christ promised to return to this earth. By looking at the book of Daniel, the book of Revelation, and other various portions of the Holy Scriptures, one can have peace in knowing that God's Glorious Kingdom is very near.

ONE-WORLD GOVERNMENT FORETOLD

In conjunction with Israel becoming a nation, Jerusalem being under Jewish control, and the present increase of every sign mentioned by Jesus Christ, we are also told that there will be a one-world government in the latter days. Yes, 2,700 years ago, God's Word revealed the fact that in the latter days there would be a final one-world empire and even identified it for us. The prophet Daniel foretold, as he was moved by the Holy Spirit, that a final world leader would arise out of the people who would crucify Jesus Christ and destroy the city of Jerusalem (Dan. 9:26). This group of people were members of the Roman Empire. The present European Union, ratified by the Treaty of Rome, is in fact the beginning of the Revised Roman Empire. Jesus, the Living Word of God, told the apostle John that the leader of this final world empire would arise and would rule the nations of the world from ten regions (Rev. 13:1). There are maps in existence today that have already divided the nations of the world into ten regions.

A CUP OF TREMBLING

Twenty-five hundred years ago, the prophet Zechariah fore-told that the LORD God would make Jerusalem a cup of trembling for all nations in the latter days (Zech. 12:2). Worldwide tension over the control of Jerusalem is mounting daily. Israel has made it clear that Jerusalem will always be its undivided capital, while the Palestinians declare that Jerusalem shall be their capital. God's Word declares that there will be a temple of the LORD in Jerusalem before the mid-point of the final seven years of this age. This has not been the case since 70 A.D., at which time the temple was destroyed by the Romans. Today there is a great movement in progress to rebuild the temple. Much of the furniture and articles that will be used in this future temple have already been prepared, along with the priestly garments. There is one problem, though, and that problem is that the Biblical location of Israel's past temple is now occupied by one of Islam's holy shrines, the Dome of the Rock. Both the Jews and the Muslims realize that the "Dome of the Rock" and the "Temple of the LORD" are not meant to be together. Growing tension over this situation is leading up to the end-time wars, as described in the Holy Bible.

END-TIME WARS

God, through the prophet Zechariah, not only foretold that Jerusalem would be a cup of trembling in the latter days, but also foretold that Jerusalem would be the location of the last war of this age. Before this final battle of Armageddon occurs, there will be another war in which Russia, along with a confederation of Islamic nations, will invade Israel. The aligning of these nations is presently taking place, exactly as prophesied in the Holy Bible. Every sign the Lord Jesus mentioned is in place. The final seven years of this present age, which are commonly referred to as the 70th week of Daniel, are very near (Dan. 12:11–12).

THE SEVENTIETH WEEK OF DANIEL

As we learned, Jesus Christ's description of the last seven years of this age, known as the 70th week of Daniel, is found in the twenty-fourth chapter of the book of Matthew. Jesus foretold that prior to His return, many would appear and claim to be Him. Jesus said that there would be wars, rumors of wars, famines, pestilences, and earthquakes. Following these things, Jesus said, his disciples would be killed for His Name's sake. Because of this, he warned his disciples to flee Judaea when they see the abomination of desolation. This event will occur when a false Christ will enter the future Temple of the LORD in Jerusalem and declare that he is God. Jesus then talked to His apostles about the Great Tribulation, His Return to this earth, the great harvest, and the outpouring of God's Wrath upon the unrepentant.

GOD'S TWO WITNESSES

God illustrates to us in His Word that after the measurements of the new temple in Jerusalem are made, He will empower two witnesses to prophesy. These witnesses are said to be clothed in sackcloth and ashes (Rev. 11:3), which is symbolic of repentance. These two witnesses will warn the Jews about the future tribulation. They will tell them that they must be "born again" in order to enter into the Kingdom of God, and that Jesus Christ will soon come to set up God's earthly Kingdom. Those that attempt to kill these witnesses will themselves be killed. As did God's early prophets, these witnesses will have the supernatural power to stop the rain, to turn waters into blood, and to smite the earth with all plagues (Rev. 11:6).

THE ANTICHRIST

The seventieth week of Daniel will officially begin when the future leader of the Revised Roman Empire, who is referred to in the Holy Bible as the "antichrist," will confirm a seven-year peace agreement between Israel and the nations (Dan. 9:27). This leader will be controlled by Satan the devil, who has always desired to be like the Most High God. God's Word tells us that the whole world will marvel after this leader, that this leader will receive power over all people and nations, and that this leader will be worshipped by the whole world (Rev. 13:4–8). The nation of Israel will not know that this peacemaker is the antichrist when he first appears, and will therefore embrace him. His emergence to power was envisioned by the apostle John as a rider appearing on a white horse (Rev. 6:2). White in the Holy Bible represents God's Righteousness, available only through the Lord and Savior, Jesus Christ. This leader will appear as the most beautiful and wonderful person in the whole world, who has come to save the world from all its problems. In reality, this leader's main goal will be to receive the worship of all mankind, and to lead them to eternal destruction by turning them away from Jesus Christ. Never forget that God's Kingdom is being established in the Name Above all names, Jesus Christ, and that in the end there will be only two sides. One side will consist of those that trusted in Jesus Christ as their Lord and Savior, and the other side will consist of those that rejected, or neglected to receive Jesus Christ as their Lord and Savior while they had the chance.

RUSSIA WILL MARCH

Immediately after envisioning the rider on the white horse (the antichrist), the apostle John envisioned a rider on a red horse (a Russian leader) coming to take peace away from the earth. This creates a situation in which the antichrist and his armies, and the Russian and his armies desire to kill each other (Rev. 6:3). The prophet Daniel described this future event when the king of the south (Egypt and its Arab confederation) will push against Israel from the south, as the king of the north (Russia) will lead the invasion of Israel (Dan. 11:40). The prophet Ezekiel also wrote about this invasion of Israel, immediately after foretelling that the Jews would return to their land from among the nations (Ezek. 37:21). Ezekiel foretold that the LORD God would be against Gog, the chief prince of Meshech (Moscow) and Tubal (Tobulsk) (Ezek. 38:3). Ezekiel said that Russia would "think an evil thought," and would invade Israel to "take a spoil" (Ezek. 38:10–12). Many Russian people today openly support the idea of using their military power to destroy the Jews, and to take over the natural resources and the riches of Israel. In addition to Egypt and its Arab confederation, the prophet Ezekiel wrote that Persia (Iraq and Iran), Ethiopia, Libya, and Germany would also join forces with Russia (Ezek. 38:5–6). These nations are presently aligning themselves exactly as prophesied in the Holy Bible. In the meantime, Russia is continuing to build its military arsenal and underground bomb shelters.

TURN OR BURN

Before we continue our end-time study, it is important to know that the LORD God does not delight in the death of the wicked, but desires that the wicked turn from their evil way and live (Ezek. 33:11). This is why the LORD God told Ezekiel to warn the nations that would come against Israel. God's warning to those that hate the Jews and oppose the nation of Israel is to literally turn or burn. God's Word never returns void. Everything that God said would happen, has and will happen exactly as God said it would. If you are presently holding hatred for the Jews and for the nation of Israel, you can change by asking Jesus Christ into your heart before it is too late. When one receives the Love of God in his heart, he realizes that all of God's promises of Eternal Life are possible only from hearing and believing the Revealed Word of God, as recorded by the Jewish prophets, and by receiving forgiveness of one's sins through faith in the Shed Blood of Jesus Christ, the Son (True Image) of God, Who was born into this world by the Jewess Virgin Mary. Over the centuries, God's Word, the Holy Bible, written by Jews, would have lost its meaning without a Jewish people and a Jewish nation. This is why various devil-possessed rulers have tried to destroy the Jews in the past, and why present-day leaders, under the influence of Satan and his demons, are planning to exterminate all the Jews and "born-again" believers, who will not renounce their faith in the Jewish Messiah, Jesus Christ. Let us see what is going to happen.

RUSSIA & ALLIES WILL PERISH

The prophet Ezekiel wrote that Russia and her allies would be like a cloud, with all her bands and many people, and that they would ascend and invade Israel as a storm (Ezek. 38:9). He also foretold that the whole earth would shake at this time, as God in His fury rains great hailstones, fire, and brimstone upon Russia and its allies (Ezek. 38:18–22). The LORD God told Ezekiel that five-sixths of this northern army would perish on the mountains above Israel (Ezek. 39:2). The defeat of Russia may be the starting point of Daniel's seventieth week, because Ezekiel said that Israel would burn the confiscated weaponry for seven years (Ezek. 39:9–10). This is the exact time span of the final period of this age, known as the seventieth week of Daniel.

THE RISE OF THE ANTICHRIST

After envisioning the rider on the red horse, who brings war, the apostle John envisioned a rider on a black horse and a rider on a pale horse (Rev. 6:5–8). These horses and riders symbolize famine, inflation, earthquakes, and the pestilences that will result from Russia's disastrous defeat. It will be at this time that the antichrist will be noticed and embraced by Israel and by the world. Due to the fact that the apostle John envisioned the antichrist as the rider on the white horse, which precedes the red horse that will bring war, we know that the antichrist will be on the scene at this time. Whether he will confirm the seven-year peace agreement with Israel just prior to the time in which Russia invades Israel, or in the time following Russia's defeat is not certain. In either case, this leader will take credit for God's work in stopping Russia's invasion. He will offer the world the solutions to its economic, religious, and political problems, as he unites the world under his command. He will be supported by the masses as he takes from the rich and gives to the poor (Dan. 11:24).

THE FALSE PROPHET

God declares in His Word that this antichrist, who will head up the final one-world government (referred to as the beast), will bring to power with him a false prophet who will head up a one-world religion (referred to as the second beast) (Dan. 7:5). This false prophet is described as having two horns like a lamb (representative of Christianity), but inwardly he is evil because he will speak as a dragon (Rev. 13:11). As we learned, John the Baptist introduced Jesus Christ as the "Lamb of God" (John 1:29). The antichrist will use this false prophet to unite all people and all religions under the banner of brotherhood. This humanistic idea is energized by Satan's spirit of antichrist, and is a rebellion against God. God's "Will" is to bring mankind unto Himself in the Name of, and under the banner of His Image, Jesus Christ. The antichrist will use this false prophet to bring the world together in a one-world religious system. The apostle Paul foretold that there would be an apostasy (abandoning of the faith) prior to the time that the antichrist would become known for who he really is, "the man of sin" (II Thess. 2:3). This apostasy has already begun. So-called Christian leaders are meeting together, denying the Divinity of Jesus Christ, and are working towards a one-world religion, exactly as foretold thousands of years ago.

THE GREAT WHORE

This apostasy will reach its peak when the world, including many Jews and so-called Christians, will forsake God's Word, and bow to this coming antichrist, either through deception or for fear of being killed. The one-world religion, headed up by the false prophet, will deceive multitudes into worshipping the antichrist, while the one-world government will execute those that refuse to bow to the antichrist. God called this final one-world religion, the "great whore" (Rev. 17:1), with whom the kings of the earth committed fornication. God foretold that this "Mother of Harlots and Abominations of the Earth" will be carried on a government that was, is not, and that shall ascend out of the bottomless pit. This describes the Roman Empire that was, and then was not in power, and will arise to power once again. This agrees perfectly with Daniel's prophecy, which foretold that this final world leader would arise out of the people who would crucify Jesus Christ and destroy the city of Jerusalem (Dan. 9:26). This group of people were members of the Roman Empire. The apostle John continued by identifying the location of this religious system, which he called the "great whore," by stating that she sits on seven hills. Yes, this final one-world government and one-world church will have its headquarters in Rome, Italy. This is where the papal palace and government buildings known as the Vatican are located. Isn't it something that Rome is the home of the first church-controlled government, that the pope has been asked to participate in the talks over Jerusalem, and that the Vatican has been suggested as becoming the sovereign capital of Old Jerusalem? This may come as a shock to many Catholics and Orthodox Catholics who are not familiar with the Book of Revelation, and with God's warnings about spiritual adultery.

SPIRITUAL ADULTERY

The first commandment which the LORD God gave Moses states in both the original translation and the Greek translation (the Septuigent) that "You shall not have any other gods *beside* Me" (Ex. 20:3). True followers of Jesus Christ are referred to as His "Bride" (Rev. 21:9). A spotless bride is one that loves and remains faithful to her husband. She does not commit fornication with others during her engagement. In a spiritual sense, a true child of God does not pray to anyone or anything besides Jesus Christ. The LORD God's second commandment states: "You shall not make any graven image for yourself, or any likeness . . ." and that "you shall not bow to them" (Ex. 20:4–5). Those that bow down to any image, regardless if it is of the Virgin Mary, of the apostles, or of man-made saints, are committing spiritual adultery. The LORD God called the final world religion, headquartered in Rome, the great whore because she leads people into committing spiritual adultery by bowing down to others *besides* Him. The pope is presently inviting all religions to join the Catholic (which means universal) church in a one-world orgy of religions. In addition to Roman Catholics and Orthodox Catholics, there soon will be Hindu Catholics, Buddhist Catholics, New Age Catholics, Muslim Catholics, etc. Those that have doubts about this should consider the fact that the pope gathered with the leaders of the 12 major religions, and declared that they were praying to the same God. This is a lie. God's Word clearly declares that one can worship God's Eternal Spirit only in the Name of Jesus Christ. In Italy, the pope allowed his friend to replace the cross with a Buddha on the altar of St. Peter's Church, and to perform Buddhist worship there. For more information about this and about the Catholic Church, please read "A Woman Rides the Beast" by David Hunt.

FALSE PEACE

As we learned, the antichrist, the future leader of the coming one-world government, will confirm a seven-year peace agreement between Israel and the nations (Dan. 9:27). The nation of Israel (as a whole, but not all) will put their faith in this leader when he rises to power. The antichrist will use the false prophet to bring the world together in a one-world religious system, in which the Jews and all people will initially have the freedom to worship God as they please. Everything will look wonderful, and Israel will believe that their covenant with the antichrist will bring in a new age of peace and safety. It is possible that the Dome of the Rock could have fallen during Russia's invasion, and that Israel, under the terms of her seven-year peace agreement with the nations, will be granted the right to construct a new temple on this site in Jerusalem. Even if this does not happen, we know there will be a temple in Jerusalem by the middle of this agreement, because it will be at this time, three and one half years after the antichrist will have confirmed a seven-year peace agreement between Israel and the nations, that the antichrist will desecrate the temple. This will be a time of great deception as Satan and his demons are cast to the earth.

WAR IN HEAVEN

In preparation for the return of Jesus Christ, the heavens are freed from Satan and his demons. The apostle John describes a war in heaven just prior to the "abomination of desolation" in which Satan and his angels come against Michael the archangel and God's faithful angels. This war results in Satan and his evil spirits being cast out of the second heaven and onto the earth (Rev. 12:7–8). As we learned, Satan was cast out of God's (the third) Heaven before the creation of man. The prophet Daniel said that this will be a time of distress such as never was (Dan. 12:1). At this time Satan will empower the antichrist to perform supernatural signs and lying wonders (II Thess. 2:9). The apostle Paul foretold that Michael the archangel, who is the protector of God's children, would cease to restrain Satan and his demonic spirits at this time (II Thess. 2:7–8).

SATAN'S PLIGHT FORETOLD

In order to fully understand this war in heaven and what will follow, let us review Satan's history. Lucifer was a most magnificent angelic being, created perfect, and anointed by God to serve Him. He became Satan the devil when he desired to exalt his throne, which was set in the second heaven above the earth, to the height of God, so that he could be worshipped like God. In a rebellion, he tried to exalt his throne up to God's heaven (the third heaven), and was cast out along with the unfaithful angels that followed him (Is. 14:12–14). After defeating Satan and his followers, God allowed them to remain in the second heaven until a predetermined future date, in order to give the human race the opportunity to individually choose between serving Him, in the Name of Jesus Christ, or serving Satan. When Satan along with his demons are cast out of the second heaven and onto the earth and its atmosphere, which is the first heaven, Satan will have great anger because he will know that he has but a short time before he himself will be thrown into the bottomless pit. For this reason, he sets out to destroy God's children and the nation of Israel, who brought forth Jesus Christ (Rev. 7:12–13). He will possess the body of the antichrist, enter Jerusalem (Dan. 11:45), and perform supernatural signs and wonders to deceive the Jews and those in the one-world church into believing that he is their Messiah.

Remember, from the day that Lucifer became Satan the devil, he has desired to be worshipped as the True God. This is why he will enter the Jerusalem temple and proclaim that he is the True God of the Holy Bible.

THE GREAT TRIBULATION

In the midst of her seven-year peace agreement with the nations, Israel and the entire world will lose their religious freedom. At this time, the antichrist will exalt himself above all that is called God, or that is worshipped. He will falsely show that he is God by sitting in the temple of God as God (II Thess. 2:4). This event will be the "abomination of desolation," and will mark the beginning of the "great tribulation," also known as the "time of Jacob's (Israel's) trouble" (Jer. 30:7). Jesus Christ foretold that this event would happen, and warned those that will be in Judea at this time to flee as fast as possible to the mountains. Those at home are to flee to the mountains without taking anything with them, and those away from their homes are not to return for even their clothes (Matt. 24:17–18). When the apostle John envisioned this period of time, he saw the souls of those murdered for the Word of God and for confessing their belief in Jesus Christ, as they cried unto God to avenge their blood on those dwelling upon the earth (Rev. 6:10). It will be during this time that man will be given the choice either to bow down to the antichrist and receive his mark, or to die. As you can now understand, the true and final battle of this present age is a spiritual one between Jesus Christ and Satan, between those that trust in God's Word and those that trust in man-made religions. God's children are the "born-again" believers, and Satan's children are the unregenerate (those that have not received God's Spirit of Truth into their minds and hearts).

GOD'S FINAL WARNING

God gave everyone a free thinking mind, capable of accepting or rejecting Him. Each mind that chooses to be led by God's Holy Spirit and receives Christ's Spirit of Truth will have a righteous image (soul) that is molded after the likeness of Jesus Christ. Each mind that either neglects or rejects God's Word will have an unrighteous image or soul. What many fail to realize and accept is the fact that every mind belongs to God. Jesus Christ could speak the Word of His Eternal and Heavenly Spirit Mind, Who is the Father of all spirits (Heb. 12:9), and in an instant, everyone would believe and acknowledge Him as their Creator. This however would not involve a personal choice, and would therefore not be true love. When Satan is cast out of the second heaven, just prior to the great tribulation, Jesus will display this same authority, and will send strong delusion to those that have rejected Him and have enjoyed unrighteousness (II Thess. 2:11). These folks will believe Satan's lie, which the false prophet will declare. This lie will state that the antichrist is the true "Christ" or "Sent One." Those that will believe this lie will be led into the eternal torments of hell. Those that believe that they can do whatever they want to now and change their minds later may never have the chance. One must seek the LORD while He may be found, and call upon Him while He is near (Is. 55:6). Today, this very minute, may be the last chance you will ever have to turn from your sin, and ask God in the Name of Jesus Christ to cleanse you with His Shed Blood and to come into your mind and heart as your personal Lord and Savior. Everyone that sincerely calls upon God in the Name of Jesus Christ will receive the Mind of Christ and will have the Knowledge and Power to overcome the trials of the great tribulation.

GREAT TRIBULATION BEGINS

Let us now continue our scenario by looking at the final three and one half years of this present age. Three and one half years have passed from the day that the antichrist confirmed a seven-year peace agreement between Israel and the nations. Israel as a whole is saying peace and safety. The Revised Roman Empire is bringing the world together from ten regions under the leadership of the antichrist. The false prophet (pope) is head of a world-wide conglomeration of religions with its headquarters in Vatican City Rome. Satan, having been cast to earth along with his demons, will set out with great wrath to destroy Israel and the Jewish race for recording God's Word and for bringing forth Jesus Christ (God's True Image). Satan will possess and empower the antichrist to rise from a fatal wound. Having always desired to be worshipped as the Most High God, Satan, in the person of the antichrist, will enter the temple in Jerusalem and declare that he is God. Jesus foretold this so that his followers would not be deceived (I Thess. 2:3–4), and so they would know to flee to the mountains at this time. The antichrist, empowered by Satan, will enable the false prophet to perform supernatural signs in his presence. The false prophet will therefore believe that he is God's prophet and will declare that the antichrist is the true "Christ" or "Messiah" (the True Image of God's Invisible Spirit). As a result of the false prophet's signs, which will include making fire come down from heaven, many will believe this "lie" and will obey his command to make an icon, or an image to the antichrist (Rev. 13:12–14). In His Love for man, Jesus Christ commanded the apostle John to record these things so that man could overcome Satan's deception.

BOW DOWN OR DIE

The false prophet will be given the power to give a spirit to the image of the antichrist so that it can speak, and he will cause those that will not worship this image to be killed. This is why Jesus Christ warned those in Judea to flee to the mountains when they see the antichrist sit in the temple as God. As we learned, Satan's desire has always been to be worshipped as the Most High God. At this time, mankind will be given the choice either to bow down to this image, or to be killed. This of course is against God's Second Commandment, which forbids the creation and the worship of any graven image (Ex. 20:4). Those that will have rejected or neglected to receive God's Word into their hearts, will have enjoyed unrighteousness, and will have put their faith in the religious system of the false prophet will gladly bow. There is an eternal difference, even though many do not realize it, between following man-made religion and following God.

RELIGION VS. RELATIONSHIP

Man was created to have a personal and loving friendship with God, based on "Faith" and "True Love." God, through His Soul (True Image of His Spirit Mind of Love), first appeared and talked to man as the "Word" of God, and man talked directly to Him. Later God revealed His Eternal Soul to man in the Person of Jesus Christ, the Son (True Image) of God's Invisible Spirit of Love. While on earth, Jesus Christ told His disciples that they were not to Him as servants but as friends (John 15:15). Yes, God, through Jesus Christ, is establishing a group of friends with whom He will share and enjoy His Eternal Kingdom. Because true love requires a choice, God does not force anyone to love Him. Those that choose to love Jesus Christ will be those with whom He will spend eternity. Satan the devil knows how much God loves man, and uses religion to prevent mankind from talking directly to God, in the Name of Jesus Christ, and becoming friends with Him. A friendship is a relationship between minds and hearts, and is based on love and trust. Jesus Christ foreknew that Satan would use religion to lead man away from Him. Because of this, He gave us the Holy Scriptures to use for doctrine, reproof, correction, and instruction in righteousness (II Tim. 3:16–17). As we learned, Satan quoted Scripture when he tried to tempt Jesus Christ. From this we know that God's enemies are not only those that outwardly deny Jesus Christ, but also those that Satan has deceived, through religion, into disregarding His Word and trusting in man-made doctrine for their salvation.

GOD'S KINGDOM

As we learned, God's Heavenly Spirit is the Spirit of Love (I John 4:8). This is why Jesus Christ (the True Image of God's Spirit Mind of Love) is referred to in the original Greek Scriptures as the Son of God's Love (Col. 1:13). Prior to His crucifixion, Jesus Christ told Pilate that His Kingdom was not of this world (John 18:36). When Jesus Christ commanded His disciples to go and declare that the Kingdom of Heaven was at hand, He told them to shake the dust off their feet where they were not received (Matt. 10:14). By considering the above, we know that God's Kingdom is not of this world, and that God's Kingdom is not being established by force but through His Spirit of Love, in and through the Name of His Son (True Image) Jesus Christ. Those that put their faith in Jesus Christ and trust in His (God's) Written Word are being united by God's Holy Spirit, and will rule and reign for all eternity with Jesus Christ when He returns. Knowing that he would be removed from this world, Satan has been working hard through false doctrines to prevent as many as possible from personally knowing God's "Truth," Jesus Christ.

FALSE DOCTRINE

While on this earth, Jesus Christ warned man about worldly religion. He told man not to follow the Pharisees because they teach the commandments of men and not the commandments of God (Matt. 15:9). As we learned, these self-righteous hypocrites had replaced God's Word with man-made doctrines, rituals, customs, and traditions. As a result they did not have the Spirit of God's Word in their minds and hearts. Jesus said these Pharisees honored Him with their lips but their hearts were far from Him (Matt. 15:8). Jesus also said that these Pharisees would not enter into heaven, and would keep those that follow them from entering in. Modern day Pharisees are deceived and deceive others into following and putting their trust in them and their man-made doctrines, instead of in God's Word, the only True Doctrine. As Jesus warned the people not to follow the Pharisees, He gave mankind a command which identifies the present day Pharisees, who under the false prophet will unite the various man-made religions into the final one-world church government. Jesus Christ's command, which identifies the present day Pharisees and which, through force, intimidation, and deceit, has been disregarded by millions is, "call no man your Father upon the earth; for one is your Father, which is in heaven" (Matt. 23:9).

SATAN'S LIE

As we learned, Daniel foretold that the final one-world leader would arise out of the people who would crucify Jesus Christ and destroy the city of Jerusalem. This group of people were members of the Roman Empire. We also learned that 2,500 years ago, Daniel received a vision from God in which he saw an image which foretold the future world empires which would lead to the return of Jesus Christ and the end of this age. The two legs of this image symbolized the Roman Empire, which under Julius Caesar conquered the Greeks in 63 B.C. This, the first one-world church government, had its headquarters in Rome and also in Constantinople. It is no mere coincidence that the Roman Catholic Church, with its headquarters in Rome, and the Eastern Orthodox Catholic Church, with its headquarters in Constantinople, are the two religions that call their priests "Father." These religions, which were one before splitting up, have been leading multitudes away from God's "Truth" and into spiritual adultery. The lie of these worldly churches is: "We are the Way, we are the Truth, and we are the Life." Satan, through these religions, has been and is telling man to disobey God's command not to call any earthly priest "Father," and to believe that they will lead them to God. Do not be deceived! Remember, Satan promised Eve that if she disobeyed God's command, she and Adam would become as gods. Remember also that man's righteousnesses, regardless of how holy they might appear, are as filthy rags before God (Is. 64:6).

ONE SPIRIT FATHER

God tells us in His Word that man has one biological father and One Spirit Father, Who is the Father of all spirits (Heb. 12:9). The physical father is required by God to provide for the physical needs of his family. According to God, those that do not provide for their own have denied the faith and are worse than unbelievers (I Tim. 5:8). The husband, as the head of the wife, is responsible for leading his family to Jesus Christ. This is because Jesus Christ is One with and the Only Son (True Image) of God's Heavenly Spirit Mind of Love, known as God the Father, As man's High Priest, Jesus Christ is the One and Only Mediator between His Invisible and Heavenly Spirit known as the "Father," and man (I Tim. 2:5). One can know and enter into the Presence of God's Heavenly Spirit only through Jesus Christ. As we learned, Jesus Christ is the Vine of God. Those that cling to Him are the branches (God's children). Eternal Life and all of God's Blessings (Fruit of God's Holy Spirit) are given by and through Jesus Christ. When one communes with Jesus Christ, he partakes of His Divine Nature, and becomes One with His Heavenly and Eternal Spirit of Love. This is why Jesus said: "I ascend unto my Father, and your Father" (John 20:17), "I and My Father are One" (John 10:30), "he that hath seen Me hath seen the Father" (John 14:9), and "I am the Way, the Truth, and the Life" (of God) (John 14:6). Jesus said that he that loves Him is he who keeps His Commandments (John 14:21). Everyone and anyone that truly loves Jesus Christ, through the Holy Spirit, will have received the Spirit Nature that Jesus had as a man, and would never call an earthly priest "Father," a title reserved for God alone.

NOTE

Unlike God's Kingdom, which was and is being established in and by the Love of God, the Roman church was established through deceit and force. Jesus Christ labeled this church the great whore because of her unfaithfulness. Members of these churches disobey God not only by calling their priests "Father," but also by bowing and praying to statues, icons, man-made saints, etc. This is spiritual adultery. It is important to know that in 365 A.D., the Roman church changed God's Sabbath Day of worship from Saturday to Sunday, and killed those that refused to comply with their decree, which were the truly "born again" followers of Jesus Christ. You see, one cannot be truly "born-again" by force or through ritual. In order for one to be born again, one must hear and believe the Gospel of Jesus Christ, and then invite God in the Name of Jesus Christ into their heart. Do not be deceived by the Roman church's worldly size, power, and riches. The Roman church will expand by accepting and including other "so-called" Christian and also non-Christian denominations under her wings. Thus her members will be made up of the "unfaithful" and the "unbelievers." The unbelievers are those that deny that Jesus Christ is the Son (True Image) of God's Invisible Spirit. This group will bow, and receive the Mark of the Beast. Included in this group is Islam, which was also forced upon people by church-government. The common denominator between the Roman church and Islam has been their use of force and their hatred towards the Jews. God's Loving advice to mankind in regards to the great whore is "come out of her" (Rev. 18:4).

THE MARK OF THE BEAST

The antichrist will attempt to exterminate the Jewish race for bringing the Son of God into the world, and will also strive to exterminate all those who confess the Name of Jesus Christ. In his attempt to become the master of the world, he will outlaw and try to destroy every copy of God's Word, the Holy Bible. At this time, all mankind will be told to bow down and worship the beast (the antichrist), and to receive his mark, his name, or the number of his name, which is 666, on their right hand or forehead. At this time money will be worthless, and those that do not have the mark of the beast will be unable to buy or sell (Rev. 13:16–19). Only those that receive the mark of this antichrist will be able to keep their homes and possessions. For the first time in history, the technology to implant a microchip in every human being is available. This would enable a one-world leader to track every individual and to monitor all of his or her personal transactions. As we learned, during this great tribulation, many will be beheaded for the witness of Jesus and for the Word of God (Rev. 20:4). Jesus Christ said that those that endure this wrath of man shall be saved from the Wrath of God (Matt. 24:13). The apostle John heard an angel of the Lord say that endurance is keeping the commandments of God and the faith of Jesus Christ. Those that bow to the antichrist and his image, and receive his mark shall be eternally tormented in fire and brimstone. Those that refuse the mark and die having faith in the Lord Jesus Christ will be eternally blessed (Rev. 14:11). They will have overcome Satan by faith in the Blood of Jesus Christ, the word of their testimony, and by not loving their lives unto death (Rev. 12:11). These martyrs will be resurrected and will receive new glorified bodies. This is why Jesus taught His followers to fear only God, and not to fear man who can kill only one's body but not one's soul. Notice that God's "Way" of salvation is not through a worldly establishment.

GOD'S "WAY"

Jesus Christ is referred to as the second Adam (I Cor. 15:45). This is due to the fact that God, through His Son (His Soul or True Image) Jesus Christ, poured out (through His Shed Blood) His Holy Spirit (Titus 3:5–8), so that He could offer His Holy Spirit to mankind. Man would then have the opportunity to replace his sinful nature (passed on to him by the first Adam) with God's Righteousness. Those that receive God's Holy Spirit are "born again" when they are baptized (cleansed of their sin) by God's Holy Spirit. At this time they are mentally changed as they receive the Spirit Mind of Jesus Christ (I Cor. 2:16), which gives them the desire to do God's Will. When one is led or headed by the Mind of Christ, his soul, which is the true image of his mind, is transformed into the Righteous Image of Jesus Christ. This is God's Loving and Voluntary Plan of Salvation. Those that choose to believe and to worship God in the Name of Jesus Christ will receive God's Grace (Mercy). As a result, they will be saved from God's coming Judgment and will be granted entrance into God's

Eternal Kingdom. One is saved by God's Grace for believing that Jesus Christ is the True Image of God's Invisible Spirit and that He shed His Blood for the forgiveness of man's sin. Salvation is a Gift of God and is not a result of doing good things, lest any man should boast (Eph. 3:8–9).

NOTE

God through Jesus Christ (His Eternal Soul) became man so that He could take on a human mind (spirit), which He could give to mankind after ascending to His Heavenly Spirit Mind (known as the Father) and becoming fully God again. Due to the fact that the life of all flesh is in the blood, Jesus Christ shed His Righteous Spirit Mind (Nature), which He had as a man, through His Shed Blood. Those that believe that Jesus Christ is the "Truth" of God, and believe in the Power of His Shed Blood for the forgiveness of their sins, will partake of His "Divine Nature" and will become eternal members of His Kingdom, if they abide in His Spirit of Truth. As you can now understand, one can partake of Jesus Christ's Divine Nature and receive God's Mercy only through faith in the Shed Blood of Jesus Christ. Those that are looking towards and trusting in their own righteousnesses, or in a worldly establishment for their salvation are deceived. If man could have saved himself, God in the Person of Jesus Christ would not have had to shed His Spotless Blood to save mankind. God's Loving Warning to the Jews of Judaism, to the Muslims, to the "so-called" Christians, and to all mankind is that "You must be born again" (John 3:7). It is not God's Will that any should perish, but that all should inherit eternal life (II Pet. 3:9). One can be born again only by trusting in and confessing one's faith in the Shed Blood of Jesus Christ for the forgiveness of his sin, and then asking God in the Name of Jesus Christ into his heart as the Lord and Savior of his life. Jesus Christ foretold that many of His followers would face worldly persecution on account of Him, but would be eternally blessed for following Him.

FIRST CHRISTIAN MARTYRS

As we learned, prior to commanding His apostles to go into all the world and preach the Gospel, Jesus Christ commanded His apostles to "Go not in the way of the Gentiles" (non-Jews) (Matt.

10:5). This is why the apostle Paul declared that the Gospel of
Jesus Christ was "the power of God unto salvation to every one that
believeth; to the Jew first, and also to the Greek" (Romans 1:16).
It is most important to understand that the first truly "born-again"
followers of Jesus Christ were the Jews that believed and followed
Him. What would become known as Christianity began as a sect of
Jews within Judaism. These Jews recognized Jesus as their Messiah.
The majority of the Jews, however, were led astray by the Pharisees
which were the most influential sect within Judaism at that time.
Jesus Christ's Jewish apostles and followers became the first
martyrs of His Church when they were killed, by the soldiers of the
Roman Empire, for confessing their faith in Jesus Christ.

NOTE

In the fourth century, "so-called" Christianity in the form of
the Catholic Church became the head of the Roman Empire. At
this time the Roman church began the myth that they were
Christ's True Church. Millions became so-called Christians as they
were forced and coerced into joining the state church instead of
hearing, believing, choosing, and receiving Jesus Christ through
the "born-again" experience. Suddenly this man-made religion
declared that one was and could be "born again" only by joining
their worldly establishment. To hide the fact that the first "born-
again" believers of Jesus Christ were Jews, the Roman church
distanced themselves from the Jews: by changing God's Sabbath
from Saturday to Sunday; by declaring that the One LORD God
was a "Trinity;" by moving God's earthly throne from Jerusalem to
Rome; by making it illegal for the common man to possess the
Holy Scriptures; by indoctrinating Rome's pagan beliefs into their
worship services; etc. As the head of the government, the church
made it punishable by death to put God's Word before their
doctrine. Is it any wonder why for centuries, multitudes of Jews,
who relate Christianity with Catholicism, have turned a deaf ear
towards the Gospel of Jesus Christ?

JEWS RECEIVE JESUS

As this present Age of Grace nears its end, so will man's
opportunity to receive God's Free Gift of Grace. God will complete His church with those with whom He began it, the Jews. The

people of Israel are God's chosen people, because God chose Israel as His servant to bless the entire world with His Word. Many Jews are presently receiving Jesus Christ as their Lord and Savior. Unfortunately, many are also being kept away by the Jewish Pharisees. Just prior to identifying the Gentile Pharisees as those that call their priests "Father," Jesus identified the Jewish Pharisees. Jesus commanded the Pharisees "be not ye called Rabbi: for one is your Master, even Christ" (Matt. 23:8). The Good News is that many more Jews will be "born again" after hearing the Gospel of Jesus Christ as preached by the two Jewish witnesses. One of these witnesses will be Elijah (Mal. 3:1) who, as we learned, was miraculously caught up to heaven in a whirlwind (II Kin. 2:11). Many of these and other "born-again" believers will be killed by the servants of the Revised Roman Empire, as were many of the first "born-again" disciples (followers) of Jesus Christ by the original Roman Empire.

LATTER-DAY CHRISTIAN MARTYRS

God tells us in His Word that many of these end-time Christian martyrs will be beheaded by the final one-world church government of the antichrist (the Revised Roman Empire) for confessing their faith in Jesus Christ, for possessing or proclaiming the Gospel of Jesus Christ, for refusing to bow down to the beast (the Revised Roman Empire, the antichrist, the image of the antichrist), and for refusing to receive the mark of the beast upon their forehead and upon their hand (Rev. 20:4). Reports of guillotines being manufactured in the United States, and of states considering the use of guillotines as a method of capital punishment are additional signs that the Holy Bible is the Word of God, and that the time of the great tribulation is drawing near.

THE SIGN OF CHRIST'S RETURN

Jesus Christ said that for the sake of His elect, the Jews, He would cut the tribulation period short, so that they would not all be killed. Jesus foretold that there will be many false prophets during this time, which will be performing great signs and wonders, and warned His followers not to believe anyone that would claim that Christ is here or there. Prior to His return, Jesus said that the sun and the moon shall be darkened, the stars shall fall from heaven, and the powers of the heavens shall be shaken (Matt. 24:29). Jesus told the apostle John that there would be a great earthquake, the sun would become black, and the moon would become like blood at this time (Rev. 6:12). This will be the sign of Christ's return, after which He will come as lightning that fills the sky from the east as far as the west (Matt. 24:27).

144,000 RECEIVE GOD'S MARK

When Jesus Christ appears in the clouds, God's Wrath will be unleashed and will fall upon an unrepentant world. Just prior to this time, an angel—probably Michael, the guardian of Israel (Dan. 12:1)—will command the four angels, to whom it will be given to hurt the earth and the sea, to wait until they seal the servants of God in their foreheads (Rev. 7:2–3). This group will be made up of 144,000 "born-again" Jews, 12,000 from each of the twelve tribes of Israel (Rev. 7:4–8). These Jews that receive God's Mark will be the firstfruits of many more, whose eyes will be opened. These Jews will see, and will finally believe that Jesus Christ is the True Messiah, that He shed His Blood for the remission of their sins, and that with faith in His Sacrificial Blood, they will be able to abide with Him in God's soon-to-come Millenial Kingdom. This group of Jews will be virgins, in that they will not have committed spiritual adultery with the "great whore," and will not have received the mark of the beast. As a result of their faithfulness, they will now be covered with the Blood of Jesus Christ and will be protected from the outpouring of God's Wrath, as were the Israelites on that Passover day in Egypt.

THE RAPTURE OF CHRIST'S CHURCH

The apostle Paul taught that God hath not appointed Christians to wrath, but to salvation (I Thess. 5:9). Just prior to the outpouring of God's Wrath, the Rapture of the Church will take place. It will be at this time that the souls of all the physically dead "born-again" Christians will return to their former bodies. They will then come up out of their graves and, along with the living "born-again" Christians, will be caught up in the clouds to meet the Lord Jesus Christ (I Thess. 4:16–17). All this will happen in the twinkling of an eye (I Cor. 15:52). This universal Church of Jesus Christ will not be a denomination or an earthly institution.

This group will consist of all the "born-again" followers of Jesus Christ from all nations, kindreds, and tongues (Rev. 7:9). Those in this group, which were alive during the great tribulation, will have remained pure from the great whore, and will have not received the mark of the beast. As these believers are caught up in the air, their old bodies will be transformed into new glorified bodies, which shall be like the resurrected Body of Jesus Christ (I John 3:2). Even though we do not know exactly what this body will be like, we can have an idea by looking at Jesus after He was resurrected. From this we can know that we will enjoy eating, and that we will be able to appear and disappear. For more information and scriptural proof that the Rapture of the Church will occur at this time, please read "The Pre-Wrath Rapture of the Church" by Marvin Rosenthal.

NOTE

Following this Rapture, God will give His chosen people, the Jews, one last chance to receive Him in the Name of Jesus Christ. As we will learn, those that do will be caught up in the next Rapture along with God's witnesses.

THE DAY OF THE LORD

The time of God's Vengeance upon an evil world, known as the "Day of the Lord," will arrive after the 144,000 born-again Jews will have received God's Mark, and after the Rapture of the universal church of Christ. For centuries, mankind has asked, "How can God allow such suffering?" Only God can answer that question and He does. The answer is that the Lord is long-suffering toward us. He does not wish to see anyone perish, and has therefore given mankind as much time as possible to repent and to follow Him in the Name of Jesus Christ (II Pet. 3:9). As we will soon learn, everyone who has died will be resurrected and will bow before Jesus Christ. Some will bow to eternal life, and some will bow to eternal damnation. The Day of the Lord's Wrath will be reminiscent of the time Moses had approached the Pharoah of Egypt and told him that if he would not release the Israelites, God would send a certain plague upon Egypt. In the same likeness, God's two witnesses will warn mankind to repent, after which God will unleash His Wrath upon an unrepentant world, in a series of seven trumpet judgments (Rev. 8, 9).

ALL WILL HEAR GOSPEL

After the antichrist, through the great whore, causes as many as possible to commit spiritual adultery and to receive his mark, the antichrist will destroy the great whore. He will make her desolate by burning her to the ground (Rev. 17:16). The antichrist will have failed to destroy God's true children, because they will have chosen to die rather than to deny their faith in the Shed Blood of Jesus Christ. Those that obeyed the false prophet and his pharisees, will have received the mark of the beast, and will never have another chance to receive Jesus Christ and to inherit eternal life in the Kingdom of God (Rev. 14:9–11). Along with those that received the mark of the beast, there will be another large group of people on the earth that will have not received the mark of the beast. These folks will be given the opportunity to worship Jesus Christ after hearing the Gospel of Jesus Christ from an angel in the midst of heaven (Rev. 14:6–7). Those that hear and receive Christ will enter into the "Millenial Kingdom of God" upon this earth (Rev. 20:4). Jesus said He would not return until the Gospel of God's coming Kingdom would be preached in all the habitable earth (Matt. 24:14). At the end of this Age, no one will be able to say that God is not fair, for everyone will have been given the opportunity to accept Jesus Christ as their Lord and Savior.

EAST MARCHES TO ARMAGEDDON

As we learned, the Day of the Lord will begin after the Church (body of "born-again" believers) of Jesus Christ has been removed from the earth, and after the 144,000 born-again Jews will have received God's Mark, which will ensure their safety at this time. Mankind, as a whole, will not change their minds about giving glory to the True God. After the first five plagues, evil mankind will blaspheme Jesus Christ, the Name above all names (Phil. 2:9), Who alone has the Power to stop these plagues. Because of this, the great river Euphrates will be dried up to make the way for the kings of the east. These kings, along with their two-hundred-million-man army, will come against the antichrist and his armies at Armageddon. This nuclear war will occur after the eastern armies, along with the remnant of the Russian army, are influenced by demonic spirits to come against the antichrist (Rev. 16:14). One third of the earth's inhabitants will be killed during this war. Those that survive this plague still will not worship Jesus Christ, but instead will worship demons and idols, which neither see, hear, nor walk. Neither will men repent of their murders, drug usage, fornication, or their thefts (Rev. 9:20–21). Instead, they will kill God's two witnesses.

GOD'S TWO WITNESSES KILLED

It will be at this time that the two witnesses shall have completed their testimony, and they will be killed by the armies of the antichrist (Rev. 11:7). Their bodies will be left in the street of Jerusalem for all the people to see. Those dwelling on earth at this time will rejoice, party, and send each other gifts. Their partying, however, will come to an end when God's Spirit of Life enters into the witnesses, and they stand upon their feet (Rev. 11:11). Great fear will fall upon those remaining on earth when next, they hear a great Voice from heaven tell the witnesses to "Come up hither," and they watch the witnesses ascend up to heaven. God tells us that at this time, seven thousand "born-again" believers in Jerusalem will have been killed in a great earthquake, and that the remaining Jews will have received Jesus Christ as their Lord and Savior (Rev. 11:13). It is therefore probable that they will be raptured along with God's Witnesses. Those included in this rapture will also receive new glorified bodies, as they are caught up in the clouds to meet their Lord and Savior Jesus Christ.

CHRIST'S BRIDE

Jesus foretold that at the time of His return to earth, His elect would be gathered from the ends of heaven (Matt. 24:31). As we learned, one can enter into God's Heavenly Kingdom only through faith in Jesus Christ (John 14:6). Christ's Bride, those that will have received glorified bodies up to this point, will now gather together and accompany Jesus Christ, as He Personally returns to set up God's Kingdom on earth. This group, having been changed from mortal to immortal, will live and rule, as priests and kings, with Jesus Christ for all eternity. Upon Christ's return, the kingdoms of the world will become the Kingdoms of God.

REWARDS

Those of you that have asked and have received the Spirit of Jesus Christ into your hearts will want to work hard for Him now, to ensure that you will have a rich entrance into heaven (II Pet. 1:10–11). This is because every redeemed servant of God will stand before Jesus Christ, and will be judged for his good works. Even though good works cannot gain one entrance into God's Kingdom, they do determine the degree of one's reward. As we learned, only faith in the Shed Blood of Jesus Christ for the remission of sin can justify one's entrance into God's Kingdom. Good works are things that a person has done, and will do in the Love and for the Glorification of Jesus Christ. There will be great joy as Jesus Christ presents His faithful servants with a crown of righteousness for having put and having kept one's body under control (I Cor. 9:27), for turning many to righteousness (Dan. 12:3), for loving His appearing (II Tim. 4:8), for continuing to love Him during hard times (James 1:12), and for being good shepherds (I Pet. 5:4). One must remember that "Faith without works is dead" (James 2:20). Jesus warned that those that are lukewarm in their faith will be spewed out (Rev. 3:16), and that narrow is the path that leads to life and few will find it (Matt. 7:13–14).

THE GLORIOUS RETURN OF JESUS CHRIST

When Jesus Christ returns in the clouds, He will judge and destroy Satan's children. Unlike His humble entrance on that Palm Sunday almost two thousand years ago, Jesus Christ will enter into Jerusalem, through the Eastern Gate, as King of kings and Lord of lords (Rev. 19:16). This gate was sealed off by the Muslims and has remained sealed since 1517. Over 2,550 years ago, the prophet Ezekiel foretold that this gate would be sealed, and would remain sealed until the Prince of Peace would come (Ezek. 44:1–3). The prophet Zechariah foretold that the Mount of Olives would split in two when Jesus Christ returns and His feet touch the ground (Zech. 14:4). Those remaining on earth will be separated into two groups by God's angels. These two groups will be made up of those that will have received the mark of the breast, and those that will not have received it. At this time, the antichrist, the false prophet, and the kings of the nations, along with their armies (those that came against Israel), will be gathered together to make war with Jesus Christ (Rev. 19:19). When Jesus Christ returns, the antichrist and the false prophet will be cast into the eternal lake of fire, and those with them will all be killed in what the Holy Bible calls the "Winepress of the Wrath of God" (Rev. 14:19). Afterwards, one of God's angels will summon all the birds to gather for the supper of the Great God, at which time they will eat the flesh of those killed (Rev. 19:21). The other group, which did not receive the mark of the beast and were loving and helpful towards the people of Israel, will be spared. These survivors of God's Wrath will include people of all tribes and nations. This group will continue living on earth in their human bodies.

GOD'S KINGDOM ESTABLISHED

After destroying those that were destroying the world, Jesus Christ will set up God's Kingdom on earth for 1,000 years. He will rule and reign, along with those that were redeemed (those that received new glorified bodies), over those of every tribe and nation which did not receive the mark of the beast and survived God's Wrath. Christ's glorious reign on earth will begin with Satan being bound and placed in the bottomless pit (Rev. 20:1–3). Only God Himself, in the person of Jesus Christ has the right to set up a one-world government under God, and He does this at this time. Jesus will place those that He chooses in the various positions of leadership. Only God knows who is the best qualified for each position, and He will Personally appoint them. There will never again be corruption in the government. Isaiah the prophet foretold that Jesus Christ would sit on the throne of David in Jerusalem, and that the government would be upon His Shoulder. He added that at this time, Jesus would be called Wonderful, Counselor, the Mighty God, the Everlasting Father, and the Prince of Peace (Is. 9:6).

PEACE AT LAST

During the Millenial Kingdom, all the world will know that the LORD is One (Zec. 14:9). The Lord Jesus Christ will rule with a rod of iron (Rev. 19:15). At this time the world will walk in the Spirit of God's Love. The prophet Isaiah foretold that nations would beat their swords into plowshares and their spears into pruning hooks, and that the nations would never again make war with each other (Is. 2:4). Isaiah foretold that even the animals would be full of God's Love at this time. He said the wolf would dwell with the lamb, the leopard with the kid, and the lion with the calf (Is. 11:7–9). Every survivor (those that did not receive the mark of the beast) from the nations that came against Jerusalem will go up yearly to worship King Jesus. Those that refuse will be punished (Zec. 14:16–19). It will be a near-perfect society, because Satan will be bound up. The little trouble that arises will be dealt with quickly and firmly. This sin will originate from the sin nature of the remnant from each nation that will enter the millenium in their natural bodies. This group will repopulate the earth, and will enjoy a nice life under the rule and guidance of Jesus Christ and His redeemed saints. The prophet Zechariah foretold that a person that is one hundred years old during this time will be considered a child (Zech. 65:20). Some may live to be 1,000 years old, but none are guaranteed eternal life at the end of the millenium. Only those that were a part of the raptures before the millenium, and were changed from natural to spiritual (I Cor. 15:44) are guaranteed eternal life.

SATAN LOOSED FOR A SEASON

When the thousand-year Millenium comes to an end, Satan will be let out of prison, and he will go out to deceive the nations (Rev. 20:7–8). Believe it or not, he will succeed in gathering multitudes around Jerusalem to battle against Jesus Christ and the saints. This rebellion will come to a quick end, when fire comes down from God and devours them. Satan the devil will then be cast into the lake of fire, where the antichrist and the false prophet will still be burning, and will be tormented with them day and night for all eternity (Rev. 20:10). God makes it clear in His Word that there is an eternal hell, so that man will fear Him and walk in obedience to His Holy Spirit. Before the old heaven and earth are purged of all evil, the "Great White Throne" judgment will take place.

THE GREAT WHITE THRONE

The time has come for all sin and unrighteousness to come to an end. Satan will have been cast into the lake of fire for all eternity, never to tempt anyone again. Jesus Christ said that this everlasting fire, called Gehenna, is a place prepared for Satan and his angels (Matt. 25:41). This judgment is called the Great White Throne Judgment, because white is the color of God's Righteousness, which is available only through faith in the Shed Blood of Jesus Christ. At this time the sea, death (the grave), and hell (hades) deliver up the dead which are in them, and are themselves then cast into the lake of fire. At this point in time, all death will come to an end (Rev. 20:13–14). All the lost souls from the time of Adam will return to their former bodies, and will stand before Jesus Christ to be judged. Unlike the righteous souls that were judged according to their good deeds, these souls will be judged for the evil that they committed, and will then be cast into the eternal lake of fire. There they will be tormented day and night for all eternity, according to the degree of their sin.

GOD'S MASTER PLAN FULFILLED

Following the Great White Throne Judgment, the former heavens along with this old earth will be dissolved with the Fire of God. Jesus Christ gave the apostle John a vision in which John saw a new heaven and a new earth. He then saw the "New Jerusalem," the future Holy City, coming down from God out of heaven, prepared as a bride for her husband. As we previously learned, the group of "born again" believers, known as the "Church," were referred to as the Bride of Christ. Now the Throne of God's Eternal Spirit of Love, known as the Father, when Jesus, as a man, was known as the Son, will come down from heaven as a bride adorned for her husband, Jesus Christ. As we learned, Jesus Christ shed His humanity, is now fully God, and will be called the Everlasting Father when He returns, and sits upon God's Throne for all eternity. The prophet Ezekiel, 2,550 years ago, was told that this Holy City would be called "Jehovah-Shammah" which means, "The LORD is there" (Ezek. 48:35). This vision of God's Throne, Jesus Christ, and His redeemed followers is a picture of the fulfillment of God's Master Plan.

THE ETERNAL STATE

All the sacrifice and persecution, which one endures while on this earth, cannot be compared to the everlasting joy that awaits those that overcome this evil world, through faith in Jesus Christ and in His Shed Blood for the forgiveness of their sins. In God's Eternal Kingdom there will be no tears, death, sorrow, crying, or pain (Rev. 21:4). He that overcometh will inherit all things. Jesus will be his God, and he will be God's son (Rev. 21:7). There will be nothing but pleasures forevermore (Ps. 16:11). God declares that no one has seen, nor heard, nor imagined the things that He has prepared for them that love Him (I Cor. 2:9–10). Those that overcome this world will eat from the tree of life. They will be allowed to enter the Holy City through its pearl gates and travel on its streets of pure gold. Most of all, one will be able to talk face to face with his Creator, Spiritual Father, and Friend, Jesus Christ.

JOHN IS WARNED

The apostle John became so overwhelmed with these things that he fell down to worship before the feet of the angel which showed him these things. The angel stopped him and told him that he is a fellow servant of the prophets and all those that keep the sayings of God's Word: "Worship God" (Rev. 22:9). A child of God is not to bow to any man, angel, or object, and was commanded by Jesus Christ, the Everlasting Father, not to address any spiritual leader on earth as "Father." Jesus said that he will love those that keep His commandments (John 15:10).

ETERNITY

As this Age draws to an end, those that want to live eternally with Jesus Christ must judge themselves. They must look and see whether they are following and putting their faith in Jesus Christ and the Written Word of God for their salvation, or if they are following and putting their faith in worldly institutions and man-made doctrines for their salvation. Everyone will spend eternity with the master they choose to follow and obey. Those that desire to inherit the Kingdom of God must look within and ask themselves if they are trusting in the Shed Blood of Jesus Christ for the remission of their sins and if they are being led by His Holy Spirit in their daily lives. If not, they must turn from their sin, and be "born again." Jesus, in His Love for man, warned him not to be deceived into living, working, and selling his soul for the temporary things of this world. All the material things of this

present world such as cars, homes, money, etc., will pass away. The
only things that will remain, and will determine one's eternal
destiny, are the Living Word of God in one's life and the good
deeds done for and in the Name of Jesus Christ. Knowing this,
your eternal destiny is now in your own hands.

SUMMARY

I would like to begin my summary by stating that this book
was written to lead lost mankind onto the True Path of Righteousness. Its twofold purpose and goal is to lead mankind to God's
"Truth," Jesus Christ, and to provide him with a deep and overall
understanding of God's Written Word, the Holy Bible. This is the
only "Way" in which one can be freed from the bondage of drugs,
immorality, false teachings, etc. Those that receive God's Inspiration (the Holy Spirit of Jesus Christ and of His Written Word) and
live accordingly will overcome this world and will inherit Eternal
Life in the Kingdom of God.

Knowing this, are we to respect the beliefs of others by not
telling them the Good News of Jesus Christ? Should we sit quietly
by and watch our fellowman lose his or her opportunity of gaining
eternal life? The answer is an emphatic "No"!!! As we learned, it is
not God's Will that any should perish, but that all should follow
Jesus Christ and inherit Eternal Life. This is why Jesus commanded each and every one of His disciples to go out into all the
world (in their daily lives) and to be witnesses unto Him. The
message to all mankind, whether it be to a Jew of Judaism, a
Muslim, a Catholic, an Orthodox, a Jehovah's Witness, a Mormon,
a New Ager, a Christian Scientist, a Protestant, a Buddhist, a
Hindu, or to whomever else, is the same. The message in Christ's
OWN WORDS is: "You must be born again" in order to enter the
Kingdom of God.

One is "born again" when he or she receives God's Holy
Spirit. In order for this to happen, one must first hear the Gospel
of Jesus Christ. As just mentioned, this is why Jesus commanded
His followers to be His witnesses. The Gospel or Good News of
Jesus Christ is God's Promise that the Holy Spirit will enter into,
dwell with, and give eternal life to all those who, after hearing
about Jesus Christ, believe and confess with their mouth that Jesus
Christ is the Son (Soul—True Image) of God, that He shed His
Spotless Blood on the cross for the forgiveness of their sin, and

SUMMARY 211

that He rose bodily from the dead, and who then ask Jesus Christ into their heart as their Lord and Savior.

Those of every race and nationality that receive and abide in the Holy Spirit of Jesus Christ will love Him and their fellowman. You see, God in His Infinite Wisdom knew that the only "Way" to gather together a special people unto Himself, as a loving and unprejudiced family, would be to join them together in His Blood and in His Spirit of Love. Only by becoming "One Spirit Blood" with God could all races of every nationality truly love God and love each other as brothers and sisters. This is the purpose of God's Master Plan and the reason why God through His Son (Soul-True Image), Jesus Christ, shed His Spotless Blood on the cross.

As this present age nears its end, so does man's opportunity to receive God's Holy Spirit in the Name of Jesus Christ and to be born into the family of God. This is the true meaning of being "born again," and not joining some earthly church as some falsely believe. God's invitation is open to all. If you haven't yet asked Jesus Christ into your heart, I warmly urge you to do it now. Those that become children of God, through faith in His Shed Blood, will be saved from God's coming Judgment, which shall soon fall upon and purge this earth from all its evil.

Yes, Jesus Christ will soon return for those that have been faithful to Him, by refusing to pray to, trust in, or bow to anyone or anything besides Him, and who are anxiously awaiting His return. At this time, the eyes of the blind shall be opened, the ears of the deaf shall be unstopped, the lame shall leap, and the tongues of the dumb shall sing, as God's children are rewarded with new glorified bodies which shall be like that of Jesus and in which they shall eternally live in perfect peace, health, and happiness. As this glorious time draws near, we are to gather together and encourage one another. Talking and thinking about Jesus Christ with family and friends should be the everyday norm for those that love Him. It is time to stop worrying and to look up, because our redemption draweth nigh.

In His Love,
Sotirios J. Noussias

SCRIPTURE INDEX

ABOUT THE AUTHOR

The author, Sotirios J. Noussias, following a series of events and a revelation from God, was led to the Scriptures of the Holy Bible. His advantage of having grown up in a Greek speaking home enabled him to read, grasp, and convey the true meaning of the original Greek New Testament Scriptures. He has spent four years of exhaustive preparation, detailed research, and dedication for this in-depth presentation.

ORDERING INFORMATION

For additional copies ask your favorite bookstore for "MAN'S QUESTIONS—GOD'S ANSWERS," ISBN 0-9652284-0-1

or

If you wish to send a copy to a relative or friend, please send $12.95 + $3.00 S&H to:

Flower Publishing
P.O. Box 8498
Canton, Ohio 44711

(Ohio residents please add 72¢ sales tax.)